THE WORLD POLICY
OF GERMANY, 1890–1912

"OUT IN THE COLD!"

"I am like a traveller lost in the snow, who begins to get stiff while the snowflakes cover him."

Speech of Prince Von Bismarck at Friedrichsruh.

(*Punch*, February 6, 1892.)

THE WORLD POLICY
OF GERMANY
1890–1912

BY

OTTO HAMMANN

TRANSLATED BY

MAUDE A. HUTTMAN, Ph.D.

NEW YORK
ALFRED · A · KNOPF
MCMXXVII

First published in German under the title
" Der missverstandne Bismarck,"
subsequently published in enlarged form (of which
this is a translation) under the title
" Deutsche Weltpolitik, 1890–1912."

Printed in Great Britain by
Unwin Brothers, Ltd., Woking

FOREWORD

THE writer of this book, Otto Hammann, J.U.D., was born in 1852 near Weimar. He studied Law in Leipzig, Heidelberg, and Jena, and became Referendar in Weimar. Before long, however, he forsook Law for Journalism, and finally settled in Berlin. Here he attracted the attention of Bismarck's successor by his conciliatory attitude during the bitter conflicts between Friedrichsruh and Berlin over the New Course (Der neue Kurs).

In 1893, Caprivi made Hammann Chief of the Press Division of the Foreign Office, and this post Hammann occupied uninterruptedly until 1917, when he reached the statutory age for retirement. It was under the third Imperial Chancellor that Hammann reached the zenith of his activity in the Foreign Office, and he played a most important part behind the scenes. Bülow was in daily contact with his Press Chief in order to keep him informed on all important matters in foreign and domestic affairs, and he continually consulted Hammann about proposed speeches in the Reichstag. When Bethmann-Hollweg became Chancellor he too kept in close touch with Hammann.[1]

Since his retirement from the Foreign Office, Hammann has published several books on German politics since 1890. The present work is a new and enlarged edition of *Der missverstandne Bismarck* which appeared in 1921. The chief sources for that book were Hammann's own memory and his valuable notes. For this, his latest book, Hammann has also made use of the German official documents that

---

[1] Hammann was absolutely opposed to a policy of unrestricted submarine warfare, and held that Bethmann-Hollweg should have resigned rather than agree to the decision at Plese. Cf. *Bilder aus der letzten Kaiserzeit*, p. 131.

are now in course of publication.[1]   The later references to
these official documents are to chapters only, since pagination
and book divisions were not yet determined when Excellency
Hammann made use of the advance sheets of the later
documents.

The translator wishes to acknowledge with thanks the
kind permission of *Punch* to reproduce the two cartoons.
She also desires to express her appreciation of the kindness
of Dr. Theodore Lorenz, who has read a large part of the
manuscript and offered valuable suggestions.

M. A. H.

LONDON,
July 1926.

[1] *Die Grosse Politik der Europäischen Kabinette*, 1871–1914.
Throughout this work, where no title is mentioned in footnote
references, *Die Grosse Politik der Europäischen Kabinette* is to be
understood.

CONTENTS

BOOK IV

THE ENCIRCLEMENT OF GERMANY

BOOK V

THE YEARS OF CRISES, 1908–1912

BOOK VI

CONCLUSION

ILLUSTRATIONS

BOOK I

INTRODUCTION

THE WORK OF BISMARCK

WHAT especially distinguished the great master was his clear understanding of the historical origins of the relations between the European Powers; the finest sensibility for the national shortcomings and virtues of the German people; and the clairvoyance and courage to comprehend the future. In general, we might picture to ourselves the fundamental ideas that imbued his work somewhat as follows:

In the preceding centuries the two outlying countries of Europe, Russia in the east, England in the west, gradually extended their power, while in the central part, through constant wars that brought no great conquests, the boundaries shifted somewhat, now in that direction, now in this. As alliances changed under rulers and cabinets, so did the victories and defeats. While the peoples were offering bloody sacrifices and the land visited by war was laid waste, territorial possession and the balance of power remained more or less unchanged. France proved the strongest Power among the rivals in the international conflicts in Europe because she was a national unit and possessed a centralized government. But what she may have gained in land was heavily counterbalanced by the positions England gained at her expense on the other continents, in America and Asia. A similar fate overtook the Austrian dynasty. When Austria had succeeded in stemming the Turkish tide, Russia, grown powerful under Peter the Great and Catharine, stepped forward as the heir presumptive of the Sick Man of Constantinople in South-Eastern Europe. Towards the west, Russia increased her possessions by the destruction of the electoral kingdom of Poland, which had gradually become disorganized by

mismanagement and civil strife. Smaller portions fell to
Austria and to Prussia, which, during the decline of the old
German Empire, had been rising to power by its own
energy under the Great Elector, the soldier King and his
great son.

But Russia, shut off from the highways of the seven seas,
was still only a Great Power on land. England, on the
other hand, had meanwhile become the mistress of the sea ;
she had created strong bases on the coast of every continent, had acquired great colonies, and thus comported
herself on every continent as a World Power. She
was not entirely free to strengthen and develop this position
at home and abroad until she had vanquished, with the
help of the Central Powers and Russia, her most ruthless
opponent, Napoleon, and had dispatched him, a prisoner
on an English vessel, to St. Helena.

At the Congress of Vienna, the establishment of a German
Federal Diet as the central organ of the component parts
of the former Empire did not solve, but only postponed
for the future, the German problem—the creation of a
national State in which the people could participate in
determining their own destiny. It was impossible to solve
this question from the standpoint of a Greater Germany,
because that would have disrupted the Austrian State of
many nationalities. Only under the leadership of that
German State which was the most strongly knit together
and that possessed the most powerful army could this be
achieved.

When Otto von Bismarck-Schönhausen went to Frankfort
as Prussian Ambassador, he still shared the Austrian view-
point that the German problem should be solved through
a dual arrangement : Austria-Prussia. There he soon perceived that the mutual support of Prussia and Austria
was a fond delusion, and that passive and planless as was
the Prussian policy, the Gordian knot of German affairs
could not be amicably untangled by adopting the dualistic
solution, but could only be cut by the sword; and that
this could be achieved most easily in close touch with

A WISE WARNING

(Founded on the first part of an old Fable, the Sequel of which Mr. Punch trusts may never apply.)

Daedalus Bismarck, Political Parent of Wilhelm Icarus:

" My son, observe the middle path to fly,
   And fear to sink too low, or rise too high.
   Here the sun melts, there vapours damp your force,
   Between the two extremes direct your course.

   Nor on the bear, nor on Boötes gaze,
   Nor on sword-arm'd Orion's dangerous rays:
   But follow me, thy guide, with watchful sight,
   And as I steer, direct thy cautious flight."
                    OVID, *Metamorphoses*, Book VIII, Fable III.

(*Punch*, October 6, 1888.)

Russia. Acute in judging men, he got the impression during his residence in Paris, from interviews with Napoleon III, that the latter was not the *génie du mal* for which he passed in the world, but a weakling obsessed by the craze for prestige who was playing with the idea, if not of the incorporation of the whole left bank of the Rhine, at least with that of a *petite rectification des frontières*, and of an Italy entirely dependent on France, with French stations on her coast.[1] The " period of transition," [2] which lasted until the " blood and iron " speech in the budget commission in the Chamber of Deputies on September 30, 1862, was immediately followed by his first preparatory move—the assistance to Russia in the Polish Revolution, for which he has been much criticized but which happily ensured the needed protection at the rear on the Russian frontier.

A second diplomatic move, intended to provide for the future, was the moderation he wrung from King William for the terms of the Peace of Nikolsburg. The Monarchy on the Danube was spared humiliation and territorial loss and was permitted to retain its rank as a Great Power able to enter into alliances, in order to fulfil its destiny of keeping the way to Constantinople open for Central Europe and of preventing the division of Turkey's possessions between Russia and England.[3]

[1] *Gedanken und Erinnerungen*, chap. ix.

[2] " Zwischenzustand." This word is used in the Table of Contents of Chap. XI in *Gedanken und Erinnerungen*.—TRANSLATOR'S NOTE.

[3] On Near Eastern problems Prince Bismarck has given expression to different views according as his diplomatic aims were modified by the successive political constellations. That he really intended not only to forsake Austria-Hungary, but also to permit the Russians to enter Bulgaria and Constantinople, is by no means certain, the Reinsurance Treaty of 1887 notwithstanding. To Russia Prince Bismarck said : " Do what you will ; we have no direct interest there." To his ally on the Danube he gave the advice not to deploy until the Russians were actually in Bulgaria, for then Austria would have them in the grip of the shears (close of 1886). When various journals ascribed to him the programme of supporting Russia's advances on Constantinople, he instructed the *Hamburger Nach-*

The larger part of the work for national unification, with the exclusion of Austria, was achieved with the founding of the North German Confederation. Its completion was still further facilitated by the French Emperor, who, in his rôle as arbiter of the Continent, went so far as to demand the Bavarian Rhine Palatinate and Rhine Hesse, together with Mainz, as compensation for Sadowa. The result of this was the speedy conclusion of negotiations for treaties by which the south German States bound themselves, in case of war, to place their armies under the command of Prussia. The two outlying Powers of Europe allowed it to come to pass, England more willingly and easily than Gortchakov's Russia, that from henceforth the internal affairs of Germany could no longer serve as a pretext for foreign interference or ambition. After the sanguinary settlement with her restless neighbour, who had followed his traditions in being unwilling to permit the rise of [1] a

---

richten on December 17, 1892, to publish the following : " The Prince has never been of the opinion that the support of Russia's plans should be the business of German diplomats ; but he has held the view that it was not for Germany to hamper Russia in carrying out her projects. Herein lies a great difference. The business of blocking the Russian advance naturally belongs to those Powers whose interests would directly suffer from Russia's advance."

Writing to the German Crown Prince, July 15, 1880, he justified the sending of officers and officials to Turkey, with the words : " If the Chauvinists, the Panslavic, and the anti-German elements in Russia should attack us, the attitude and the fighting power of Turkey would not be a matter of indifference to us. She could never be a menace to us, but under certain circumstances her enemies could possibly become ours also."—Hohenlohe, *Denkwürdigkeiten*, vol. ii, p. 302.

" Bismarck, with his clear view of the future, was fully aware of the ever-approaching danger. Openly and covertly he blocked the Russian expansion projects, and when he appeared to encourage them, as in Constantinople and the Balkans, he did it only in order to cramp the Tsar's policy by arousing the strongest antagonism in the other Powers."—Johann Haller, *Die Auswärtige Politik des Fürsten Bülow, Süddeutsche Monatshefte*, January 1917, p. 423.

[1] " Louis Napoleon not only saw no danger to France in the aggrandizement of Prussia in Northern Germany, but rather an obstacle

United Germany, the final act in the unification of Germany was consummated in the Palace at Versailles. The French longing for the Rhine, dating from the age of the Louis's, had survived the French Revolution and the rise and fall of the Great Napoleon. It cropped up again during the Second Empire and disappeared after 1870, only to be well preserved below the surface that it might shoot up afresh at an opportune time. Many German historians believe that the strong feeling for prestige in France was much more deeply stirred by Sedan than by Waterloo or Sadowa. Consequently it is possible that the danger threatening the new Empire from the west would have existed even without the regaining of Alsace-Lorraine, the German Thermopylae, to which Bismarck consented [1] less for sentimental historical reasons than for the need of blocking the gateway to an attack on Southern Germany. In any case, the danger could only arise if France should succeed in finding allies for a new war against Germany. To prevent this was the chief task of Prince Bismarck's far-seeing policy in the two decades between the establishment of the Empire and his retirement.

to the unification and national development of Germany ; he believed that the other German States would then feel all the more need of French protection. He remembered the Federation of the Rhine, and wanted to prevent the development of a union of all the German States " (*Gedanken und Erinnerungen*, chap. xxi). In a letter of September 13, 1865, Lord Palmerston wrote to Lord John Russell : " With a view to the future, it is desirable that Germany, in the aggregate, should be strong, in order to control those two ambitious and aggressive Powers, France and Russia, that press upon her west and east. As to France, we know how restless and aggressive she is, and how ready to break loose for Belgium, for the Rhine, for anything she would be likely to get without too great exertion."

[1] In a speech in the Reichstag on March 3, 1874, Bismarck said : " We never flattered ourselves that we would speedily succeed in making the Alsatians happy, and it was not for this end that we worked for the annexation. We have built a bulwark to protect ourselves from the invasions which have been undertaken for two centuries by that passionate, militaristic nation whose only directly exposed neighbour in Europe it is Germany's misfortune to be."

Culturally the youthful Empire was attracted to the west; historically, to the east. From the west came the danger on the Rhine which rendered it desirable to continue the amicable relations existing between the Russian and German Courts, thus to ensure protection at the rear on the Russianr fontier. Russia, however, had been, and continued to be, a State bent on conquest with repellent Asiatic and barbaric methods of government. The work that Bismarck had created required peace both for its preservation and its internal rounding out. Russia, on the other hand, wanted war because without it the Tsarist despotism over a multitude of subjected peoples could not endure. The Three Emperors' League of 1872, for the time being, allayed his anxiety to divert the course of the Russian neighbour's aggressive tendencies away from Central Europe and at least to postpone, if not to prevent, an alliance between him and the ancient enemy in the west. But as early as 1876, Prince Bismarck was asked by the Russian Chancellor, Gortchakov, who, in the previous year, had tried to pose as the saviour of the peace of Europe, whether in the event of Russia going to war with Austria-Hungary over the Eastern Question, Germany would remain neutral. The purport of the reply was that if the integrity of Austria-Hungary were endangered, Germany would be forced to come to the assistance, for Germany could not allow Austria-Hungary to suffer an injury that might endanger her existence. Bismarck's counter-inquiry as to whether Gortchakov for support in the east would be willing to enter into a treaty guaranteeing Germany's possessions met with a flat refusal.[1]

Favours could not bind Russia permanently to Germany. Bismarck always clearly realized that it was through the maintenance of the friendliest possible relations with England that the value of Germany's friendship must be brought home to the Russian despots and their Panslavic entourage. Inversely the case was exactly the same : an

[1] Cf. L. Raschdau, " Der deutsch-russische Rückversicherungs- Vertrag " in the *Grenzboten* of April 12, 1918, p. 27.

open disagreement with Russia would have made Germany dependent on England. Therefore he opposed every attempt of England, whether open or covert, to get Germany to sacrifice the Russian for an English friendship and endeavoured to avoid a prematurely definitive choice of one country or the other. As he had foreseen, the Russian Colossus, advancing across the Balkans up to the " cornerstone of the world " during the Turkish War, ran up against the opposition of the World Power, England.

At the Congress of Berlin, Bismarck was at the height of his diplomatic skill ; but in spite of all his honest brokerage, Prince Gortchakov left the Congress with his ambition unsatisfied. It was shortly after this that for the first time the cry was sounded in the Panslavic Press—" Constantinople must be conquered in Berlin " ; this afterwards, used in slightly altered form by Skobelev, became a shibboleth. Prince Bismarck had said in the Reichstag on December 5, 1876: " Only the Imperial Russian Government itself could possibly create a rift in the friendship between itself and the Prussian Government that had stood the test for a century." And during the Congress in 1878 he had remarked to Gortschakov in Berlin : " Do not force me to choose between Russia and Austria-Hungary." The contingency referred to in this warning became an actual fact by 1879.

The circumstances under which Bismarck felt himself compelled to hasten the conclusion of an alliance with Austria-Hungary have been cleared up in all details by the publication of the diplomatic documents of the Berlin Foreign Office. In a report to William I, from Gastein, September 15, 1879, the Chancellor confesses his alienation from his old partiality for a Russian alliance and the mistrust of Russian policy with which he has become imbued since the Congress of Berlin. A letter of the Tsar Alexander II to his nephew, the German Kaiser, dated August 15, 1879, containing threatening passages, he considered only symptomatic of a *mood*.[1] The explanations offered by the

[1] Vol. iii, p. 81 *seq.*

Tsar and his Ministers for this letter, on the occasion of the meeting of the Russian and German Emperors in Alexandrovo, September 4, 1879, seemed empty words to Bismarck, invalidated as they were by actual facts such as the Russian armaments, the posting of troops on the German border, the inflammatory anti-German articles in the Russian Press, the preliminary arrangements for big loans, the sounding of Paris in regard to an alliance, according to information supplied by the French Minister, Waddington. The most effective means for warding off the danger of isolation threatening Germany seemed to Bismarck to be a " defence insurance " with Austria-Hungary. He thought that this might be conducive to a continuation of amicable relations among the three Imperial Powers. Austria-Hungary was at that time willing to conclude such a defensive treaty.

The Minister for Foreign Affairs, Count Andrassy, who possessed Bismarck's confidence, was on the eve of retiring, but he postponed his withdrawal from office in order to put his signature to the treaty. Bismarck, on an understanding with the Crown Prince Frederick William, Field-Marshal Moltke, and the Prussian Ministry, urged the conclusion of the treaty in his anxiety not to miss so favourable an opportunity, which might be only transient, for providing for Germany's safety. When William I opposed the treaty he threatened to resign, and on October 5, 1879, the German Emperor withdrew his opposition.

Far more difficult in the second decade after the founding of the Empire was the task of protecting the now Allied Central Powers from the danger of an alliance between the Gauls in the west and the conquest-hungry Slavs in the east. Prince Bismarck throughout the term of his Chancellorship suffered more and more from the nightmare of coalitions. At first he succeeded by means of the good relations existing between the Prussian and Russian dynasties in drawing Russia once more to the side of the Central Powers. In the spring of 1880, the Russian Ambassador, Saburov, was instructed by the Tsar, Alexander II, who admitted that his threatening letter had been a piece of stupidity, to enter into conversations with the German Imperial Chancellor concerning the problems of the Near East. Prince Bismarck desired Austria-Hungary's participation, and after long opposition on the part of the Vienna Cabinet, he brought about the realization of the secret tripartite agreement of neutrality, at first for a term of three years. Bismarck himself fifteen years later, long after the treaty had expired, revealed it to the world, and it still survives to-day as a subject of controversy among statesmen and scholars.

The admission of Italy into the Central European Alliance proved to be a more effective measure than the above for preventing a war on two fronts. The flank protection ensured to the Triple Alliance by England on account of her Mediterranean interests, and who was at variance with France, after occupying Egypt, made it easier for Bismarck, exercising due caution and wisdom, to acquire colonies in the Pacific and in Africa. Nevertheless, the Russian shirt was nearer to his heart than the English coat. When Russia was threatened with a serious conflict after her attack on Merv, Bismarck did her a great service by bringing pressure to bear on the Porte so that the Dardanelles should remain closed to warships.[1]

Not until Prince Bismarck's last years in office, when the French eagerness for an alliance with Russia became more and more evident and Panslavic hostility was flourishing among the upper classes in Russia, did the indications of a leaning towards a closer friendship with England increase. It was the time of Boulangism in France, the beginning of the gigantic French financial oblation to Russia, the first armament orders placed by Russia in France. Compare the two speeches of Bismarck in support of the bill of the autumn of 1886, dealing with the increase in the peace strength of the German Army. In the first of these, delivered in the Reichstag commission on January 11, 1887, he still did not accept the assumption

[1] L. Raschdau, *op. cit.*

that Russia was looking for alliances and that Germany would have to face a Franco-Russian coalition, and he declared there was as little doubt as ever about Russia's friendship. He said the greatest danger was that the lawsuit between Germany and France pending for three hundred years was not yet settled, and that, under the pressure of energetic minorities, which in serious crises always determined the final decisions, and which were at that time moved by the *feu sacré de la Revanche*, a fresh passage at arms was threatening that would be the last because it would end by bleeding white at least one adversary. Italy and England were mentioned only to complete the survey, because there was no reason why " we should not have towards both Governments, and they in their turn towards us, the utmost good will." The second of these speeches, the most famous of all Bismarck's speeches, delivered on February 6, 1888, is in quite a different tone. There are complaints over the geographical fate that God had placed the French, the most militaristic and restless nation, on one side of Germany, and that on the opposite side in Russia He had allowed warlike tendencies to grow apace. Here for the first time there was mention of a national war waged with *furor teutonicus* on two fronts, and here, according to historical memoirs, the pithy words flashed out: " We shall no longer sue for love, neither in France nor in Russia. We shall not obtrude ourselves. We have endeavoured to regain the old intimate relations (with Russia), but we run after no one! " Italy and England are not mentioned save in an historical reflection or two.

Between the time of the first and the second speeches, the Treaty with Italy had been extended and a military convention added to it after Crispi's visit to Friedrichsruh ; and above all, Bismarck had written his personal letter on November 22, 1887, to Salisbury. In this he denied that there was any truth in the idea that the policy of the future Heir to the German Throne was, on principle, anti-English. He referred in general terms to the Panslavic intrigues and the internal conditions of the Russian

Empire as threatening the peace of Europe, and he invited England to form an alliance with Germany's two allies for the preservation of the *status quo* in the Near East. In his reply, Lord Salisbury abandoned his objections to England's participation in an Oriental [1] alliance on account of the possible anti-English disposition of Prince William, but he evaded Bismarck's veiled invitation for a further exchange of views concerning the Russian menace. Just as Bismarck desired to keep his hands free as long as possible, so Salisbury fought shy of a formal compact. What he was prepared to offer was at most moral support to the Triple Alliance, which Bismarck repaid and strengthened at the same time by thwarting the repeated Franco-Russian attempts to create difficulties for the English occupation in Egypt.

In spite of the reserve shown by Salisbury in 1887, Bismarck, even to the end of his Chancellorship, clung to the idea of a formal Anglo-German Alliance. The published secret documents of the German Foreign Office show that while the German Ambassador to England, Count Hatzfeldt, was his guest at Friedrichsruh early in the year 1889, Bismarck requested him to seize the first opportunity for a confidential conversation with Lord Salisbury, the British Prime Minister, in order to propose in Bismarck's name an Anglo-German treaty for a definite term of years, as mutual protection against a French attack. On January 12th, an order signed by Bismarck himself was sent to the Ambassador, now back at his post, instructing him to suggest to Lord Salisbury, without too much insistence, that he examine impartially and confidentially the feasibility of the idea of such an alliance from the English point of view. Salisbury took up Hatzfeldt's suggestion with full understanding of the significance of Bismarck's proposal and he promised to give the matter further consideration.

[1] The *Entente à trois* came into existence 1887–8 ; not indeed in the form of a treaty which would have had to be laid before Parliament, but in accordance with Salisbury's wish, through an exchange of secret notes.

He expressed to the German Secretary of State, Count
Herbert Bismarck, during the latter's visit to London in
March 1889, his appreciation of the Chancellor's suggestion,
and said he hoped still to live to see the time when the
general trend of affairs would permit him to take the matter
up.[1] He repeatedly expressed his regret that he was
hampered at the time by his dependence on Parliament
and democracy. This attempt on the part of Germany
to make connections with England did not result in discord.
On the contrary, it brought about a willingness on Salisbury's
part to go hand in hand with Germany in as demonstrative
a fashion as possible until an opportunity for closer co-
operation should present itself. As far as Bismarck is
concerned, the documents prove that in his anxious consideration of the question of Germany's security he had
already reached the point where he was seriously considering
a temporary compact with the Powers on the west flank,
and where he was revealing this desire to the English
Government confidentially and frankly by proposing a
regular treaty of alliance.

Further light is thrown on Bismarck's attitude towards
England at the close of his official career by a statement of
the Prussian Minister, Baron Lucius von Ballhausen, in
his *Bismarckerinnerungen*[2]: In a session of the Prussian
Ministry on August 17, 1889, Bismarck said, in reference to
the general political situation, that the whole end and
object of the German policy for ten years had been to win
England over to the Triple Alliance. That, he said, was
only possible if Germany constantly re-emphasized her
indifference to the Eastern Question. If Germany did
not do this, if she embroiled herself with Russia over this
question, then England would sit quietly and comfortably
back and allow someone else to pull the chestnuts out of
the fire for her. Furthermore, he complained of the German
colonial humbug which was stupidly disturbing Anglo-
German relations.

[1] Vol. iv, p. 405.
[2] Stuttgart and Berlin, 1920.

This roughly is the picture we get from the acts of the great realist. We see his greatness in the conception of his aims, and also in his resourcefulness in finding appropriate ways and means for changing conditions. In the first half of his political life what stood out most conspicuously were his bold ideas and courageous decisions; in the second half it was rather his wise moderation and his never flagging caution. In the beginning Bismarck had grappled with the problems of lack of unity in his own country, and with the racial faults of the German Fatherland; but later, after completing the structure of the new Empire, he wrestled with that destiny which the historian Hintze has summed up as follows: "Our geographical position constitutes our historical and political destiny." Therefore his policy till the very end was always directed towards Europe, and in spite of the ruthless use of blood and iron it was never a policy of prestige; but he always felt that Germany's greatness depended on her internal strength.[1]

The watchword "blood and iron" has led foreign critics repeatedly to draw the false conclusion that the essence of Bismarck's policy and its success consisted in the use of force as its means. In connection with this, the error has arisen of classing Bismarck as an imperialist. He was a royalist, not an imperialist. In spite of the hesitating and cautious steps taken by Bismarck to acquire extra-European possessions, Germany remained an inland Empire, strong in her military and intellectual ability but without any

[1] We find the following guiding principle in his political memoirs : " We must, as far as possible, prevent or limit a war, keep for ourselves the last hand in the European game of cards and not permit ourselves to be dragged prematurely from our temporizing course into one of action by any impatience, by granting any favours at the country's expense, by any vanity or by friendly provocation ; otherwise *plectuntur archivi.* . . . My ideal, after bringing about our unification, has ever been to win the confidence not only of the smaller European States, but also of the Great Powers, that the policy of Germany, after repairing *injuria temporum,* the loss of national unity, shall be peace-loving and righteous " (*Gedanken und Erinnerungen,* chap. xxx).

imperialistic ambition to compete in naval armament with
the older Great Powers, least of all with Great Britain,
who ruled the highways and coasts of the seven seas.
Just as in judging Bismarck's remarks we must not overlook
the actual aims and objects of his policy at the time of the
remark, so we can evaluate his acts correctly only by taking
into account the age and the task set him by History.
Germany was impotent at home and abroad, and needed
a strong man of action if she were to become a unified
Empire with national representation of the people. Whoever is inclined to condemn the expression " blood and
iron " should read over Carlyle's famous letter to *The Times*
of 1870, in which he shows that Bismarck pursued far
higher aims than did Napoleon with his land hunger and
overweening ambition. About the same time Ranke, the
master of the dispassionate writing of history, wrote to
Thiers that Germany was making war on Louis XIV.
Bismarck had fought for an idea that was as much a
humanitarian idea as that of the abolition of slavery—the
idea of unifying a nation that for centuries had been rent
and torn to pieces. Other peoples in similar case, e.g.
Italians, Serbs, Poles, have not attained their aims either
without blood and iron.

BOOK II

THE NEW COURSE

CHAPTER I

PRINCE BISMARCK IN RETIREMENT

WITH Bismarck's compulsory resignation, Germany entered
the new epoch that will always be known in history as
" The New Course." It covers roughly the eight years
between 1890 and 1897, from the dismissal of the first
Imperial Chancellor to the retirement of Baron von Marschall
as Secretary of State shortly before Bismarck's death.
There was an almost uninterrupted development of political
currents within the German nation during this period, under
influences arising from Bismarck's fall or from his attitude
in retirement, which was actually one of war with the
Kaiser and the new men in the Government. Bismarck
had been wounded by the way in which his unexpected
and unwelcome separation from work, for which he felt
he still possessed the energy, had been effected. With
the spirit of a valiant hero of old, he defended himself with
all his powers as pitilessly as he had waged all his political
battles.

Among the political parties, the joy at being freed from
the mighty opponent with his enormous official power
at first outweighed every other feeling of the Social Democrats, the Bourgeois Left, and the Centre. But even in
these camps the politically thoughtful, while having the
sense of liberation, were displeased that the German people
had been deprived by the will of a single person of this
greatest statesman, whom even his opponents in internal
affairs considered as still indispensable in the Empire's
foreign affairs. Bismarck's dismissal was not contrary
to any legal prescription of the imperial constitution
which he had himself created. But for the imperial

power to interfere so roughly with the creator of the Empire was a thing unheard of. Foreigners, who learned that the existing constitution gave the German Kaiser the right to dismiss the leading statesmen without the concurrence of the Bundesrat and the Reichstag, drew the conclusion that such a constitution gave wide opportunity for absolutism. As a matter of fact, the lack of constitutional check for the Crown's decision in the case of Bismarck's dismissal has had a disastrous effect on the later course of the internal and external fate of Germany. There was something unhealthy in the way the absolutism of the Kaiser developed by leaps and bounds ; under Bismarck's successors the position of Chancellor never recovered from the blow which the Kaiser had dealt it by his high-handed treatment of Bismarck. As seen from abroad, the Imperial Chancellor, the Bundesrat, and the Reichstag very soon disappeared behind the Kaiser, of whom Bismarck, after his dismissal, coined the phrase: " He wants to be both Kaiser and Chancellor." At the moment when he was separating himself from the surpassing adviser of William I, the Kaiser telegraphed to the Grand Duke of Weimar: " The post of commanding officer on the ship of State has fallen to me. The course remains the same—' Full steam ahead ! ' "

It was in opposing this declaration that the common expression " The New Course " arose. The Bismarck Fronde, which grew out of the opposition to the personal behaviour of the Kaiser and to his policy, fought this course with increasing bitterness. In general, the contest was carried on in accordance with the wishes of the resentful hermit at Friedrichsruh, and in essential details according to his personal instructions. There was no possibility, nor was there any intention, that this should remain concealed. But as the gigantic figure of the old Prince himself appeared again and again behind the almost daily Press battles, the Fronde gained many members from the host of faithful supporters for whom the veneration of Bismarck signified an estimable form of opposition to the Kaiser's

WILLIAM THE SILENT AND WILLIAM THE GARRULOUS

Guillaume le Bavard : "C'est tout de même drôle qu'en se taisant on puisse devenir un grand homme !"

(J. Braakensiek, in *Weekblad voor Nederland*.)

new method. Professors and students in the universities, the teaching staff of the gymnasia, and even of the primary schools, stood in the foreground in demonstrations of this sort ; but the leaders of the agrarian interests, united under the common name of Agrarians, became the picked political troops of the Bismarck Fronde. They organized their followers into an offensive and defensive Farmers' Alliance against the policy of commercial treaties inaugurated by Bismarck's successor, Caprivi.

When General Leo von Caprivi, General Staff Officer in the Franco-Prussian War, later Chief of the Admiralty and Commander of an army corps, succeeded Bismarck, he realized clearly that he would be always overshadowed by his great predecessor in the Chancellorship. In the early days of his retirement Bismarck spoke very favourably of the personality of the new Chancellor to foreign journalists. This lasted, however, only a short time, for very soon, both in conversations at Friedrichsruh and in articles in the *Hamburger Nachrichten,* more or less sharp criticism of Caprivi's actions set in. On the occasion of the first treaty concluded after Bismarck's retirement, by which Germany acquired the little island of Heligoland, lying off the German harbours in the North Sea, in exchange for the recognition of England's rights to Zanzibar, the criticism from Friedrichsruh was still fairly moderate. The *Hamburger Nachrichten* did indeed approve the excellent intention of cultivating relations with England, but it asserted that Bismarck would not have concluded the treaty in that way.

During the negotiations over the Colonial Agreement with England, the Ambassador at London, Count Hatzfeldt, had had opportunity to display his unusual diplomatic ability. He had the especial advantage of knowing intimately the peculiarities and habits of the English Prime Minister, Lord Salisbury. The task was not easy. It was made particularly difficult because public opinion in England was dominated by the idea that Zanzibar was an English creation which was insufficiently protected by a

c

weak Government and that English trade there was suffering severely from the presence of German traders. It was believed that the English merchant came into constant conflict with German interests and that every settlement between the two Governments would lead only to further limitations to English expansion. Lord Salisbury had the idea of settling the rival land claims of both parties by arbitration. The colonial chauvinism of both countries stood in the way of a delimitation of spheres of influence. Salisbury's further endeavours to bring about a treaty were rendered more difficult by Stanley's inflammatory speeches. In order to bring about a happy conclusion, Hatzfeldt proposed to Salisbury that they should for once, not as officials but simply as " private gentlemen," discuss the matter fully and frankly *sans aucun préjudice*. Salisbury at once agreed, and the result of that highly confidential conversation was embodied in the following main points : England was to take over the protectorate of Zanzibar ; Germany was to renounce Witu in favour of England. Germany was to receive certain territorial advantages on the lakes of Nyassa and Victoria Nyanza ; further, the full possession of the coast on the mainland, whose administration only had hitherto been granted to Germany by the Sultan of Zanzibar; and, finally, by an Act of Parliament the island of Heligoland. The final difficulties in the way of the achievement of the treaty arose in the English Cabinet, which had to decide on the question of the cession of the island of Heligoland. According to a report of Hatzfeldt of June 11, 1890, some of the Ministers stubbornly opposed the Prime Minister, partly because they feared a possible reaction on the position of the Cabinet, " partly because, strange as it may sound, they thought they must attach real value to the possession of Heligoland." [1]

Bismarck did not set a high value on the possession of Heligoland. Even in his *Gedanken und Erinnerungen* he looked upon the acquisition of Heligoland as a burden laid upon the German Empire. He preferred—strangely

[1] Vol. viii, p. 25.

enough—to have Heligoland protected by English neutrality
rather than to have it made the easy point of attack for a
French squadron.   He thought only of a French blockade;
the possibility of an English one never entered his mind.
In this connection it is to be noted that even under Bismarck
the question of a transference of the island to German
hands had been weighed.[1]   As a matter of fact, Heligoland
was of greater value to Germany than the acquisition of
Zanzibar could have been, for the island filled a gap in
Germany's defences.   As early as 1883 Caprivi had stated
in a memorandum that the North Sea Canal could not
acquire its full value for purposes of war until Heligoland
passed into Germany's possession.   But we see how little
Bismarck had trained his Germans in foreign affairs by the
fact that it was just the Zanzibar-Heligoland Treaty which
served as the impetus to the founding of the General
German League (Allgemeiner Deutscher Verband), which
was formed by those who opposed the cession of Zanzibar
to England as a relinquishment of German territory.   This
League was the forerunner of the Pan-German League
(All-Deutscher Verband).   Karl Peters was chosen as its
first president; however, he soon returned to East Africa
as Imperial Commissioner.

In 1883, on his return to Berlin after a somewhat lengthy
stay in England, he published an article in the *Gegenwart*
in which seriously and passionately he exhorted all Germans
to join the Anglo-Saxons in the contest for overseas
possessions.   The conscious antagonism towards Anglo-
Saxons has remained a fixed characteristic of the Pan-
German movement.   These Anglophobes wanted Germany

[1] The idea of exchanging Heligoland for colonial advantages was
first mentioned by Chamberlain in a conversation with the Secretary
of State, Count Herbert Bismarck, when the latter was sent to London
in March 1889 to discuss an offer of alliance with Salisbury.
Cf. *supra*, p. 26.   Chamberlain was not at that time a member
of the Government, but he exercised great influence both on Parliament and the public.   His suggestion was to exchange Heligoland
for Angra Pequena and its Hinterland.

to pursue a World Policy not only without England, but even directed against England, quite untroubled by the fact that the friendship of England, as well as that of the United States, was indispensable for the German Empire, whose supply of raw materials and foodstuffs was inadequate.

Nevertheless, the skirmishes between Friedrichsruh and Berlin, between the old and the new Chancellor, were still carried on with a tolerable degree of consideration after the publication of the Anglo-German Colonial Agreement, June 1, 1890. Then came the journey to Vienna. What the editor of *Die Neue Freie Presse* published as the direct statement of Prince Bismarck, who had gone to Vienna for the wedding of his son Herbert, was in fact a passionate declaration of war on his successor. " I did not enter the Reichstag (Bismarck, after his retirement, had been elected a member of the Reichstag) because I had to attack the Government *en visière ouverte*, as leader of the Opposition so to speak. It is true, though, that I have no personal obligations towards the present members. The bridges have been demolished." Finally, he complained that the personal confidence of the Tsar was gone and that the wire that had connected Germany and Russia had been broken.

At first it was not clear what had caused this shrill and irritated tone, nor how one was to explain why Prince Bismarck had so compromised the German Government before the whole world. But the outburst of a deep resentment that had assumed the proportions of a personal hostility became comprehensible and even excusable when Caprivi's order of June 9, 1892, to the Viennese Ambassador, Prince Reuss, appeared in the *Reichsanzeiger*.

Caprivi had been deserted by his good genius when he put his name to that telegraphic order to Prince Reuss. Its contents were objectionable and deeply insulting to Prince Bismarck. Its object was to prevent an audience of the Prince with the Emperor Francis Joseph. Furthermore, the Ambassador was instructed not to attend the wedding of Count Herbert Bismarck if he received an invitation; and Prince Reuss was to advise the Austro-Hungarian Minister of Foreign Affairs, Count Kalnoky, that the German Kaiser would take no notice of the wedding.

After the publication of this so-called Uriah letter there was a storm of enthusiasm for the offended old Chancellor. The homeward journey from Vienna became a real triumphal progress for the Prince and a horrible tempest for his successor.

Caprivi was a soldier through and through. Immediately upon taking office he had made a strategic plan for the relations with his predecessor, the outline of which was as follows: The Kaiser had exercised an uncontestable right when he dismissed Prince Bismarck. Consequently there could be no question of a dispute between the Kaiser and the former Chancellor. If the Prince, in spite of this, should lift the battle-axe against the Emperor, he would be in the wrong. Most generals, if called from their own field to that of politics, would be tempted to attach more value to the strict delimitation of the different spheres of competence and to the classification of tasks according to departments and boxes rather than to the art of handling men. The psychological insight necessary for conducting public business was to General Caprivi foreign ground, where he moved with difficulty, hampered by his military rigidity. This explains the clumsy blunder of the Uriah letter, which was contrary to the nature of Caprivi, who was a gentleman at heart, and which did him great harm.

While Bismarck's followers were to be found in all bourgeois camps, and their political powers were also weakened by the struggle about Bismarck, the Social Democrats did their utmost to make themselves as strong as possible both in doctrine and in organization.

The Social Democratic movement increased enormously. Its dominant ideas determining course and end were Communism and Internationalism. At the Erfurt Congress in 1891, a new programme was drawn up that put an end to the old strife between the two main groups called respectively by the names of Lassalle and Marx. The Halle

Congress of 1890 had voted that "Scientific Socialism" should receive its due in their programme. By "Scientific Socialism" was meant essentially the "Communist Manifesto," which Karl Marx and Friedrich Engels had written shortly before the February Revolution of 1848, and which had been translated into many languages: first into English, then into French, Polish, Russian, Danish. Therefore, Friedrich Engels could venture to describe it in the fifth German edition of 1890 as the most international work in the whole of socialist literature, as the general programme of millions of workers in all lands from Siberia to California. In it the Materialistic Conception of History, according to which the life of nations is dominated only by economic motives, was erected into a system for the first time. Even before Marx, German and French Socialists had occasionally shown that politics were dependent on economics, that the predominant principle of history was that of economic class conflicts, and that the only revolutionary element in the world was that of the relation between rich and poor.

According to an aphorism of Goethe, general concepts and great self-conceit are always bringing about frightful calamity. The masses of the workers have never at any time up to the end of the World War manifested a more unrestrainable sense of power than in the middle of the last decade of the previous century. Fresh attempts to suppress the movement by applying drastic measures could therefore be only more dangerous for the internal peace of the Empire.

Prince Bismarck did not allow any grounds for uncertainty after 1890 as before, as to his not being afraid of a violent solution. Shortly after his retirement he spoke of a "bloody cataclysm" that would suppress the socialist disorders, and this in the near future. According to a well-authenticated statement, in the very year of his death he wanted to deprive the Social Democrats of political rights, of the suffrage, which could not be brought about without a *coup d'état*. In his address at Jena, July 20, 1892, Prince Bismarck had said he would like to assist Parliament

in regaining a permament majority and authority; he
himself, he said, had unconsciously contributed to bring
about a decline in the Reichstag's influence. In the same
speech he declared it a dangerous experiment to strive
after absolutist ideas and velleities in Central Europe.
Therefore, he wanted a Parliament with a political will of
its own that would oppose absolutist inclinations. And
at the same time was the Democratic Party to be crushed
by absolutist measures? To fight not only against the
upper forces of Kaiser, Court, and Army, but also, at the
same time, against the lower ranks of the masses of prole-
tarians, lower middle-class people, and intelligentsia who
were dominated by the idea of international brotherhood—
that was beyond the powers of a Parliament in which the
middle class and the junkers, broken up into a dozen
parties, and groups large or small, were confronted by the
united Social Democrats.

Under the third Chancellor, the aged Prince Hohenlohe-
Schillingsfürst, who had been called from Strassburg to
Berlin, devious efforts continued which, under the guise
of fighting a revolution from below, were actually aimed
at bringing on a revolution from above. Blind followers
of Prince Bismarck and the East Elbe supermen, who had
highly applauded the call "To arms! in the name of
religion, morality, and order, against the parties of revolution" which had been sounded by the Kaiser at Königsberg,
were joined by courtiers and ambitious dignitaries offering
suggestions and plans for adopting drastic measures against
the democratic demeanour of the Reichstag. Of all these
irresponsible advisers the former Chief of the General Staff,
Adjutant-General Count Waldersee, exercised the greatest
influence on the Kaiser. In an official report which
Waldersee as Commander of an army corps had to make,
as did all Corps Commanders, respecting the penetration
of socialist ideas into the standing army, he proposed a
political programme of the following points: the drafting
of a bill dealing with attempts at revolution and empowering
the Government to impose a penalty of banishment; if the

Reichstag should refuse to pass this, it should be dissolved, more than once if need be ; if the federated Governments did not consent to the *coup d'état*, Prussia should leave the federation and form a new one.   There was even the suggestion not to shrink from foreign complications in order to reach the goal in internal affairs.   However much the spirit of this proposal might agree with the Kaiser's dreams, yet he was clever enough to recognize the danger of such a hazardous enterprise.   The third Chancellor made a special effort to urge moderation upon the Kaiser.   From one passage in his diary, where he speaks of the eagerness for the fray displayed by place-hunters of high rank,[1] it is clear that he opposed the *coup d'état* as had his predecessor, Count Caprivi.

Great as were still the differences at that time between Social Democracy and middle-class Liberalism on account of the extreme theory dominating the former, nevertheless the Kaiser himself gradually brought it about by his many speeches that Eugen Richter, the old leader of the Radical Party and author of a widely circulated pamphlet, *The Erroneous Theories of Social Democracy*, emulated in the Reichstag August Bebel, the herald of the approaching " great crash,"[2] in condemning the personal rule very severely.

Other bourgeois speakers' criticisms of the autocratic behaviour of the Kaiser differed from the sharp attacks of Bebel and Richter only in tone ; and even a representative of the Right, the old leader of the (Liberal-Conservative) Imperial Party, von Kardorff, had to admit that the monarchical stock was going down.[3]

But the capital of royalist sentiment, especially in Prussia,

[1] Fürst Hohenlohe, *Denkwürdigkeiten*, vol. ii, p. 523.

[2] " Grosser Kladderadatsch."

[3] For the personal rule and its attendant phenomena *vide* Johannes Haller, *Aus dem Leben des Fürsten Philipp zu Eulenburg-Hertefeld*, Berlin, 1924, where new historical material on the Government crises, adjutant politics, and diabolical intrigues is given from the literary remains of this friend of the Kaiser.

was at that time still so great that every attempt at a
revolutionary uprising would from the very start have
suffered a sanguinary defeat. The deep exasperation
aroused in the working class by certain sayings of the Kaiser,
such as " a rabble not worthy to bear the name of Germans,"
was kept in check by a faith in the mysterious force of
development, or more exactly by the discernment that the
chief task of revolutionary Social Democracy was first
to organize the working masses. Furthermore, as early as
towards the close of the century some educated men
recognized, and some clever workers in the lower class felt,
that the Marxian theory adopted in the Erfurt programme
did not contain the last word of Wisdom. Especially
was the Marxian theory of the division of society into two
classes, that of the exploiter and that of the exploited,
and the idea of labour's degradation into a commodity,
bound to lead gradually to internal conflicts and finally to a
revision of the party dogma.

CHAPTER II

THE WIRE BETWEEN BERLIN AND ST. PETERS-BURG AND THE DUAL ALLIANCE

So long as Count Caprivi was Chancellor the public did not know what really lay at the bottom of Bismarck's Vienna indictment [1] of his successor: that he was responsible for breaking the wire to Russia. It is true that as early as June 3, 1891, the *Hamburger Nachrichten* had censured the Government because, whereas Germany had hitherto had two strings to her bow, now the Russian string had been cut without ado. And besides, on January 24, 1892, the same paper made a still clearer allusion to "a certain agreement no longer in existence." But the Press at home and abroad was still far too busy with the personal conflicts between the young Kaiser and the fallen old Chancellor and did not notice the reference to a change in the relations with Russia made by the new Chancellor. In the deliberations over the Army Bill of November 23, 1892, Caprivi merely answered the reproach that the Government had destroyed the wire with the brief observations: "We have done our utmost to preserve this wire. We only desire that it shall not divert the current from the lines that connect us with Austria-Hungary and Italy." The few touches that Caprivi added to the figure Bismarck had made use of were not sufficient to show up the real background. It was not until an article appeared in the *Hamburger Nachrichten* on October 24, 1896, that more light was thrown on this obscure matter. According to this article both Empires of Russia and Germany were mutually pledged to benevolent neutrality in case either was attacked by

[1] *Vide supra*, p. 36.

a third Power. If, for example, France should undertake an offensive war against Germany, the benevolent neutrality of Russia might be expected, and vice versa that of Germany if Russia had to defend herself from an unprovoked attack. The concluding sentence of the article was as follows: " Thus originated Kronstadt with the Marseillaise and the first rapprochement between absolutist Tsardom and the French Republic, brought about, according to our opinion, exclusively by the blunders in Caprivi's policy."

Being interpellated by the Centre, Prince Hohenlohe declared in the Reichstag that after the most careful examination of available material he could not but recognize that the motives which at that time guided German policy were of decisive weight. Marschall discreetly raised the question whether the Reinsurance strengthened the Insurance, and whether the Imperial Government in the event of a conflict between Austria-Hungary and Russia would not be in a difficult position in having to decide which was the assailant and which the assailed. Why all this twisting and turning if the agreements amounted only to a simple formula of neutrality ?

A mountain of political and historical literature has accumulated in the decades following the disclosure of the *Hamburger Nachrichten*, in which the generally prevailing view is that the renouncement of the treaty was an incomprehensible mistake, because but for it the fatal division of the Continent into two strong groups of Powers, which finally brought on the World War, might not have occurred. This view rested chiefly upon the supposition that the *Hamburger Nachrichten's* statements concerning the contents of the secret treaty were correct and complete, although the attitude of Hohenlohe and Marschall had already given rise to a suspicion to the contrary. The greater part of this literature, which for the most part overrates the Treaty of 1887, has become worthless since the text of the treaty has been published.[1]

[1] Dokumente aus den Russischen Geheimarchiven bis zum 1. Juli 1918. Auswärtiges Amt, Berlin.

Through the alliance with Austria-Hungary the German Empire had run the risk of becoming entangled in a war with Russia, merely to protect Austro-Hungarian interests on the Lower Danube. To guard against this danger Bismarck in 1881 brought about among the three Imperial Courts a secret agreement whose centre of gravity was not so much the neutrality clause of the main treaty (dealing with the possibility of a war with a fourth Great Power), but rather in the recording of an understanding concerning conflicting interests in the Balkans.

According to this understanding, Austria-Hungary was to be free formally to incorporate Bosnia-Herzegovina "at an appropriate time," and, furthermore, the prescriptions of the Berlin Treaty touching the Sanjak of Novi-bazar were to remain in force. Turkey was not to be permitted to occupy Eastern Rumelia and Balkan territory, provided Bulgaria and Eastern Rumelia avoided provoking Turkey in any way. Bulgaria was to be permitted to unite with Eastern Rumelia—but, on the other hand, was to be hindered from making any attack on neighbouring territory, especially Macedonia.

The treaty was concluded for three years, and in 1887 was extended for another three years. At the expiration of this second term neither St. Petersburg nor Vienna felt any inclination further to extend the treaty, because both sides felt they had grounds for ill-humour on account of the Serbo-Bulgarian War and the change in sovereigns at Sofia. On the other hand, at the desire of Russia the "Courts" of St. Petersburg and Berlin continued to observe the conditions of the treaty. The main treaty in its new version recognized the rights Russia had acquired in the course of history on the Balkan Peninsula, and especially the legality of her preponderant and decisive influence, "*influence prépondérante et décisive*," in Bulgaria and in Rumelia; likewise the binding character of the principle of closing the Straits, with the addition that both parties would consider the guarantee of Turkey's territorial possessions contained in the Treaty of Berlin as forfeited in the event of her violation of this principle. There was a still greater divergence in the new appended protocol from that of 1881. The earlier delimitation of the Balkan interests of Russia and Austria-Hungary was entirely omitted, and in the question of the Straits the Imperial German Court promised benevolent neutrality and moral and diplomatic support, even in case the Tsar should consider it necessary to take measures to defend the entrance to the Black Sea " in order to keep the key of his Empire in his own hand."

Moreover, besides the Reinsurance with Russia there was still another agreement that did not coincide with it, but might, under certain circumstances, run counter to it. This possibility is intimated in the illustration Count Caprivi used in a conversation with his predecessor when the latter advised extending the secret treaty with Russia: The Bismarck insurance system is like performing with five balls, which is done successfully only by an artist whose hands and eyes have been specially trained.[1] The fifth ball was Rumania. Between that State and Austria-Hungary an alliance had been concluded by Bismarck's advice in 1883, providing for reciprocal military assistance in the event of an unprovoked attack by a third party, and therefore containing also protection in the rear against Russia. King Carol thought it very important that there should be a similar alliance with Germany, because it would counteract the opposition of those Rumanians who were Pro-Russian and promoters of Rumanian Irredentism in Siebenbürgen. Hence Germany entered into the Austro-Rumanian Treaty, and Italy did likewise. The treaties were renewed in 1892, again in 1902, and finally in 1913.[2]

[1] According to Julius Eckardt's *Aus den Tagen von Bismarcks Kampf gegen Caprivi*, Leipzig, 1920, Caprivi's reply ran thus : " A man like you can perform simultaneously with five balls, while other people do well to be satisfied with one or two balls. However, I must inquire further into the matter."

[2] The text of the treaty of February 5, 1913, and that of Germany's explanation of February 26, 1913, as to why she entered into the treaty, are published in Appendix III of vol. iv of *Die deutschen Dokumente zum Kriegsausbruch*.

From the published documents of the German Foreign Office extending over the period from March 20 to June 9, 1890, it is clear that the driving-power for the non-renewal of the treaty with Russia came from von Holstein, the Senior Councillor in the political division of the Foreign Office. He did his best to convince the new Chancellor, Caprivi, as well as the new Secretary of State, Baron von Marschall, that the content of the treaty was incompatible with the treaty allegiance due to Germany's allies, Austria-Hungary and Rumania. Marschall took exception especially to the fact that the treaty pretty unequivocally promised the Straits and Constantinople to Russia as compensation for her neutrality in certain cases of war. Holstein succeeded also in finally changing the opinion of the Ambassador at St. Petersburg, von Schweinitz, during his stay in Berlin, although hitherto he had favoured the renewal of the treaty. It was the Treaty of 1883 with Rumania that turned the scale for Schweinitz, for it seemed to him at variance with the Russo-German treaty.

After his return to St. Petersburg the Ambassador reported on April 3, 1890, that the Foreign Minister, von Giers, " displayed some consternation " on learning of Germany's refusal, but that he was still clinging to the hope that they might yet succeed in concluding the treaty, perhaps through a change in the wording.

There were subsequently two more conversations in May, of which the second, that of May 15th, was by far the most important in the whole affair.[1] Von Giers explained assiduously and somewhat informally to the Ambassador that he was disturbed by the idea that after June 18th there would be no longer any written agreement in force between Russia and Germany; he said he did not attach any value to the extensive stipulations in the appended protocol nor to the strong adjectives, *préponderante et décisive* (in regard to Bulgaria), in the main treaty; his concern, pure and simple, was that there should be something in writing between the two countries.

[1] Vol. vii, pp. 17 *seq.*

Holstein at once recognized the weak point in Giers's proposition. In disclaiming obligations, he had not included the one over which Germany had felt the greatest hesitation, that of influencing Constantinople to close the Straits permanently—that obligation therefore was to stand. The impression that the Ambassador, von Schweinitz, got from the communications of the Russian Minister is shown by the following words: "According to my judgment the moment is favourable for us to secure the neutrality of Russia in the event of an attack by France, without the renewal of the obligations that are incompatible with our stipulated engagements towards other Powers." As a matter of fact, the Russian proposal in its new form, softening down to a considerable degree as it did the terms of the old treaty, was calculated to lessen the misgivings arising from the treaty allegiance due Austria-Hungary, Italy, and Rumania, and to allow full weight to the great advantage of Russian neutrality in a Franco-German war.

But there continued to be fears of Russia's indiscretion. Holstein noted on May 20th: "If we do at this time extend the clause dealing with the Straits, we do so on the assumption of secrecy on the part of Russia in a matter which, if disclosed to the English, would drive a wedge of mistrust between England and Germany." Furthermore, he referred to the fact that Italy had the right, according to the text, to be informed "*sur nos propres dispositions, ainsi que celles d'autres puissances.*" The Chancellor, von Caprivi, agreed with Holstein, as the following words indicate: "All of Herr von Giers's suggestions amount really to secret agreements, whether the form is that of a treaty, or an exchange of notes, or an exchange of letters between the monarchs. Such a secret would lay a mine underneath the Triple Alliance, to which Russia might any day put a match." The new Chancellor could also refer to the fact that von Giers had refused to renew the treaty with Austria-Hungary in 1887, because he felt that the accountability to the Russian people and to History would be too great "*si jamais la chose s'ébruitait.*"

The decisive factor in coming to a decision as to whether there should be a new treaty, or whether Russia's proposals should be rejected, was therefore the fear that an acceptance of the clauses dealing with the Straits, if disclosed, contained enough inflammatory material to irritate England and to blow up the Triple Alliance.

After unbiased examination we must acknowledge that Caprivi, who was a novice in diplomacy, did not decline to renew the treaty through stupidity or obstinacy. Although Marschall, in the interpellation debate in the Reichstag on November 16, 1896, denied that Germany had at any time ever agreed to anything that was not consonant with existing treaties, that was only a piece of sophistry necessary to allay the excitement aroused in Austria-Hungary and Italy by the revelations in the *Hamburger Nachrichten*. Unquestionably the secret clauses of the old treaty with their biased favouring of Russian claims were, from the point of view of loyalty, not above suspicion. Bismarck himself, in a memorial presented to Kaiser William II on August 19, 1888, acknowledged that a situation had been created by the Russian Treaty which might under certain circumstances become difficult.[1] That could not frighten Bismarck, who never was at a loss as to ways and means ; he was fully conscious he could always in the final analysis, in case conflicting interests grew too strong, prevent any injury to the vital interests of the Powers allied with Germany. With the experience of a long diplomatic career, and possessing the prestige of being the greatest statesman of the whole century, he had incomparably greater chances of achievement than any of his successors could possibly have. Caprivi was, therefore, not a simpleton because of the fact that he did not boast of the same consummate skill and similar achievements! As a matter of fact, the state of affairs was exactly as the then Under-Secretary of State, Count Berchem, described it in the opinion he rendered on March 25, 1890 : "So complicated a policy (as that of Bismarck), of whose success, moreover, there has

[1] Vol. vi, p. 342.

always been a question, we are not able to continue since the retirement of the statesman who was able to profit by his successes of thirty years and his really magical influence abroad." [1]

Thus we arrive at the apparently paradoxical conclusion: the refusal to renew the treaty would have been a mistake if Bismarck had continued in office; it was a necessary act of precaution since he had retired.

Had there really been a causal connection between the non-renewal of the Reinsurance and the conclusion of the Franco-Russian Alliance, as was Bismarck's opinion published in the *Hamburger Nachrichten*? From the document it appears that it was not so much Germany's refusal to renew the Reinsurance as the renewal of the Triple Alliance in 1891 that had influenced the Russian Government in an anti-German direction. Without a doubt the Russo-German Secret Treaty had formed a barrier against the fraternization of Republican France, thirsting for *la revanche*, and Russia's Panslavic and nihilistic forces. Nevertheless, the barrier had been weakened between the years 1886–90 as a result of the great progress in the Franco-Russian rapprochement. We need only to recall that in 1887 France delivered to Russia 500,000 Lebel rifles on receiving the promise that they would not be used against France, and that she began to place at Russia's disposal billions upon billions of francs for armaments. Whether the Dual Alliance might not have been concluded even if the Russo-German Treaty had continued can neither be absolutely asserted nor conclusively refuted.

The Russo-German Secret Treaty could not exert any influence on the temper of the Russian people. The establishment of the Dual Alliance all depended on whether Alexander III could or could not be induced to abandon his abhorrence of the Republican Government of France. How difficult it was to cure the Tsar of his antipathy to an alliance with Republican France may be seen from the following incidents.

[1] Vol. vii, pp. 4 *et seq.*

On May 27, 1891, Schweinitz reported from St. Petersburg
having heard from his Italian colleague, Baron Marochetti,
that France's attempt to obtain the Tsar's assurance of
co-operation in case of war had failed. According to a
note recorded by the Chancellor, Caprivi, the Minister
of Foreign Affairs, von Giers, told him during a call,
November 25, 1891, that at the banquet given in honour
of the French squadron at Kronstadt on July 25th of that
year the tune of the "Marseillaise" had been played, but
that the words had not been sung, and that after the first
measures had been played, the Tsar had said "Assez." [1]

From many passages in official German reports we get
the impression that German diplomacy was inclined to
build too securely on the Tsar's antipathy to an alliance
with France. The Ambassador, von Schweinitz, is an
exception, for after the interchange of demonstrative
courtesies, especially that of conferring the highest Russian
order on President Carnot,[2] he noted a change in the
situation.

But the retired warrior full of resentment was a very
different person from the Bismarck at the height of his
power, who was thoroughly distrustful of Russia's internal
conditions, and who could trust himself to perform the
trick with the five balls without danger of one ball's coming
into collision with the others and falling to the ground.
In his reminiscences and admonitions he lingered longer
over the experiences of the sixties and the seventies of
the last century than on those of the last decade of his
official career. The old friendly relations of the time of
Tsar Alexander II were revived in his mind, and both the
disagreeable experiences with Russia in the period following
the Congress of Berlin, and the teaching of the "picture
of forty years" in his speech of February 6, 1888, sank
almost entirely into the background. The counterpoise
was lacking to the aged Imperial Chancellor's authoritative
statements about the necessity of leaning on Russia. What
had been, towards the close of his official career, the end

[1] Vol. vii, pp. 207 and 227   [2] Ibid. p. 204.

and object of his policy for Germany, to win England,[1]
seemed now to have become valueless, or to have been
forgotten.

Therefore, at Bismarck's death the impression survived
among the German public that his most valuable legacy to
the nation was the friendship with the Tsar which his
successor had not sufficiently cultivated, although with
moderate skill it might have been preserved. This dogma,
faithfully cherished by the bulk of the followers of the old
Chancellor, offered the most serious obstacle in every attempt
to bring about a reliable adjustment of the differences
between the strongest Continental Power and England
with its world power.

The eyes of the seer in the Saxon forest had grown dim
and weary during the bitter experience of the eight years
following his retirement, and on July 30, 1898, they closed
for ever. At first his contemporaries in Germany remembered from his political legacy much more vividly the
utterances of his last years of suffering than the doctrines
of his long and incomparably rich creative period ; and his
most ardent followers would not recognize that the old
system of courtly secret diplomacy with its Machiavellian
acts was no longer serviceable at all in the new world that
was arising.

[1] *Vide supra*, pp. 25 *seq.*

CHAPTER III

THE TRANSITION TO WORLD POLITICS

EVEN before the close of the official career of the first
Imperial Chancellor there were signs that Germany was
developing along other lines than those planned by
Bismarck. The growth of industrialism, the inevitable
attendant increase in the number of factory workers, the
necessity of selling German products overseas, the great
importance in the national economy claimed by business
and maritime interests—all these facts denote the transition
to a line of development which the highly successful champion of Germany's continental policy did not in his heart
desire and yet was not able to prevent. Along the path
of this development Germany was to run into sharp
competition with sea-going States, chiefly with England.
Germany's relations with England, which Bismarck always
considered in general as ranking second in importance to
Germany's connections with her continental neighbours,
especially France and Germany, assumed a significance in
themselves, which gradually was to overshadow everything
else. Neither Bismarck nor any of the civil statesmen who
followed him sought to create in Germany antagonism
against England. The splendid achievements of German
manufacturers, engineers, technicians, business men, and
mariners in fields where in former times England had led
or completely dominated, caused a rivalry which at first
was non-political but which later aroused antagonism. It
was not due to any ambition or desire for aggrandizement
on the part of princes or statesmen, but to the urge of their
own inner power, that the German people ceased to find

Europe the centre of gravity of their life. As a result they needed a greater measure of protection than that afforded by a purely European policy.

Even if it now seemed imperative to go beyond the extensive frontiers of Bismarck's policy, nevertheless Germany's World Policy, both in origin and character, of necessity differed fundamentally from the imperialism which had driven and was still driving other Great Powers older than Germany to found great colonial empires. Russian imperialism was seeking to expand still further its enormous territory in the direction of the highways of the sea by the political domination of European and Asiatic peoples. France's expansion movement, abetted by Bismarck, was not due to over-population ; on the contrary, in her acquisitions in North and West Africa, at all events, a contributing purpose was that of augmenting the French Army by means of available coloured troops. It was not so much the need of exporting goods as the existence of surplus capital available for lucrative enterprises that influenced the method by which her colonies were both acquired and governed. While Spain's old colonial power was gradually falling into decay, England had been building up a world empire by reason of her control of the seas. It had territory with climate suitable to colonization, and possessed colonies producing raw materials and colonial wares, and offering excellent markets for the exchange of foreign industrial products ; it possessed bases and coaling stations on all the highways of the seas. Political power and economic interests were closely interwoven. For Germany, on the other hand, neither political nor military interests played any decisive part in her colonial expansion. Her chief concern was due to her constantly increasing population, for which as yet there was very little land overseas. The prosperity of the German people was dependent upon the increase in home production and in foreign sales. Her commerce was seeking footholds on foreign shores, distant protectorates as sources for colonial products and raw materials, and finally, as many open

doors as possible in all independent States. In this respect
German economic interests were the same as those of
England.   Whoever is inclined to judge Germany's World
Policy only from the trumpet-blasts of the Kaiser will do
it an injustice.   In reality, in accordance with her deepest
nature, she has not been prompted by any zeal for acquiring
political power, and she has been far less imperialistic than
the other Great Powers.[1] We shall see further on that
even English statesmen at first took the German Kaiser's
pompous proclamations for what they actually were, the
dreams of an impetuous world-benefactor ; and England
took no defensive action until the dreams received a real
basis through the building of a great fleet of battleships.

The first step in World Politics that the Empire took
under the third Chancellor appeared to be the policy of
the Free Hand for the extra-European world, which seemed
inconsistent with the alliance policy for Europe.   Germany
joined the opponents of the Triple Alliance, Russia
and France, in protesting against the Peace Treaty of
Shimonoseki, with which a victorious Japan had saddled
China, April 17, 1895.   The protest was directed against
the provision of the treaty by which Japan was to receive
not only the island of Formosa, but also the southern part
of the peninsula of Liau-tung, with the fortified harbour
of Port Arthur.   They did not wish Japan to set two
" sentinels " at the commercial highways leading into China
and so to obtain the economic and political ascendancy
over the Middle Empire.   Since the three Powers persisted
in their protest even after the ratification of the Peace
Treaty, May 8, 1895, Japan yielded to pressure and
renounced the peninsula of Liau-tung.

Russia, of all the three Powers, had the strongest political
reasons for protecting herself against the transference
of the peninsula of Liau-tung to Japan.   In Russia's
endeavour to prevent Japan from acquiring Liau-tung,
she could confidently count on the support of France, her

[1] Cf. O. Hintze, "Deutschland und das Weltstaatensystem" in
Deutschland und der Weltkrieg, Leipzig, 1915.

new ally in Europe. For plainly it was not a matter of political indifference to France, the possessor of Indo-China, that China was to be subjected to the controlling influence of Japan. At first, however, Germany's reasons for becoming the third party in an East Asiatic Alliance were not clear, and were the subject of controversy. It is true that German commerce had acquired a position in China that was already stronger than that of Russia and of France. Of the foreigners in China, the Germans had the second greatest number. Many of the leading commercial houses in the Chinese treaty ports were German firms. The German-Asiatic Bank had been in existence seven years, and a German mail-steamer service nine years. But the German Empire was not politically interested in the same way as were the two other associates in the protest; on the contrary, from the very beginning there was the chance of losing something of political value—for Japan, hitherto friendly and grateful, might be alienated from Germany.

In the light of the published documents from the German Foreign Office, the preliminary history and the course of the East Asiatic Triple Alliance were as follows:

During the eighteenth century violent conflicts occurred repeatedly between Japan and China in regard to the legal status of Korea. China claimed sovereignty and treated Korea as a tributary State. According to a treaty of 1885, China and Japan both were to have the right, in case of fresh disturbances in Korea, to send troops there, only, however, after mutual agreement. When, in 1894, China sent troops into Korea, Japan, maintaining that Korea was an independent State, declared war on China. There was no doubt from the very start about Japan's extraordinary military superiority. The important question now was, what attitude the Great Powers with East Asiatic interests would take towards the triumphal progress of the Japanese, and what peace terms Japan would demand. It was generally feared that Japan could not be checked in her rapid advance, and that she would conquer continental territory of China. The first Great Power to suggest an

exchange of views was England.   The English Ambassador,
Sir Edward Malet, presented a note of the date of October 7,
1894, to Berlin, in which the question was raised whether
Germany were prepared to intervene with England, France,
Russia, and the United States on the basis that Japan
should receive reparation for the cost of the war, and that
the independence of Korea should be declared and guaran-
teed by the Powers.   The suggestion was treated in Berlin
as premature, and then was dropped also by the British
Prime Minister, Lord Rosebery.   The Japanese Ambassador,
Viscount Aoki, keenly appreciated Germany's loyal attitude.
Japan had at this time not yet announced her peace terms.
The Japanese military party was demanding the cession
of Port Arthur with its Hinterland.   The German Secretary
of State, Baron von Marschall, the English Secretary of
State, Lord Kimberley, and the Russian Minister, Prince
Lobanov, were all of the opinion that such a cession would
eventually be equivalent to a protectorate over China.
Germany offered as a programme the preservation of the
status quo on the continent, for otherwise China's existence
would be endangered, and European Powers might be expected to make territorial acquisitions there from which
there might result not only a shifting of power in East Asia,
but even the danger of a European war.   Therefore,
Germany joined in the protest now proposed by Russia
against continued occupation of continental territory in
China.   At first the Kaiser had made no secret of his
admiration of the military achievements of the Japanese,
and as late as April 2, 1895, he did not consider the Japanese
claims excessive.   Directly afterwards his mood changed,
the horrible spectre of the " Yellow Peril " emerged and
disturbed the mind of William II.   He saw in the East
Asiatic conflicts the prelude to a new Mongolian assault
upon Christian Europe, under the sign of Buddha.   But it
was less the catch-phrase itself than the peculiar fervour
with which the Kaiser seemed to make the antagonism
towards the yellow race a German question that injured
Germany in the eyes of Asiatic peoples.   The picture that

was all too familiar, which represented the gentle, luminous Buddha as a horrible idol enthroned above blood and fire, was a challenge to do battle for the Cross, as were the Kaiser's own words : " Nations of Europe, guard your holiest possessions ! " It was not difficult for Asiatics to see that this mistaken programme was an unjust challenge from a ruler who himself placed his Cross of Christ along-side of the Turkish Crescent.

On March 6, 1895, instructions were sent to the German Minister in Tokio to recommend to the Japanese Government that they should hasten the conclusion of peace and show moderation in the terms, since China had asked the Great Powers of Europe to intervene. " The more the Powers claim from China as the price of their trouble, just so much less will be left for Japan." Japan's demands on the mainland, it was added, were especially likely to bring about intervention. Through some oversight in Tokio, this good and friendly counsel did not come promptly to the knowledge of the Minister-President, Marquis Ito.

In the meanwhile Japanese military operations had continued. At the beginning of April, Japan made known her peace terms. Port Arthur, with its Hinterland for the purpose of securing Korea's independence, constituted, together with Formosa and Pescadores, the chief feature. The English Government, who had remained continuously passive since their premature suggestion of a joint intervention, resolved, in a Cabinet meeting of April 8th, that English interests were not injured enough by Japan's peace terms to justify intervention. By this clever decision England at the outset secured Japan's gratitude and kept the door open for the alliance she concluded with Japan in 1902. Finally, on April 17, 1895, China, completely powerless and fearful of the fate of her capital, Pekin, consented to sign the peace treaty of Shimonoseki in spite of Japan's harsh terms. On April 23rd, the three intervening Powers lodged a protest in Tokio, as agreed upon, against the peace treaty. Moreover, as bad luck would have it, the German protest turned out to be harsher and more emphatic than those of France and Russia.

The German Minister in Tokio, who was no friend of the Japanese, exceeded his instructions, for he presented as the German note an almost literal transcription of the brief statements that had been cabled to him simply to guide him as to what he should say. These statements were in marked contrast to the courteous language of both the other intervening Powers, and provoked much ill-humour in the Japanese Government, reverberations of which the German Ambassador, Baron Mumm von Schwarzenstein, had to acknowledge as late as 1907.

According to the German official documents it appears as though von Holstein had had little share in the official handling of the question of intervention. Not until the above-mentioned piece of bad luck did he take a more prominent part. Just those first years of Prince Hohenlohe's Chancellorship was the time when this eccentric person, highly gifted, of encyclopædic knowledge, but misanthropic and full of whimsical suspicions, was able most easily to exercise his influence. From his almost daily conversations with me at this time, I know that in the establishment of the East Asiatic Triple Alliance Holstein was actuated by thoughts of Europe. His chief concern was to prevent the Franco-Russian Alliance from receiving a baptism of blood. The danger of a baptism of blood was, he believed, dispelled by Germany's joining in the interference in East Asia. Another dominant motive was that of supporting Russia in her plans in East Asia, which meant obstructing the Panslavic yearnings for expansion in Europe. But, it might be objected, the same result might have been achieved, without running the risk of losing Japan's good will, by following England's example of maintaining benevolent neutrality. Still, Holstein was within the bounds of the Bismarckian traditions in his fundamental notion that European politics were what chiefly mattered. As a matter of fact, Bismarck had expressed his opinion con-

cerning Germany's participation in the new Triple Alliance
in the *Hamburger Nachrichten*, where he said that he feared
" a straining after prestige " was playing a part in this
" leap in the dark." The commendable aim of proving
that Germany had no desire of interfering on England's
behalf in the Russo-English antagonism could certainly,
he said, have been accomplished by a declaration of
benevolent neutrality. Germany's conspicuous change to
an anti-English policy in Eastern Asia seemed to him
symptomatic of the constant lack of that important faculty
of being able serenely to bide one's time.

After the realization of its immediate object, that of preventing a Japanese Gibraltar at the entrance to the Gulf
of Petchili, with its political and economic consequences,
the East Asiatic Alliance, formed for a special purpose by
Russia, France, and Germany, fell apart.

The service done to Russia had given Germany a natural
claim to participate, in the same ways as the other partners
of the East Asiatic Alliance, in the Chinese loan which was
necessary to meet the Japanese war debt, and which amounted
to about a billion marks. Instead of which, the negotiations
between the financiers of the three intervening Powers, who
had been joined by the English Rothschilds, were frustrated
by a partial loan of 310 million marks, made with the
sanction of Witte, the Russian Minister of Finance. Paris
banks supplied the gold on Russia's guarantee of the prompt
payment of interest. In this way both partners, quite by
themselves, without Germany's assistance, played the rôle
of benefactor to China, and the impression was borne out by
the facts : that Germany had only secured advantages
for Russia by her protest against the Japanese peace terms,
and that she herself had gone away empty-handed. After
France had obtained a rectification of her Indo-Chinese
boundary from China, German newspapers insisted with
increasing fervour that Germany ought to demand compensation for her co-operation in protecting China, if possible
in the form of a base for her navy and commerce. The
economic interests were already so important that German

diplomacy could see profit in the task of acquiring a base. The favourable opportunity for achieving this end occurred after the murder of the two German Catholic missionaries in Southern Shantung in the autumn of 1897.

The acquisition of Kiao-chau as a base for Germany's navy and commerce was not consummated so smoothly and so independently of high politics as persons contemporary to the event believed at the time. For this reason we wish to examine more in detail contemporary official statements and reports.

In a letter to the Tsar, dated April 26, 1895, the Kaiser not only offered his support in the great task of defending Europe against an invasion by the yellow race, but also expressed in the following words his desire for a reciprocal service for protecting Russia's rear in Europe : " You will please see that Germany, too, is allowed to acquire a harbour somewhere that is not inconvenient to you." The Tsar's answer to this letter is not among the German official documents, but from the memoirs of Prince Hohenlohe [1] we know that during his visit to Peterhof, September 11, 1895, the Tsar spoke of the Kaiser's letter of April 26th, and observed that his reply at the time was quite in the affirmative. In a telegram of September 1, 1895, from Werki, his Russian estate, Hohenlohe communicated to the Secretary of State, Baron von Marschall, a dispatch which he had received from the Kaiser, who declared that the moment had arrived for occupying Wei-hai-wei. He reminded Hohenlohe at the same time that as far back as the previous spring he had made sure of the Tsar's consent, in writing, to the occupation of some place in China. The Secretary of State, von Marschall, succeeded in making clear to the Kaiser the " incalculable import " of such an act. Wei-hai-wei at that time was occupied by Japan as security for China's payment of the war indemnity. The Kaiser's eagerness to acquire a base on the coast of China was still further excited by newspaper reports, according to which England was planning action in Chinese waters

[1] *Denkwürdigkeiten*, vol. ii, p. 521.

on account of the murder of English missionaries in August 1895. The year 1896 passed in discussions and investigations in official quarters in Berlin, as well as on the spot in Eastern Asia, as to the choice of a place suitable for naval and commercial purposes. The coaling station originally demanded by the navy gradually transformed itself into a naval base that could at the same time serve for the founding of a German colonial settlement. The choice of a landing-place fell upon the Bay of Kiao-chau (August 1897).

The execution of this resolution was hastened by the news that two Catholic missionaries under German protection had been attacked and murdered in Shantung, November 1897. " Now or never," telegraphed the Kaiser to the Foreign Office, November 6, 1897. Von Diedrichsen, the admiral in command, received orders instantly to sail with the whole squadron for the Bay of Kiao-chau and to exact full expiation. Even before the squadron arrived there, the Kaiser, by telegraph, once more asked the Tsar for his consent, and received the reply that he, the Tsar, could neither sanction nor oppose Germany's action, since Kiao-chau had been only temporarily, during 1895 and 1896, in Russia's possession. From the Tsar's answer, therefore, it could be assumed that Russia was no longer interested in Kiao-chau. Nevertheless, during the meeting of the two Emperors at Peterhof in August 1897, Count Muraviev, the Minister of Foreign Affairs, broached the subject of Russia's *droit du premier mouillage*, and put this in writing. He now, on November 10, 1897, transmitted a note to Berlin in which he asserted Russia's prior right to the use of the harbour of Kiao-chau, and at the same time announced that Russian ships were being sent there. Probably the Minister had no knowledge of the Tsar's answer to the Kaiser's announcement of November 7th, that the German squadron had been sent to Kiao-chau. The lack of agreement between the Tsar and his Minister, which could easily have led to serious tension between Berlin and St. Petersburg, caused the Chancellor, Prince Hohenlohe, to sound Lord Salisbury, through the Ambassador in London. Count Hatzfeldt got the impression from his conversations with the English Premier that the latter would raise no difficulties on account of Kiao-chau and, what was more, that the German occupation of the bay was not unwelcome. The Russo-German tension ended all at once when, on December 4, 1897, the Russian Ambassador, Count Osten-Sacken, presented to the German Foreign Office the transcript of a telegram from his Government stating that in view of the German occupation of Kiao-chau, the Tsar, after obtaining the consent of the Chinese Government, had ordered the Russian squadron to proceed to Port Arthur and to remain there until further notice. The Tsar, it was added, was convinced that Russia and Germany could and should go hand-in-hand in the Far East. After that there was no more talk of Russia's right of anchorage in the Bay of Kiao-chau. In Berlin it was believed that this sudden favourable change, which was scarcely to be expected after the difficulties raised by Count Muraviev must be ascribed to the influence of Witte, the Russian Minister of Finance.

The formal conclusion of the treaty by which China leased to Germany the whole bay and some square miles of land, with the conveyance of sovereign rights, dragged on until March 6, 1898. In the meanwhile a rash step of the Russian Government had threatened anew the peace of the Far East.

On January 1, 1898, the Russian Ambassador, Count von Osten-Sacken, had presented to the German Secretary of State, von Bülow, a promemoria that contained a programme for the future of the northern domains of the Chinese Empire. Russia demanded nothing less than that she should exercise exclusive influence not only in Manchuria, but also in Tschili and in the Chinese portion of Turkestan; furthermore, that all foreign military instructors should be withdrawn from these regions. Russia herewith announced her claims to the inheritance of a huge territory comprising the lands between the boundaries of Afghanistan and the Japanese Sea. This Russian scheme, which constituted a challenge to all the Great Powers, especially to England and to Japan, was not taken seriously in Berlin. And, indeed, Russia herself was satisfied for the time being with the demand for the permanent occupation of Port Arthur and Talienwan, and for the concession of a branch-line for the Manchurian Railway by way of Kirin and Mukden (the Russo-Chinese Treaty of March 27, 1898). Wei-hai-wei, following an understanding with Japan, passed into the possession of England, whose Government guaranteed Germany's rights in a friendly declaration. During the discussions following the German occupation of Kiao-chau, Lord Salisbury had not allowed himself to be influenced by the indignation aroused in the English public over the Krüger Telegram, and on the whole he behaved in no way unfriendly to Germany.[1] The Berlin Government gladly followed his constant advice to make the regulations for international commerce as liberal as possible when making the bay a free port.[2]

A glance at the course of events in Eastern Asia after the intervention of Russia, France, and Germany in regard to the Peace of Shimonoseki shows the existence of a continuous connection between the interests of the Great Powers in Europe and their claims in the Far East. The watchword, " The East and the West are no longer separable," became a rule in politics.

Let us come back once more to Europe and the Near East. In Asia Minor bloody atrocities had again been perpetrated against the Christians in Armenia. The reforms demanded by the English, French, and Russian Ambassadors were at first bluntly refused by the Porte, but were afterwards conceded when a British squadron appeared off Beirut. It was to be feared that the massacres would be repeated. After the parliamentary defeat towards the end of June of Rosebery's Ministry, in which Grey had been the Under-Secretary of State for Foreign Affairs, Salisbury formed a Government in which he was both Premier and Minister for Foreign Affairs. Others in his Cabinet were

[1] *Vide infra*, p. 67.   [2] Vol. xiv, pp. 3–181.

the Duke of Devonshire, Balfour, Chamberlain, and Lansdowne, the last as Minister for War.

Shortly after taking over the affairs of the Foreign Office,
Lord Salisbury, in a conversation with Count Hatzfeldt,
raised the question of an Anglo-German Agreement that
should deal with the partitioning of Turkey if there were
a collapse of the Sultan's rule some time or other.   Among
other things, he suggested that Italy might receive Tripoli,
and for certain claims on the Somaliland coast might be
compensated with Albanian territory.   Berlin was at
first dumbfounded by this suggestion.   If Holstein had
apparently held aloof during the handling of the protest
against the Treaty of Shimonoseki, he now undertook the
rôle of secret director.   In this question of high European
politics he felt quite in his element.   Private telegrams
passed back and forth between himself and the German
Ambassador in England.   Salisbury must have been conscious of the tremendous difficulties connected with his
project.   To the objection that Germany did not want to
aggravate the antagonism between her two allies in the
Adriatic, and that Germany's relations with Russia might
be endangered by unrolling the Balkan Question, Lord
Salisbury replied that he was prepared to accord to Russia
an ample share of Turkey's estate.   Nevertheless, Holstein
was quite certain that Salisbury's real object was to involve
the Continent in wars in which England could play the
part of an unconcerned spectator.

Hatzfeldt, on the contrary, believed that it was the sincere
intention of the English Prime Minister to take precautionary
measures in due season to provide for the eventual break
up of Turkey, at the same time paying due regard to the
conflicting interests of France, Russia, and the Triple
Alliance.   The Ambassador's request to be permitted to
enter into further parleys with Salisbury was refused.   Von
Kiderlen, who accompanied the Kaiser to the Cowes Regatta,
was instructed to see to it that His Majesty (William II)
should not discuss anything when he met Salisbury.

Some of the London papers greeted the Kaiser with

cutting comments and advice such as to remember his maternal origin and to abstain from diplomatic experiments. Public opinion was still excited over the protest of the German Foreign Office against the article in a treaty between England and the Congo State by which a strip of land fifteen miles wide along the frontier of German East Africa was to be leased to England for a Cape to Cairo telegraph line.

After the Queen's banquet in Cowes, on August 5, 1895, Lord Salisbury explained to the Kaiser his ideas for the partition of Turkey. The Kaiser, however, refused to accept the view that Turkey was thoroughly rotten, and rejected the notion of a partition.[1]

Now even if Salisbury's proposal was not actually inspired by the desire to get some other Power to pull the chestnuts out of the fire for England, still there is no doubt that any attempt to destroy " rotten " Turkey would have been a most dangerous enterprise, involving too many delicate questions, with consequences that could not be calculated in advance ; a grandiose idea, but scarcely to be realized without severe storms and convulsions. Lord Salisbury himself, without much ill-humour, let his scheme drop. After fresh massacres in Constantinople and Trebizond a promise of reform was wrung from the Sultan by means of a naval demonstration by the Great Powers near Constantinople.

During the flights of German politics in Eastern Asia between the years 1895 and 1897 the general situation in Europe had perceptibly altered. In the Central Bloc rifts were visible that could easily widen into a breach. The French Government missed no opportunity of putting financial and economic difficulties in Italy's way, and of injuring her position in the Mediterranean. In July 1895 the Italian Minister for Foreign Affairs, Baron Blanc, drew up a promemoria which contained complaints about the insignificance of Italy's benefits from the Triple Alliance, and which demanded that the Alliance be vivified and made effective. Baron Blanc further pointed out that in asserting

[1] Book X, pp. 1–57.

E

her protectorate over Abyssinia, Italy could expect no support from her allies ; also that England had not granted Italy's desire during the war against Menelek for a right of way through British Somaliland by the Zeila-Harar route, and that the Dual Entente looked upon the Abyssinians as a people at war and not as rebels.[1] In February 1896 the French Prime Minister, Bourgeois, told a special envoy of the Italian Prime Minister, Crispi, that no French Government could afford to show favours to Italy, but must rather strive to make her existence as difficult as possible so long as Italy remained in the Triple Alliance.[2]

Moreover, Germany's other ally, Austria-Hungary, was not satisfied either with the Triple Alliance during the term of the third Chancellor of Germany, since it offered protection only in case of a hostile attack. Austria-Hungary desired something definitive—in other words, assistance in widening her sphere of influence in the Near East. Prince Hohenlohe's attitude towards the claims of Count Goluchowski, the Austro-Hungarian Minister, can be most clearly seen in a note written by himself on March 2, 1896, which concludes as follows : " We adhere to the Triple Alliance, but we must refuse to let it be used as a means for the realization of indefinite schemes on Austria's part in the East. Austria will have to be satisfied with the defensive character of the Triple Alliance if she does not want to perish."

All these difficulties within the Triple Alliance could have been endured and overcome if the German policy could have succeeded in preserving the old friendship of Great Britain for the German Empire and the Triple Alliance. The opposite occurred. Indeed, it needed very little to bring about a complete rupture between Great Britain and Germany. The danger came from South Africa.

In the London Convention of 1884 the independence of the Boer Republic in the Transvaal was curtailed by the stipulation that no treaty with a third State could be concluded without England's consent. According to England's interpretation, the Republic was to be autonomous in

[1] Vol. x, pp. 3 *seq.*   [2] Book XI, p. 288.

regard to its internal affairs, but in its foreign relations
it was to be under the supervision of the English Government. Thenceforth, in the eyes of every Englishman, the
Transvaal was little more than an English colony to which
self-government had been granted.

In South Africa exceptionally grave material interests
were at stake. The appropriation of the diamond fields
by the Chartered Company was intended to be followed
by the incorporation of the Transvaal with its gold mines
in British South Africa. Public opinion in London saw
in Cecil Rhodes the Napoleon of South Africa, and looked
upon Germany's spirit of enterprise in Delagoa Bay and its
Hinterland, and also on her repeated espousal of the Boer
cause, as the most troublesome impediments in the way
of British financial and commercial interests. When the
Kaiser's telegram was published on January 3, 1896, an
unprecedented storm of indignation burst in England.
In this dispatch President Krüger was congratulated on
having succeeded in an engagement at Krügersdorp in
repelling the invasion of Dr. Jameson's armed bands " by
his own energy, without appealing to the aid of friendly
Powers." This sounded as though the German Kaiser
had been ready to interfere in the South African quarrel
on behalf of the Boers.

The origin of the Krüger Telegram is not *fully* explained
in the documents now published in the *Grosse Politik der
Kabinette*. It was already well known that the text of the
telegram had been approved by the Chancellor and the
Secretary of State for Foreign Affairs, Baron von Marschall,
and hence must be considered a Government document.
On the other hand, there was no documentary light on the
question as to how far the Kaiser insisted upon sending
congratulations of this sort. Weighty reasons seemed to
indicate that neither Prince Hohenlohe nor Marschall
but the Kaiser himself had been the originator, although
in his book, *Ereignisse und Gestalten*, he tries to throw all
the blame on Hohenlohe and Marschall.

Volume XI of the collection of documents entitled *Die*

Grosse Politik der Europäischen Kabinette, 1871–1914, which contains all the documents of the Foreign Office covering the period of the Krüger Telegram, appeared in the winter 1923–4. That the documents relating to the days of the genesis of the famous telegram would contain a full account of the transactions and the decision arrived at was not to be expected, for the simple reason that the events in the Transvaal followed one another in rapid succession and because no minutes were kept of the discussions and resolutions. The Conference at the Chancellor's residence on January 3, 1896, occurred on the spur of the moment.

The fact that the contemporary documents failed to shed full light on the question of the real authorship of the telegram disturbed the co-editor of the collection, Dr. Friedrich Thimme, and incited him to make every possible effort to get at the whole truth of the matter. Of all those who had taken part in the discussion at the Chancellor's, not one was still living except the Kaiser. Therefore it remained to find out whether the gaps in the official documents could perhaps be filled from papers left by these participants. Dr. Thimme has given the most important results of his researches in the periodical *Europäische Gespräche* for May and June 1924. The most important evidence is to be found in the diary of Baron von Marschall, which the Baroness placed at Dr. Thimme's disposal upon his request. The following entry was made on the day on which the Krüger Telegram was sent : " January 3rd. At 10 o'clock conference with H.M. ; present the Imperial Chancellor, Hollmann (Secretary of State for the Navy), Knorr (Commanding Admiral), and Senden (Chief of the Naval Cabinet). H.M. unfolded *somewhat astonishing projects. A protectorate over the Transvaal, but I talked him out of that at once. Mobilization of the Marine Infantry. The dispatch of troops to the Transvaal. And upon the Chancellor's objection*: '*That would mean war with England*,' H.M. replied, '*Yes, but only on land.*' Then it was resolved to send *Scheele* (Colonel Baron von Scheele, Governor of German East Africa until February 1895) to the Transvaal to reconnoitre. *Also an unfortunate idea. Finally H.M. at my suggestion sent a congratulatory dispatch to President Krüger.* The joy over England's defeat is universal. Sir Frank Lascelles, who was received after the conference, confirmed the report of Jameson's defeat."

The light thrown into corners dark until then is glaring and painful. It shows clearly that although it was Marschall who proposed sending the congratulatory dispatch to Krüger, his urgent reason for doing so was to prevent something worse. The Krüger Telegram was the way out of a dilemma, an emergency exit, a compromise. What the Kaiser really desired was something far in excess of a mere congratulation.

But Dr. Thimme, in his researches concerning the Krüger Telegram, made still another valuable discovery, namely, a connection with the then so-called " unlimited naval programme." The source for this is a diary of the Chief of the Naval Cabinet, Baron von Senden and Bibran. Here we learn from an entry of January 7, 1896, four days after the Krüger Telegram was sent, that von Tirpitz considered that the psychological moment had arrived for increasing the naval estimates of 1896–7, and therefore presented a petition to the Kaiser. This shows us how ready the Admiral was to jump at every chance to realize the great ambition of his life. As we already know from the memoirs of Count Waldersee, Tirpitz had so influenced the Kaiser that he wanted to have a naval bill brought in for three hundred million marks ; a plan which, if carried out, would certainly not have been conducive to cooling the overheated feelings in England. According to Senden's diary, it was thanks only to Chancellor Hohenlohe's intervention that the Ministers in a session on the 8th decided to be satisfied with a bill for one hundred million marks. But Tirpitz in his unabated zeal contrived to have Senden sent to Friedrichsruh on January 10th to see if the old Chancellor would not come forward as the advocate of an increase in the naval estimate. Senden's notes, which are not entirely clear at this point, are supplemented by an article from

Bismarck's pen in the *Hamburger Nachrichten* of the 27th of the same month. In this article, which was probably inspired by Senden's visit, Bismarck spoke in favour of increasing the number of cruisers but not of battleships; but for this it was not necessary to exceed the existing estimate. Thus the grand old man in the Sachsenwald once again sought to curb Germany's naval policy.

Both Governments strove quietly and circumspectly to get over the thorny incident. From the very first Lord Salisbury did not want it to come to a break with Germany. He therefore begged Count Hatzfeldt, January 1, 1906, even before Dr. Jameson's defeat at Krügersdorp, to avoid every word that might sound like a threat. He instructed the High Commissioner in Cape Town to recall Dr. Jameson, and to express to the Pretoria Government his emphatic disapproval of the raid. On the other side, Prince Hohenlohe opposed with unwonted severity the yearnings of William II to interfere.[1]

To sum up in a few words the general impression obtained from the published documents, it is evident that Hohenlohe and Marschall in their official policy were labouring hard to preserve the independence of the Transvaal as defined in the London Convention of 1884, and to safeguard Germany's growing economic interests in South Africa. But none the less, in their relations with England in conformity with the reports from the Ambassador, Count Hatzfeldt, prudence governed their policy; whereas the Kaiser was willing to send a corps for disembarkation in Delagoa Bay and to listen to demands for territory. This was evident soon after the Krüger Telegram, as seen in the following incident:

The Kaiser wired to the Chancellor on January 6, 1896, three days after the sending of the Krüger Telegram, that the Transvaal representative, Secretary of State Leyds, had told him during an audience that, according to secret information from Lisbon, the Portuguese, under pretence of being forced, had as good as promised to allow the English to occupy Lorenzo Marques. He had replied that

[1] Book XI, p. 37.

he would not allow this ; that if there were a change in the ownership of the harbour, it must pass only into German or Boer hands. The Consul in Pretoria, as well as the Commander of the cruisers lying off Lorenzo Marques, were secretly to be informed of this and provided with instructions. Prince Hohenlohe, in a telegram of January 7th, pointed out that Leyds was a Hollander to whom a German protectorate over the Transvaal would be an abomination. In uncompromising language, in whose framing Holstein perhaps had a hand—the draft of this is not found among the official documents—the Chancellor continued as follows : Isolated Germany cannot go to war with Great Britain ; our chief diplomatic task is more and more to gather about us those who have like interests, and on no account to take a step alone, or to do anything that might increase the number of England's friends. It now rests with the Transvaal Government itself to take the initiative with the Powers, in order to obtain guarantees against the recurrence of similar attacks. If the Transvaal should make proposals of this nature the German Government will support them. *" This remains to be seen."* [1] Every initiative on our part is for the time being out of the question if we are not to incur the danger of being more and more shoved against England by France and Russia. At the close of his admonition the Chancellor entreated the Kaiser to refrain from any measures in Delagoa Bay. At the top of this document is the comment of the Kaiser: " I differ but acquiesce "; and at the end, also in the Kaiser's hand, " This forfeiture or non-acquisition of Delagoa Bay will have to be heavily paid for in the future, and we shall some day deeply regret it. "

In Paris, the anti-English feeling after the Transvaal Raid of the Chartered Company was as strong as in Germany. This inspired the German Government with the unfortunate idea of attempting a rapprochement with France. As was to be foreseen, London did not remain in ignorance of this step, which helped to prevent the indignation over the Krüger Telegram from dying down.

[1] Underscored in the original.

Paris papers issued the *mot d'ordre* : anything rather than such alliances ; the enemy is Germany, not England. Hatzfeldt's advice not to drive England into the arms of France was in vain.

The first to suffer from the acute Anglo-German tension were the two partners in the so-called Oriental Triple Alliance which Bismarck, in his famous personal letter of November 22, 1887, to Lord Salisbury, had suggested as a measure against the Panslavic menace.[1] For when in 1896 Austria-Hungary proposed in London that the *Entente à trois* be renewed in a more durable form, London, alluding to current feeling in England, sent a cool refusal. Thus another valuable link in Bismarck's system of alliances was lost.

It only remains to mention from the later days of the New Course the Cretan Revolt and the brief Græco-Turkish War. Crete was in itself only a small piece of the Oriental cake which Greece was greedily longing to consume. The most noteworthy feature in the progress of the diplomatic discussions concerning the Cretan Question was the gradual emergence of a rapprochement of the two great continental Powers that were chiefly concerned in Balkan affairs, Austria-Hungary and Russia. It found its expression during the visit of the Emperor-King, Francis Joseph, to St. Petersburg at the end of April 1898, not only in the cordial tone of the toasts proposed by the two monarchs, but also in a joint political action on the part of their respective Ministers, Goluchowski and Muraviev. From St. Petersburg they issued duplicate notes to the Austro-Hungarian and the Russian representatives in Bucharest, Sofia, Belgrade, and Cetinje, in which they expressed the gratification of the two monarchs at the calm attitude of the four Balkan States during the Græco-Turkish War. After Greece had explicitly rescinded the annexation declaration of February 14th, while recognizing the future autonomy of the island, the mediation of all the Powers in Constantinople could take place.

[1] *Vide supra*, p. 25.

It was advantageous for Germany's policy that Russia at that time wished to avoid a general conflagration in the Balkan peninsula, for England might perhaps have preferred to see Russia engrossed in the Near East and so diverted from her enterprises in the Far East. Baron Rosen, an excellent judge of Japan and, like the Minister of Finance, Witte, not blind to weaknesses and dangers in the Tsar's Government, directly after entering upon his duties as Russian Ambassador in Tokio, in the summer of 1897, wrote in the same strain as in an earlier promemoria : " We must be absolutely prepared for an inevitable crisis in our Japanese relations the moment we become involved in any European complications." [1]

*   *   *   *   *

A survey of the political situation at the close of the New Course presents the following picture. The German people, deeply disturbed by Bismarck's dismissal and his attitude in retirement, impressed outsiders as being on the downward path. The military strength of Germany was as great as ever, and had even been increased by Caprivi's reform introducing the two years' service. The relation of the Powers had considerably shifted, and certainly to Germany's disadvantage. Alongside of the Triple Alliance there had appeared a second strong combination of Powers, that of Russia and France. Within the Triple Alliance conflicting interests had emerged. The Italian ally was striving to strengthen her position in the Mediterranean and Red Seas. Austria-Hungary was doing the same in the Near East. Germany was warding off innovations and insisting on the defensive character of the Triple Alliance. France was busily engaged with Russia in trying to undermine the Triple Alliance. England, in view of the public's anti-German feelings, which had been intensified by the Krüger Telegram, refused to renew the Oriental Triple Alliance, and withdrew into her splendid isolation. The direction of England's destinies passed

[1] Prince Trubetzkoi, *Russland als Grossmacht*, 2nd ed., 1917, p. 53.

gradually from Bismarck to Lord Salisbury. The frictions within the divided continent of Europe afforded Salisbury a free hand, and he used it with great prudence. The intervention undertaken jointly with the Dual Alliance after the Peace of Shimonoseki brought to Germany, it is true, the Chinese port of Kiao-chau. But this acquisition while the Kaiser was raving against the " Yellow Peril " left behind it a long-continued feeling of hostility in Japan towards Germany.

It is still a great question whether Germany's participation in World Politics did not cause her to neglect to pay attention to the danger in the west, and whether the fire of *la revanche* still glimmering in the French nation was not fanned by the new political alinements favourable to France, and consequently endangering peace.

BOOK III

AT THE TURNING-POINT IN WORLD POLITICS

CHAPTER I

ATTEMPTS AT AN ANGLO-GERMAN RAPPROCHEMENT, 1898–1900

In the closing years of the last century the English Cabinet had an exceptional number of diplomatic and military disputes and difficulties to settle in the colonies. In Eastern Asia the integrity of China, where England had hitherto possessed preponderating influence, was threatened by Russia. England's offer not to seize any harbour on the Gulf of Petchili on condition that Russia would forgo the occupation of Port Arthur was declined. Russia went to Port Arthur with the obvious design of gradually separating Manchuria from the Chinese Empire, and consequently a counterpoise had to be created in Wei-hai-wei. The German lease of Kiao-chau was allowed to pass without dispute because its object was an economic one only, and, as Balfour said in the House of Commons, it would propitiate public opinion in Germany. In India a sanguinary expedition against the tribes of the northern frontier was in progress. After the death of the Emir of Afghanistan it was to be feared there would be disturbances and an increase in Russia's influence. In the Sudan there was the conflict with the Mahdi. The scheme to establish secure communication between Lower Egypt and the British possessions on Victoria Nyanza conflicted with France's endeavours to extend her sphere of influence from the Congo across Africa to the French colonies on the Red Sea. After his victory at Omdurman, Kitchener hastened to Fashoda on the White Nile, and ran up the Anglo-Egyptian flag alongside of the French one that had previously been hoisted by Marchand. This kindled a hot diplomatic dispute (October 1898). A similar race for first place had occurred in February 1898 in the Hinterland of Lagos and Dahomey, where English and French expeditions had come into threatening proximity at several points in the bend of the Niger. In the south-east of the Moroccan Empire, early in June 1898, the French, by their occupation of the oases of Tuat, made a beginning at direct communication from Algiers to Dahomey by way of Timbuktu ; and perhaps also at the penetration of Morocco up to the coast. Spain, already very feeble and involved in a war with the United States, could not prevent England from strengthening her garrison at Gibraltar. Finally, in South Africa the baro- meter indicated stormy weather. In the notes exchanged between President Krüger and the Colonial Secretary, Chamberlain, relative to the Uitlander Question, which were laid before the English Parliament, there was a solemn warning : " Her Majesty towards the South African Re- public holds the relation of a suzerain who has accorded to the people of that Republic self-government upon certain conditions, and that it would be incompatible with that position to submit to arbitration the construction of the conditions on which she accorded self-government to the Republic."

Acute diplomatic disputes with two Great Powers, campaigns in India and in the Sudan, a conflict imminent with a stubborn, courageous people of the white race well provided with excellent arms—here were reasons enough and to spare for making the effort, in spite of all economic rivalries, to conclude a formal treaty of friendship with the strongest military Power in Europe.

On March 25, 1898, the Chancellor of the Exchequer, Arthur Balfour, who was at that time acting for the Prime Minister, Lord Salisbury, expressed the desire for a rapprochement with Germany. A few days later the Colonial Secretary, Joseph Chamberlain, reverted to the same idea of an Anglo-German understanding. He said that the English Government was standing at the parting

of the ways, and that England could not continue her policy
of isolation but must look about for allies. He particularly
feared serious complications with France on account of
friction in West Africa, and he was also apprehensive about
Russia's endeavours at expansion, which menaced England's
important commercial interests in Asia. After lengthy
arguments Chamberlain said plainly that what he had in
mind were binding political agreements with Germany and
with the Triple Alliance.

This proposition of the two English Ministers at first
met with a sceptical reception in Berlin. The Secretary
of State, von Bülow, expressed his doubts as to whether
England, as an ally, would offer prompt and energetic assistance in case the adversaries of Germany and the Triple
Alliance should elect to follow the old rule of the Horatii
of fighting their enemies singly, and should direct their
first attack against Germany. In any case, he said, we
could not conclude a treaty unless it had been ratified by
the English Parliament, as otherwise, if there were a change
in the Ministry, England could easily elude her treaty
obligations if there were a war. Lord Salisbury, upon his
return from the South, where he had gone for his health in
the spring of 1898, explained to Count Hatzfeldt on June 2nd,
during a confidential conversation, that although he agreed
in the abstract with Chamberlain in desiring a rapprochement with Germany, he considered it more advisable for
Powers whose similar interests suggested joint political action
not to reduce their understanding to a formal treaty until
a case of necessity arose through some serious menace to
their interests. While Chamberlain was urging the conclusion of a treaty of alliance, Salisbury was playing the
part of Fabius Cunctator, who wished to keep the door to
peace open until the last moment. Finally, it was agreed
that the most important task of both Governments was
gradually to dispel the ill-humour still prevailing between
the two countries, by showing a spirit of accommodation
in minor questions, and thus to prepare public opinion on
both sides for a definite political agreement. The German

Ambassador, Count Hatzfeldt, was able further to report that not only all the members of the Cabinet but also the leaders of the Opposition, Lord Rosebery and Sir William Harcourt, were in sympathy with the proposals of Balfour and Chamberlain.[1] The idea of an alliance was therefore to remain " a possibility of the future," as Bülow expressed it. Shortly afterwards Salisbury, answering the inquisitive inquiry of the Russian Ambassador, Baron Staal, concisely summed up the situation in the words : " *Alliance*, (with Germany) *non ; rapprochement, oui.*"

It was easy to understand that the cool and hesitating attitude of the Foreign Office was largely due to the very natural fear of injuring the good relations with Russia. Bülow, the Secretary of State, became more suspicious and cautious than ever when he learned of the Tsar's letter of June 3rd to the Kaiser. This letter was in answer to one of the Kaiser of May 30th,[2] in which, after speaking of the enormous offers made by England in return for an alliance with Germany, he put the question to Nicky : " What will you offer me if I refuse ? " In his reply the Tsar paid him back in his own coin. He said that several months before England had made unprecedented offers in St. Petersburg with a view of destroying " in a masked way " the Russo-German friendship.[3] The Tsar's assertions were exaggerated, no doubt, but that they were not pure fabrications may be inferred from the following. On June 10, 1898, the Russian Ambassador in Berlin, Count von Osten-Sacken, told the Secretary of State, von Bülow, on the strength of information received from Count Muraviev as he passed through Berlin, that England had actually made far-reaching proposals to the Tsar.

There is also a slight connection between England's secret proposals to Russia and the famous speech which Chamberlain made in Birmingham on May 13, 1898, at the very time when he was working for an Anglo-German

[1] Vol. xiv, p. 204.
[2] *Briefe Wilhelms II an den Zaren, 1894–1914*, Berlin, 1920.
[3] Vol. xiv, p. 243.

agreement.   During the first months of 1898, the Salisbury
Government had to defend itself against violent attacks
on the part of the Liberal Opposition, on account of the
precarious situation in China.   Grey spoke in the House
of Commons of the preposterous policy of the Government
that was seriously damaging England's prestige.   In refuting
the charge that the Government had been inactive, Balfour
referred to the proposal not to take possession of any
harbour in the Gulf of Petchili on the condition that Russia
would renounce Port Arthur and Ta-lien-wan, a proposal
which the Russian Government had refused.   In his
Birmingham speech Chamberlain said : " As to the way
in which Russia secured that occupation, as to the re-
presentations which were made and repudiated as soon as
they were made, as to the promises which were given and
broken a fortnight afterwards, I had better perhaps say
nothing except I have always thought that it was a very
wise proverb, ' Who sups with the Devil must have a long
spoon.' . . . We have in the future to count with Russia
in China, as we have to count with Russia in Afghanistan,
and with this difference—that in China we have no army
and no defensive frontier.   But what was the alternative ?
What more could we have done under the circumstances
at the time, being, as we were, entirely isolated ?—for that is
the point on which I want to lay emphasis.   Some of
our critics say, ' Oh, you might have come to an understanding with Russia.'   It is easy to say that, but an
understanding takes two parties to the bargain, and Russia
wanted what we did not want and we had nothing to offer
her to induce her to desist from her plan.   And if we made
an understanding with Russia, who would guarantee that
the understanding would be kept ? "

These trenchant sentences seem to indicate that Chamberlain's object actually was, with the help of Germany, to
foil Russia in her schemes of conquest in Eastern Asia.
Therefore, after Chamberlain's idea of an Anglo-German
Alliance had been rejected, the Governments of both
countries immediately set about to create a warmer atmo-

sphere in Anglo-German relations through a spirit of mutual accommodation in issues of minor importance. The first question to be taken up in this way concerned certain colonial ambitions of Germany in Africa.

The Transvaal affair of 1896 had already made it plain that Germany was powerless to prevent England from absorbing the Boer Republics. But a fresh complication was bound to arise from the proximity of both countries to the Portuguese possessions in Africa, and this danger could be avoided by means of an Anglo-German agreement. Portugal was in great need of money ; to the detriment of her creditors, the payment of interest had been suspended ; Portuguese financiers were seeking assistance in London, Paris, and Berlin, and were offering the Portuguese colonies in Africa for sale or as collateral for a loan. In these offers England had the first option, since by an earlier treaty she had guaranteed the integrity of the Portuguese possessions.

On June 8, 1898, Count Hatzfeldt received instructions to enter into friendly discussion with Lord Salisbury about the matter as soon as possible. To this order was appended a list of desiderata representing the wishes of German colonial circles. Among others the following places were specified : in West Africa, a naval station on the Canary Islands ; Angola, including Benguela, and Walfisch Bay ; in East Africa, Zanzibar ; in Asia, Portugal's portion of Timor Island ; in the Pacific, the Samoan Islands. This list showed how far the German advocates of colonization had already progressed in their demands and needs during the few years since Germany's transition to World Politics.

The idea that England would cede Zanzibar could not seriously be entertained for one moment. The question of Timor presented no difficulties, but otherwise these conversations, which later on were conducted on the English side by Balfour, proved rather irksome. They turned chiefly on Angola and Mozambique. Both colonies were divided ; Delagoa Bay, with the harbour of Lorenzo Marques and the railroad to the Hinterland, fell within the English sphere. This put an end to the Kaiser's dreams about the Boer protectorate. The question of Samoa was for the moment not raised. As for Walfisch Bay, Salisbury was not averse to ceding it, but not without the Cabinet's assent. In the Cabinet, however, there was a majority that opposed the cession on the ground that it would seem unjustified in public opinion.[1] The treaty was concluded August 30,1898, and ratified by both parties September 26th.[2]

The great expectations which Bülow pinned to the agreement, with its prospect of a vast increase in colonial territory, were not realized. The situation necessary for making the agreement operative did not arise, for the anticipated loan to Portugal, with the Portuguese colonies as collateral, was not made. The agreement remained purely ornamental for both parties, but with this difference : England, from her old friendship with Portugal, could always count on Portugal's willingness to oblige as each case arose regarding railroad building, commercial enterprises, coaling stations, or rights of way, while Germany, on the other hand, could not.

Faith in England's political honesty would have been destroyed in those days of universal enthusiasm for the Boer cause if the Press had got wind of another secret treaty made between England and Portugal in 1899. The German Government also remained in ignorance of this so-called Treaty of Windsor. In its essence it was a confirmation of earlier treaties by which England and Portugal had mutually bound themselves to protect each other's possessions. The new compact did not, of course, necessarily prevent Portugal from burdening her colonial possessions by contracting obligations in return for loans necessary for her financial salvation, nor from inviting foreign assistance in their exploitation. But even with the most liberal interpretation it cannot be denied that the Treaty of Windsor encouraged the Portuguese to refrain

[1] Vol. xiv, p. 292.
[2] The text of the agreement, together with a secret note, is found in vol. xiv, pp. 339 *seq*.

from encumbering their colonies in this way, and therefore ran counter to the cardinal idea underlying the Anglo-German Agreement, that Portugal was not in a position profitably to administer her colonies alone.

As early as January 1, 1899, it was announced in the Speech from the Throne that the colonial possessions of Portugal must be maintained in their complete integrity as a sacred heritage of the nation, and in February 1900 the Chamber of Deputies rejected a proposal to sell the colonies. The sole advantage left Germany was that England was prevented by the secret treaty from acquiring independently economic and political rights in those parts of the Portuguese colonies abutting on German colonies in Africa.

The next occasion that exemplified the English Government's spirit of accommodation arose at the beginning of 1899 from complications resulting from the election of a new king of the Samoan Islands. At the Samoan Conference in Berlin, 1899, a triumvirate was created, consisting of the United States, Germany, and England. In the tropics, far from home, under the influence of rivalries which were daily renewed among members of the different nations within that confined space, it was impossible for the officials appointed by the three Powers at every step to keep within the limits set by the Samoan Compact and to remain at harmony with one another. Their frictions were occasionally as serious as the petty jealousies and conflicts among the native chiefs. In the election of a king, after the death of Malietoa, his old opponent, Mataafa, received a majority of votes. A short time before, with the consent of the American and the English consuls, he had been brought back from banishment to Samoa on a German man-of-war. The American Chief Justice, Chambers, decided, however, in favour of the minority's candidate, Tana, son of Malietoa. A revolt broke out in Apia, in which the followers of Mataafa were victorious. Chambers took refuge on an American battleship; whereupon the president of the municipality of Apia, a German,

Dr. Raffel by name, closed the supreme court. Even the commanders of the battleships were not in agreement. While the German commander held back, the English and the American commanders used their cannon to interfere in the conflict in Apia. There was, therefore, quite a dangerous muddle caused by arbitrariness and excited interference.

Under such conditions the triumvirate could no longer be maintained. After the principle of absolute separation had been accepted by the three Governments, Germany had to consider the question as to which were preferable : the acquisition of the chief island, Upolu, while England received compensation from Germany's colonial possessions in the Pacific Ocean ; or the transfer of the islands to England in return for definite compensations to Germany. The majority of the Colonial Council preferred compensations for Germany ; Bülow nevertheless, on account of the imponderable interest which the German nation took in Samoa, that child of affliction, decided to assert the old claims.

The diplomatic negotiations between England and Germany turned out to be even more difficult than those concerning the Portuguese possessions in Africa. They were carried on in London by Lord Salisbury and his representative, Arthur Balfour, and on the part of Germany by her Ambassador, Count Hatzfeldt. In a note of August 31, 1898, Hatzfeldt was requested by his Government to begin parleys on the basis that the Samoan Question could be solved only by dividing the islands among the three Powers. The American President, McKinley, from the beginning favoured the idea of division, whereas the English Government expressed the fear that the cession to Germany of one of the islands, particularly if it were Upolu, with the capital, Apia, might make bad blood in Australia. Lord Salisbury to the very end preserved the attitude of the experienced business man, who favours the convenient tactics of delay when dealing with a young competitor. His representative, Balfour, who on no account wanted a breach to occur, proved to be franker and more accommodating. There was speedy agreement to the proposition that each of the three Powers should send a commissioner to Samoa, who should be especially authorized to re-establish order, but there was a long dispute as to whether resolutions of these commissioners must be unanimous in order to be binding or whether they should require only the support of the majority. Lord Salisbury decidedly opposed the principle of unanimity desired by Germany. In the meanwhile new incidents had occurred in Samoa, and public opinion in Germany began to rebel. At last the Secretary of State, von Bülow, made a final proposition on April 11, 1899, to the effect that besides the commissioners, a joint arbitrator representing all the three Powers should be sent to Samoa to decide in cases where the commissioners disagreed. Should this proposal also be rejected, Count Hatzfeldt was to announce the severance of diplomatic relations with England until such time as she should alter her views regarding the observance of ratified treaties (the Samoan Treaty was meant).[1] Hatzfeldt did not carry out the instruction, but it probably came to the knowledge of some member or other of the Cabinet. Lord Salisbury, on April 12, 1899, accepted Germany's proposal in an altered form which contained no essential modification, only avoided reference to the Samoan Treaty.

Count Hatzfeldt's omission to carry out the instructions of April 11th, with their threat of rupture, was, it must be confessed, an unwarranted assumption of authority but not a mistake. In a personal letter of April 22, 1899, to Holstein, he wisely remarked : " You can really take it for granted that I understand fairly well the men and the situation, and therefore you can believe me that the only thing that makes an impression here is cool imperturbability and reserve without any sort of threat." [2]

The impression which Cecil Rhodes had brought back from his visit to Berlin had likewise something to do with

[1] Vol. xiv, p. 590.   [2] Ibid. p. 600.

bringing about the favourable conclusion of the negotiations by which Germany secured the islands of Upolu and Savaii, together with a piece of the neutral zone in the Hinterland of Togo, in return for her renouncement of extraterritorial rights on Zanzibar. Rhodes, who was President of the British South Africa Company, was at that time pushing his great scheme of the Cape to Cairo Railway, which was to go through German East Africa instead of the Congo State.[1] The Governor of German East Africa, General von Liebert, urgently recommended an interchange of ideas with Rhodes. In return for Germany's facilitation of the construction of the railroad, Rhodes should pledge himself to employ only Germans as signalmen in the German territory, to use German material, and to build a line to Tabora. On March 11, 1899, Rhodes was received by the Kaiser and the Secretary of State, von Bülow, who endeavoured to get him to interest himself in inducing England to meet Germany's wishes in the Samoan Question. This Rhodes actually did after his friendly reception in Berlin. While he was still in Berlin, an agreement was reached for a cable line which was to pass through German territory and to be further extended through Asia Minor to Constantinople. This plan, however, was frustrated through Turkey's opposition.[2]

Just about the time of the settlement of the Samoan Question the Boer War broke out. For a small nation like the Boers the war could, of course, be nothing but a struggle of desperation. They had the sympathy of the world, but from no quarter could they expect assistance. England could fully utilize in any way she chose her great advantage, her absolute command of the seas. America was not materially affected by the conflict. Russia had not moved a finger to help her ally during the acute Anglo-French disputes in Africa, and she displayed only faint sympathy for the hard-pressed Boers. France was still hot over the humiliation of the Fashoda Incident, and the nation, disregarding the fact that discretion was desirable on account

---

[1] *Vide supra*, p. 65.   [2] Vol. xiv, p. 560.

of the Paris International Exposition, showed more passionate indignation against England than did any other country. The Paris comic papers especially were unsurpassed in their cruel insults. But the new Minister for Foreign Affairs, Delcassé, who had taken it upon himself to recall Marchand from Fashoda, was already busy demolishing the whole far-reaching colonial programme of his predecessor, Hanotaux, and was turning the attention of his countrymen once more in the old direction, towards the gap in the Vosges Mountains. In defending himself in the Chamber of Deputies, November 24, 1899, he was more benevolent towards England than towards Germany, and by his reference to the well-known hopes of France regarding the Rhine he quickly silenced the noisy, chauvinistic champions of the Boers. He took delight in the fact that the work of French politicians favouring *la revanche* was furthered by the senseless fury against England in Germany, which was by no means confined to Pan-German circles.

In Prince Bismarck's Reichstag speeches, and in articles in *Die Norddeutsche Allgemeine Zeitung*, one can still read how harshly at the time of the Bulgarian Battenberg affair he condemned mixing morals and politics and the propensity of Germany to play the schoolmaster to the whole world. In the Egyptian Question, too, he dealt severely with the newspapers that made irresponsible attacks on England. Yet the occupation of the Nile country by the English was certainly of far greater significance for the European situation than England's fight against the independence of the Boer Republic in South Africa. Bülow preferred to take the bull by the ears rather than by the horns ; in other words, he always treated the Pan-Germans with a kind of indulgence in his speeches, humorously rather than seriously. Bülow lacked the incomparable authority of a Bismarck with which to oppose emotional politicians. Besides, the Pan-Germans were the most enthusiastic supporters in the agitation for the navy, and the statesman could not do otherwise than put up with the fact that his foreign policy must pay the penalty for many things they were saying and doing in their ardour for the building of warships.

The hostility towards England was naturally much intensified when, at the beginning of 1900, several German mail-boats were stopped by English battleships on the suspicion of having contraband on board and towed into the port of Durban. Bülow protested so strongly against this action that Lord Salisbury in a note complained of his harsh tone. Within three weeks' time the incident was happily disposed of. It had not been so much a matter of doing an ill-turn to Germany on the part of the Government, as of acts of self-assurance on the part of the British Navy which ruled the sea. The English Cabinet preferred to treat the affair not as a question of sea power but as one of maritime law, and in all essential points complied with the German demands.

The policy of the German Government towards the Boer War was from the very beginning that of preserving the strictest neutrality. The Imperial Chancellor precisely defined Germany's position in a note intended for the Foreign Office : " For reasons of general policy, for instance, in view of the Anglo-German Treaty (dealing with the Portuguese colonies), we must, of course, prevent ourselves from being drawn into a false position either towards England or towards the Transvaal during this present turmoil in South Africa."

The Kaiser had already several days previously noted on the margin of Hatzfeldt's full report from London on the critical acuteness of the situation : " We keep out of this ! Let the Hague Peace Conference take it up." [1] The State Documents also contain the following drastic statement of the Kaiser :

In the autumn of 1901 the German people were highly excited over the reports that thousands of Boer women and children were herded in concentration camps, where they were treated as prisoners. A well-known philanthropist, the clergyman von Bodelschwingh who supported

[1] Vol. xv, p. 365.

large charitable institutions in Westphalia, conceived the idea of obtaining five million signatures to a petition to the Kaiser requesting him to take action against England and, if necessary, to draw the sword. Becoming aware of this, the Kaiser ordered the Cabinet Chief, von Lucanus, and the Imperial Chancellor to send for the clergyman and " so to polish him off, that for some time to come he will have the goodness to refrain from encroaching upon imperial privileges by plebiscites in the form of conventions headed by clergymen, junkers, and elderly countesses." [1]

Through the Press the Foreign Office at that time did all that it could to quell the useless outbursts of anti-English sentiment. In the slurs the two nations cast at each other the ugly sides of the national character of each stood out conspicuously : in Germany malicious moralizing and rejoicing over the insults ; in England domineering, brutal arrogance. This behaviour did not make Germany more politically wise nor England more moral. The English Government, however, had the advantage over Germany of a long political education that had taught the people that during a campaign, even if only a diplomatic one, a soldier must stick to his colours.

Of all England's colonial wars the most difficult and bloody was perhaps that which she waged against that stubborn white nation in South Africa. Since the English Army was able only gradually and after many reverses to break the stubborn resistance of the Boers, the European Powers that had disputes with England in other continents sought to take advantage of England's embarrassment. The United States was the only Great Power from whom England did not have to expect unfriendliness. Secretary of State Hay, with much feeling, expressed to the German Ambassador, von Holleben, on January 2, 1900, his concern over England's situation. In a second conversation on February 2nd of the same year, he declared it would be a universal calamity if England's military situation in South Africa were to become more serious. There could, therefore,

[1] Vol. xvii, p. 187.

be no idea that America would participate in any intervention against England. On the other hand, it was to be expected that Russia would not remain a quiet or entirely benevolent spectator.

At the outbreak of the Boer War the Russian Minister for Foreign Affairs, Count Muraviev, stopped in Biarritz and in Paris and then accompanied the Tsar from Wolfs-garten on his day's visit to Potsdam on November 8, 1899. During this meeting of the two Emperors there was no mention either of mediation or of intervention in the war. But even before this, Paris newspapers had announced, during Count Muraviev's stay in Paris, that Russia would intervene. Russian papers, too, as early as October, had talked of a Franco-Russian understanding with regard to England. In all probability, therefore, this had been the subject of Count Muraviev's conversations in Paris with the Minister for Foreign Affairs, Delcassé, and from the silence of the Tsar and his Minister at Potsdam we can infer only that they did not consider the time favourable to mention it. The Foreign Office in Berlin, at all events, expected that sooner or later Russia would put out a feeler.

On January 12, 1900, the Ambassador, Count Osten-Sacken, inquired of the Secretary of State, Count Bülow, what attitude Germany would be likely to take towards concerted action in the event of an English advance in Delagoa Bay. (Munitions and war supplies were imported by way of the harbour of Lorenzo Marques.) He said that in St. Petersburg the answer was awaited with intense interest. Bülow replied that Germany was certainly much interested in the question, but first of all he expected an equally candid answer to his counter-question : " What is France's attitude towards the idea of a concerted protest against England's seizure of Delagoa Bay ? " At the same time, at the Russian New Year, Count Osten-Sacken said to the Kaiser, during his call at the embassy, that it seemed as though affairs in Afghanistan were becoming so involved that Russia would probably be obliged to intervene there in the interests of peace. The Kaiser replied that he would

no more stand sentinel for the Dual Alliance in East Africa
than for England in India. The Ambassador stated further
that in the judgment of the Russian Admiral, Marakov,
the English Navy, which he had recently visited, was just
as inefficient as the English Army ; whereupon the Kaiser
ironically advised the Ambassador to get the Greeks, the
Portuguese, and the Danes to attack the British fleet.[1]
Russia's watchword therefore was : Pressure on England,
either by means of a European coalition or by a new advance
in the direction of the Indian border.

Another diplomatic step in the Transvaal Question
followed on March 3, 1900. By the Tsar's order Count
Muraviev had a note presented to Berlin, proposing concerted mediation by Russia, France, and Germany. France
and Germany were to unite in applying friendly pressure
in London, and Russia was then to join them. Count von
Bülow replied that Germany must be careful to avoid any
chance of entanglement with other Great Powers, especially
other maritime Powers, so long as she was not sure of
France's attitude. This security could only be afforded by a
treaty in which the contracting Powers mutually guaranteed
each other's European possessions for a long term of years.
Thereupon Muraviev first tried a very poor subterfuge
to the effect that negotiations preliminary to such a treaty
would be long drawn out, and then on March 22, 1900, he
caused his proposition of mediation to be withdrawn
altogether.[2]

In the meanwhile both Boer Republics had declared themselves ready to make peace on condition that their independence be preserved ; a proposal which Lord Salisbury
characterized as not discussable. Moreover, the Heir to
the English Throne came forward with a noteworthy statement which proved that in London they appreciated fully
and gratefully Germany's discretion. The words addressed
by the Prince of Wales to a group of Members of Parliament
were to this effect : The German Emperor and his Government had repeatedly given proof of their sympathy for

[1] Vol. xv, pp. 493–502.   [2] Ibid. p. 500.

England, and they clearly understood that the war in South
Africa was not over the Transvaal gold mines, but over
the question whether England were to continue to be the
dominant Power in South Africa. They should not forget
what England owed to the attitude of the Kaiser and his
Government. The Prince obviously based his statements
on the recent correspondence of the Kaiser with his grandmother and himself.[1]

Just at this time pacifistic ideas were very popular at
the Russian Court. For had not the young Tsar, captivated
by the ideas of the famous pacifist, Ivan von Bloch, personally instigated the First Hague Peace Conference ? The
civilized world took a lively if sceptical interest in it, but
the positive results were slight. The Hague discussions,[2]
which lasted from May 18th to June 19, 1899, in which
representatives of twenty-six States took part, resulted
merely in agreements regarding rights and usages in war
on commerce, in the extension of the principles of the
Geneva Convention to naval warfare, and in a convention
for the arbitration of international disputes. From the
first the Conference itself had aroused the Kaiser's liveliest
interest, as his numerous and occasionally very tempera-
mental notes on the margin of the official documents bear
witness. But in opposition to the chief of the German
delegation, the Ambassador to France, Count Münster,
the Kaiser represented a point of view unfavourable to the
aims of the Conference, because he suspected that one of
the points in the programme for the limitation of armaments
was directly aimed at Germany   But in other countries, too,
no great importance was attached to the endeavours of the
Conference. This is evident from the frank remarks of
the English Admiral Fisher to one of the German naval
delegates, Captain Siegel, to the effect that in case of war
the English Government without any doubt would not
consider themselves bound and would disregard every
agreement. It is significant that Italy felt herself in no
way moved to support the German position. Although

[1] Vol. xv, p. 502.   [2] Ibid. pp. 135-351.

the Conference had opened with a definite programme, of which the Russian Foreign Minister, Muraviev, proudly claimed to be the author, this was not adhered to. And when England attempted to carry through an agreement for an obligatory court of arbitration for all international disputes, the antagonisms within the Conference, latent until that moment, emerged for the first time. The German as well as the Rumanian delegates declared the proposition unacceptable to their respective Governments, and through their united efforts they also succeeded, with the assistance of the Austrians, in making the courts of arbitration only optional. Until quite recently there were attempts again and again to lay the blame on Germany for having sabotaged the idea of the Peace Conference from the beginning. But a study of the English Press, and especially of the American Press, at the time of the Conference shows that in the Anglo-Saxon countries the pacifistic ideas were just as bluntly rejected, the only difference being that it had been done more cleverly.

Shortly after Russia's attempt at intervention a new Anglo-German special understanding was concluded, in addition to the Portuguese and the Samoan. Its background was created by the joint action of the Powers towards the attacks on foreigners in China that broke out during the winter of 1899–1900. The external impetus had been given by Russia's display of power in Manchuria after her occupation of Port Arthur. At first scarcely noticed by the legations, the movement became menacing when hordes of Boxers in the spring of 1900 advanced to the very gates of Pekin. The common danger to all foreign representatives in Pekin led to joint action by all the Great Powers possessing interests in Eastern Asia. This was the first occasion that the United States, that had just been brought into World Politics by the acquisition of the Philippines, directly interfered side by side with the Great European Powers and Japan in Chinese affairs. The German position was from the start much the same as the French and the American, namely, merely to co-operate as a civilized Power for the protection of general interests without opposing Russia's advances into Northern China.   A colonial army was formed of Europeans, Americans, and Japanese, to which the Russians supplied the largest quota.   An ultimatum to the commanders of the forts at Taku was answered by the bombardment of the foreign warships assembled there, and at the storming of the forts German blood, too, was shed. Tien-tsin had to be protected by corps of marines ; a detachment commanded by Admiral Seymour was sur-rounded by a superior force of Chinese troops while on its way to the relief of the foreign legations shut up in Pekin and therefore could not reach its objective, and was rescued only after heavy fighting.

During the miscarriage of this undertaking the German Ambassador, Baron von Ketteler, was shot dead by a Chinese soldier.   The state of anxious suspense lest all foreigners in Pekin might be slaughtered lasted for weeks, since all communication with Pekin had been interrupted and only unreliable reports reached the coast.   By the end of July 1900, the total number of foreign troops in China, strengthened by the addition of contingents from the different Powers, was estimated at 115,000 men and 300 cannon.   The troublesome question then arose as to which Power should appoint the commander-in-chief.   According to the number of her combatants, Russia should have had the prior right to the chief command, but England and Japan had no desire to increase still further her already existing superiority.   Next by force of numbers to Russia was Japan, but her rival, Russia, was opposed to giving her the command   Russia was equally disinclined to place herself under an English commander-in-chief.

The Kaiser was burning with desire to see the combined forces in China placed under the supreme command of Field-Marshal Count Waldersee.   In this way he hoped to see his imperial words realized that he had spoken at the launching of a ship of the line on July 4, 1900 : " The sea is indispensable for Germany's greatness.   But the sea proves also that no longer can important decisions upon it or far beyond it be made without the German Emperor."

But the Kaiser's object could be attained only in a roundabout way. The possibility of a German supreme command was first mentioned very casually by Count Aoki in a conversation with the German Ambassador in Tokio. St. Petersburg made the condition that under no circumstances would she place her troops under an English or a Japanese or an American commander-in-chief. Paris indicated that it would not approve giving England the supreme command. After this it seemed as though the fulfilment of the Kaiser's wish were possible. But in the other interested countries the ambition of important generals was soon aroused, and General Kuropatkin and Lord Wolseley appeared as aspirants for the post. England was very strongly opposed to the idea of a joint supreme command ; Lord Salisbury especially disputed the necessity for such an arrangement. The German Government at first kept as much as possible in the background, foreseeing the inevitable complications, and did not take up the whole matter until after the Kaiser, in a telegram to the Tsar, had proposed sending Count Waldersee. After this impulsive step the German Government was obliged to stand by its imperial master. The Tsar assented to the Kaiser's proposition. In a telegram to the President of the French Republic, and in a communication to the English Government, however, William II ascribed the choice of Count Waldersee to the initiative of the Tsar. This act had undoubtedly something to do with the fact that Field-Marshal Count Waldersee's mission was made more difficult by the later behaviour of the Russian forces in China.

The Kaiser made another memorable utterance on the occasion of the departure of the first contingent of German troops for China : " Set an example of discipline to the whole world. You will have to do battle with a crafty, barbarous foe. If you come upon him, remember, no quarter will be granted, no prisoners taken ! " The excited behaviour of the Kaiser in this Chinese crusade was as inglorious as the laurels earned by the " World Marshal " were scanty. The campaign was, however, finally directed more or less by the Concert of Powers, where there was already sufficient discord. Shortly after the taking of Pekin, Russia proposed its early evacuation, although the provinces which had been stirred up by the Boxers had as yet been in no way tranquillized. The Russian Government obviously wanted to bring the joint campaign to an end as quickly as possible in order to be able to protract the occupation of the conquered territory of Manchuria, namely Harbin and Nin-chwangh, by negotiations with the enfeebled Government of China. Generally speaking, the chief difficulties came from Russia, and the newspapers had more to report about diplomatic disputes than military achievements, a condition of affairs which ultimately benefited China. The reports made to his Foreign Office by von Mumm, the German representative, bear eloquent witness to the difficulties, often of the paltriest sort, that occupied the attention of the representatives of the eleven Powers in Pekin.[1] It was especially hard to reach an agreement about the question of penalties, since the differences of opinion between Germany on the one hand and Japan and Russia on the other made themselves most strongly felt in this matter.

To Count Bülow and to every observer concerned about Germany's future, this military business in China could not be unwelcome. A change in Chancellors was imminent on account of the advanced age of Prince Hohenlohe. Except for Bülow, Waldersee, a thoroughgoing believer in a *coup d'état*,[2] stood first in line as candidate for the succession on account of his close personal relations to the Kaiser and his own political ambitions. It was, however, a difficult task for the new Chancellor to answer the severe criticisms of the Kaiser's theatrical behaviour on the occasion of the Chinese expedition which were made in the Reichstag in November 1900 by Bebel and Richter, the leaders of the Social Democrats and of the Radical People's Party (Die

[1] Vol. xvi, pp. 155 *seq.*
[2] *Vide supra*, pp. 39–40.—TRANSLATOR'S NOTE.

G

Freisinnige Volkspartei) respectively. The Chancellor contested the notion that the supreme command had been forced upon the other Powers ; on the contrary, it was the Emperor of Russia who had put it into Germany's hand. The offensive watchword, " No quarter will be given," the new Chancellor excused on the ground that the Kaiser was naturally very excited when he made his speech at Wilhelmshaven, having heard only ten minutes before of Ketteler's assassination. In the same way he tried to smooth over the Kaiser's tirades about the German Emperor's decisive rôle in happenings in the uttermost parts of the earth, and by employing wit and irony against his assailants, he succeeded in winning the applause of their opponents in internal politics.

In the meantime the exchange of Anglo-German notes on October 16, 1900, the so-called Yang-tse Treaty, was published and gave the impression of an important event in World Politics. The agreement acquired its name from the river along whose valley and mouth was located the greater part of the foreign commerce in China. In close touch with the consulates in Shanghai, both Viceroys on the lower Yang-tse had kept their provinces free from Boxer disturbances. England up to this time had been the leading Power in this territory. As late as the beginning of 1900, the Under-Secretary of |State, Brodrick, had spoken in the House of Commons of the leading position that was England's due in that very region.

As the Chinese Navy had withdrawn to the upper course of the Yang-tse, the question had to be decided definitively whether England, who had hitherto treated the Yang-tse territory as her own sphere of influence, should alone or together with the other Powers keep this navy under surveillance. At the desire of the other Powers Germany took the initial step in London towards an agreement dealing with this important territory of 220 millions of inhabitants. Finally, after overcoming considerable opposition on the part of England, who was deeply interested in the railroads of the Province of Tschili, especially on account of capital invested, the above-mentioned agreement was concluded, on October 16, 1900, in which both Governments mutually pledged themselves that in the Yang-tse basin commerce and any other legitimate economic enterprise should be free and open to all nations. Not only in the Yang-tse basin, but in all districts of China " where they were able to exercise influence," both Governments expressed themselves as desiring to observe the principle of the Open Door. The German Government, following the suggestion of France and Russia, and contrary to the efforts of America, had from the first energetically advocated this point of view. In addition, the contracting parties mutually promised to maintain the territorial integrity of the Chinese Empire ; and if other Powers should acquire territorial privileges, to come to an agreement with each other before taking any step in the matter.

England, therefore, valued the partnership of Germany in the business of protecting the integrity of the Chinese Empire, which at that time was threatened only by Russia, highly enough for her to be ready to drop her former claims to special rights. The other Powers assented to the agreement, and even Russia could do so without scruples, since she had already proclaimed the principle of the integrity of China and had promised to evacuate Manchuria at some future time. It is true that not much value was to be placed on this promise, owing to the customary lack of consistency between word and act in Russian policy. Indeed, in acceding to the agreement Russia made it clear that she would change her attitude according to circumstances if any other Power should violate the principle of the Open Door and of the integrity of China.

Naturally the Anglo-German understanding did not at all suit the Pan-Germans' rule of calling everything done in company with England bad, and everything done in company with Russia good. The politicians who thought they were following in Bismarck's steps were much concerned at the possibility of an estrangement from Russia. Bülow seized the first opportunity in the Reichstag, during the budget discussions, to calm their excitement. While warmly extolling the Tsar, he asserted that an irreparable breach could never occur between German and Russian policies provided they were both intelligently directed. "We have no intention of acting as lightning-conductor for any other Power."

Upon the publication of the Anglo-German Treaty there followed, in March 1901, a lively epilogue that was enacted in the Parliaments of London and of Berlin, and to which we shall later revert.

First of all we must go back and take up the Anglo-German Agreement. It is true that it came to nothing, but it ought not to be overlooked, on account of the great importance of its subject, the Morocco Question.

Morocco, on account of its position on the Atlantic, at the gates of Europe, was an especially coveted country. The reason that up to the close of the last century it had not passed under the suzerainty of a civilized Power is accounted for mainly by two circumstances : firstly, the terrible internal conditions of the country, which had made it almost inaccessible to foreign influence ; and, secondly, the mutual jealousies of the Southern and Western European States.

The foreign ambassadors were stationed at Tangier, far from Marrakesh and Fez, where the Sultan held his Court. In the interior there were bloody conflicts over the succession and expeditions against rebellious tribes almost without end. What elsewhere was styled government was there a system of blood and extortion. From an instinct of self-preservation the Government was intent on preventing the inhabitants, mostly Mussulmans, from coming into contact with the outside world. There was no postal nor telegraph service in the country.

Spain's relations with Morocco were the oldest in Europe, reaching back to the days of the Moors. But with the collapse of her colonial power, her ability to compete with other European Powers in Morocco necessarily declined. France, on the other hand, by her conquest of Algiers had become the next-door neighbour of Morocco and was assiduously working to secure a passage from Algiers through the Hinterland of the Shereefian Empire to her possessions on the Senegal. Rivals, however, were not lacking. There was England with her maritime interests; Italy, too, the ancient torch-bearer of civilization on the north coast of Africa; and lastly, Germany with her commerce and her young colonies. The French occupation of the oasis of Tuat was followed in 1900 by that of the oasis of Tafilet, at the eastern declivity of the High Atlas range. Tuat might perhaps have been considered as ownerless, but Tafilet, which was peopled by Berbers and Arabs, had up to this time been regarded as Moroccan territory. Thus, taking advantage of England's difficulties in South Africa, France had begun the partitioning of Morocco, in a region, it is true, that was least accessible to the other nations. She was in the fortunate position of having the lead in the game. The further shaping of affairs depended on the shuffling of the cards in Europe, and particularly on Great Britain's mood as dealer of the cards.

Even before the settlement of the dispute over the Samoan Islands, the Morocco Question was frequently alluded to in the discussions in London—in the first instance by Lord Salisbury himself, although only casually. In a report of June 29, 1897, Count Hatzfeldt depicted the following scene. In a conversation over the Mediterranean Question, Lord Salisbury quite casually and almost in an undertone inquired: " Have you nothing at all then ? But what about Morocco ? " Astonished, Hatzfeldt replied : " Morocco ? Why, you have already laid claim there to the choicest morsels for yourself." Whereupon Salisbury observed that he laid no claim to Tangier nor to Cape Jube, but that he would claim another position. Hatzfeldt laughingly rejoined that he supposed it was to be a position from which it would be possible to join hands with Gibraltar and thus to close the Mediterranean, which Salisbury in no way denied.[1]

[1] Vol. xvii, p. 16.

In November 1899 Chamberlain declared that if the
southern part of the Moroccan coast came under the
supremacy of Germany, he would raise no objections.
Detailed discussion of the question was deferred. On
April 27, 1900, Bülow instructed the Ambassador in Paris,
Count Münster, to declare that Germany was interested
in the fate of this " nerve ganglion of our planet." Delcassé
replied to this that France had no intention of making any
sort of attack upon Morocco. Tuat, he said, lay 750 miles
south of the northern boundary of Morocco, and the occupation of the oasis of Tuat was simply for purposes of commerce. It would have been strange if the statement of
the German Ambassador had not inspired Delcassé with
the determination to prevent any German participation
in Morocco and to steal a march upon Germany.

At all events, it was high time for Germany to come to
an agreement with England over the Morocco Question.
Count Hatzfeldt, with clear insight, urged in a report of
May 21, 1900, that there be no further delay ; Chamberlain
was ready to negotiate and asked for definite proposals.
After an unsuccessful attempt to get England to take the
initiative, Hatzfeldt proposed to his Government that
Germany clearly announce in London her claims to the
southern Atlantic coast of Morocco. But Berlin preferred
the roundabout way through St. Petersburg. The Russian
Government was requested to warn France against taking
further steps in Morocco. After this the English statesmen,
dreading to become involved in bitter diplomatic quarrels
in addition to their difficulties caused by the unfavourable
course of the Boer War, postponed negotiations with Germany
about the Morocco Question until the Greek Kalends.
Once more a favourable opportunity for a hand-in-hand
policy with England was lost.[1]

[1] Vol. xvii, pp. 295 *seq.*

CHAPTER II

ENGLAND'S OFFER OF ALLIANCE IN 1901

SHORTLY after the English election in October 1900, from which the Conservatives and Unionists reappeared in their former strength in the House of Commons, Lord Salisbury made a change in the Foreign Office. Hitherto he himself had been Foreign Secretary, but now, in order to lighten his burden, he appointed the former Secretary for War, Lord Lansdowne, to that post, and kept in his own hands only the direction of the general policy of the State. Lansdowne was not a diplomat by training. Before entering upon the direction of the War Department he had occupied several posts in the Colonial Government, in Canada and in India. The Liberal Press expressed its satisfaction that Salisbury had preferred Lansdowne, with his calm and judicial temperament, to Chamberlain, the imperialistic hotspur. It was soon evident that Chamberlain in his efforts for an understanding with Germany was supported by the new Secretary of State for Foreign Affairs. Both in the adjustment in the Samoan controversy and in the affair of the seizure of the German mail-steamers, Chamberlain had shown a conciliatory spirit.

On January 18th Baron von Eckardstein reported a conversation that he had had with Chamberlain during a visit at the country house of the Duke of Devonshire. Chamberlain intimated that the time had come for England to abandon her policy of isolation and to link herself either with Germany or with Russia and France. He said he preferred a rapprochement with Germany, and in his opinion a beginning could best be effected by a secret agreement concerning Morocco. If the German Government should refuse, England would be obliged to make a treaty with Russia, even at the cost of great sacrifices in China and on the Persian Gulf.[1]

The reasons that had led Chamberlain to make his first offer to Germany in the year 1898 still existed in altered form in the year 1901. The antagonism towards France in Africa, it is true, had decreased after her withdrawal from Fashoda ; but on the other hand Russia's bearing in the Far East had assumed a threatening aspect, in the first place to Japan and China, but in its further implications to England's interests also. After the proofs of good will that England had given in the settlement of the Samoan dispute and during the Chinese complications over the Yang-tse Agreement, Chamberlain had reason to expect a better reception of his confidential proposals than that accorded in 1898. But in the meantime the South African War had occurred, and it looked as though fighting were to begin again : Boer contingents were still in the field facing superior English forces, and the storm of indignation still continued among the German people. Official circles in Berlin were in a bad humour over the public festivities in Lisbon in honour of an English squadron, for the King of Portugal had extolled the alliance with mighty Albion, a compact of ancient standing that had been recently reconfirmed and that had thereby blighted Germany's hopes of the speedy fulfilment of the Anglo-German Treaty in regard to the Portuguese colonies. The cordial relations between Russia and the United States, as well as the vigour with which the latter had insisted on setting aside the old English rights regarding the construction and protection of the Panama Canal, served to strengthen the belief that England was absolutely deserted.

On January 21, 1901, the Kaiser hurried to the death-bed of his grandmother. His warm reception at Court and by the people of London led him to prolong his visit after the death of the Queen until February 6th. The

[1] Vol. xvi, p. 15.

King conferred upon him the title of a British Field-Marshal, and in after-dinner speeches expressed his wish for the long continuance of the existing "friendly" and "excellent" relations between Germany and England. Lord Roberts, recently returned from his supreme command in South Africa, received the Order of the Black Eagle. The Kaiser's conversations with Salisbury, Lansdowne, the Lord Mayor of London and other distinguished personages added to the general mood of cordiality. There was no mention of an alliance. On the advice of Count Bülow the Kaiser avoided any reference to the subject and confined himself to the suggestion that England take sides with the Continent in the event of a Russo-American agreement.

Before we consider the discussions concerning the alliance proposed by Chamberlain, we must mention two questions relating to Eastern Asia that emerged during an early stage of these discussions and had an influence on their course. Representatives of the Russian and the Belgian Governments had each taken possession of a considerable stretch of the left bank of the Pei-ho opposite the European settlements near Tien-tsin, and in doing so Russia had even resorted to arms. While the Belgians, probably under pressure of the Powers, soon abandoned the whole adventure, the Russian agents announced that they had seized the river territory as "conquered property." It was even rumoured in the Press that Russia meant to erect fortifications there, and the English Government was deeply disturbed. The issue was finally settled through the mediation of the German Government. From the beginning Germany had taken the position that since no Power was at war with China there could consequently be no question of conquests, but at most of a settlement or of a concession. The Russian Government, therefore, declared officially she wished only to obtain "a concession under the usual conditions."

In addition to the Tien-tsin Question there was still another which showed even more clearly Russia's territorial intentions in Eastern Asia. Japan had communicated to the English Government that Russia was putting great

pressure upon Pekin to bring about the ratification of a
secret agreement arrived at by the Russian General Alexejev
and a Chinese general, which threatened European interests
in North China. In this case as in that of Tien-tsin, Russia
succeeded in harnessing the industrial interests of Belgium
to her own political chariot. The Japanese Government
proposed that the two Governments make identical declarations in Pekin, thus stiffening the back of the Chinese Government. To Lansdowne's inquiry as to the attitude of the
German Government in the matter, the answer was made
in the middle of February 1901 that the Anglo-German
Yang-tse Treaty contained no obligations affecting Manchuria, but that the German Government was ready to
caution the Chinese Government against promising financial
or territorial concessions to any third Power. It was suggested that the German representative officially notify the
Chinese Government " that according to the view of the
Imperial Government the Chinese Government ought not
to enter into any separate agreements of a financial or
territorial character with any States or corporations whatsoever until she was in a position to gauge her obligations to
all the Powers, and until there was an assurance of the
fulfilment of these obligations." [1]

Without going into the interpretation of the Yang-tse
Treaty, Lord Lansdowne at first expressed satisfaction at
Germany's willingness to join in the warnings to Pekin.
But it did not remain a secret to the Foreign Offices that
there were differences of opinion concerning the interpretation of the treaty, for the matter was aired in the Press
and in Parliament. First the London papers sounded
the alarm over the pressure that Russia was exerting on
Pekin. Then questions were asked in Parliament in reference to the Yang-tse Treaty. In the Reichstag on
March 15, 1901, the Chancellor contradicted the rumours
that there were secret clauses in the Yang-tse Treaty, and
added : " The treaty has nothing to do with Manchuria ;
we have left no doubts of this in our negotiations. . . . As

[1] Vol. xvi, p. 321.

to the future of Manchuria—well, gentlemen, I really do not know anything that can be more unimportant to us." In the further course of the debate the Chancellor declared : " I wish to state most emphatically that we are looking exclusively after German interests in China, and are leaving it to England to safeguard her own interests there." A few days later, answering a speech of the deputy Prince Bismarck the younger, Bülow stated : " Since the previous speaker has broached the subject, I am happy to be able to announce that I received two hours ago a telegram from our Ambassador in St. Petersburg, according to which the Russian Minister for Foreign Affairs has expressed to Count Alvensleben his satisfaction over my recent utterances in regard to China."

In the diplomatic disputes over the interpretation of the Yang-tse Treaty, Bülow was absolutely right in one essential point. The new English Under-Secretary of State, Lord Cranborne, evidently was not sufficiently acquainted with the earlier history of the treaty when he stated in the House of Commons that the agreement did not contain any limitations and therefore applied also to North China. The difficulty lay in the words : " where they can exercise influence." Lord Salisbury himself, during the negotiations, had designated the 38° latitude as the northern boundary of the territory affected by the treaty. Later this definition was replaced by the words quoted above, which were calculated to veil Germany's indifference to affairs in Manchuria. This was done out of consideration to public opinion in England, which would have been less favourably disposed to the treaty if Manchuria had been explicitly excluded. Lord Lansdowne acknowledged that the clause " where they can exercise influence " did constitute a limitation, but he wished to have it understood as applying only to the first article of the treaty, that dealing with the Open Door, and not to the second, dealing with the integrity of China. So an ambiguity did exist after all. After the public airing of the differences of opinion in the English Cabinet and in the German Government, Japan

hastened to proclaim through a statement of her Minister
for Foreign Affairs in Parliament that she had unreservedly
assented to the treaty and would pay no regard to subsequent interpretations. Now let us turn to the main
subject : the discussions over an Anglo-German treaty.

At the outset a brief statement of a few remarks of
leading personages will suffice to indicate the spirit with
which Chamberlain's advances were received in Berlin :
Count von Bülow, January 20, 1901 : " Wait—let England
take the initiative " ; the Kaiser in London, January 20th,
after Eckardstein had communicated to him Chamberlain's
suggestions : " So they are coming, are they ? just as we
wanted " ; Bülow, January 21st : " We must take the
greatest care neither to discourage the English nor to let
ourselves be prematurely bound. We must not appear too
eager. It would be a masterstroke if we could keep the
English hopes alive without being tied down ourselves.
The threat of joining the Dual Alliance is only a bogy
with which to intimidate us. The sacrifices England would
have to make for an understanding with the Dual Alliance
would be too great, and they would only postpone for a
short time England's struggle for her very existence " ;
Holstein on the same day in a personal telegram to Metternich : " Threat of an understanding with France and
Russia absolute humbug. We can wait ; time is on our
side. England must be first made to realize clearly her
serious *embarrassement* " ; also in a telegram to Eckardstein,
January 21st : " The threat of withdrawing from China
and from the Persian Gulf is nothing but nonsense, humbug.
There is nothing in it for France, who will be moved by no
concessions to hand Tangier over to England ; if England
strengthens her enemies she will make her struggle for
existence all the more inevitable." In this connection it
must, however, be observed that from the first Holstein
aimed at an ultimate understanding with England, as he
repeatedly explained to me at that time. He fully realized
that since German policy had widened into a world policy,
it could no longer live by the Russian friendship alone,

but must come to terms with the World Power of Great Britain. His desire for a treaty is further shown by his sending to London, shortly after the opening of the discussions, a copy of Bismarck's letter of November 22, 1887, to Salisbury,[1] and by having it brought to the memory of Chamberlain and Lansdowne. It will be seen from these examples that Germany's reception of the English offer was anything but encouraging, and that it did not argue well for the favourable progress of the negotiations.

Count Hatzfeldt, whom Holstein held in high regard, did his utmost to talk Holstein out of his distrust of Lord Lansdowne and the other English supporters of the alliance. On February 10, 1901, he vouched for the honourableness of Lansdowne's intentions. He said that the Germanophile Ministers were inspired by the dominant idea that England could make no further progress against the difficulties threatening in China and elsewhere without a strong continental alliance, and that a German alliance was the most desirable. If this were not attainable they would be obliged immediately to set to work to give a different direction to England's World Policy and even at the cost of great sacrifices to come to a friendly understanding with Russia in China and elsewhere. Hatzfeldt even sent a draft of the instructions that should be sent him. The draft was couched in cordial terms, but at the same time it insisted that if Germany were to incur dangers at the hand of her powerful neighbours, it would be justifiable to provide for stronger defences for the Central Empire. Holstein answered with violent invectives against Lord Salisbury's " unbearable personality " ; he revived the memory of his " beautiful project " for the partitioning of Turkey and referred to the total lack of perspicacity in his Portuguese policy. He even thought the English Premier capable of straightway communicating a German offer of alliance to St. Petersburg with the query, " What is your offer ? "[2]

It stands to reason that with such clumsy advances

[1] See above, p. 24.   [2] Vol. xvii, pp. 30 seq.

Salisbury could not have improved England's position towards Russia, and probably would only have encouraged her to further advances in Asia. In Central Asia a so-called test mobilization of the Caucasian troops was in progress under the direction of Kuropatkin, Minister for War, extending as far as the fortified post Kushk, opposite Herat.

On March 27, 1901, Lord Lansdowne informed the German Ambassador that he had drawn up a promemoria, and had shown it to Balfour first and to Lord Salisbury. After its careful perusal, the Prime Minister had stated that he approved of a strictly defined defensive alliance, but that all contingencies must be scrutinized and ways and means discovered for disposing of the difficulties which a long-term treaty was bound to create in Parliament.[1]

The greatest actual obstacle was the German demand that not only Germany but the Triple Alliance *en bloc* must be received into the compact; in return for which Great Britain, along with all her colonies, would also enjoy its protection, and also that the negotiations must be carried on not in Berlin but in Vienna. The inclusion of Austria and Italy seemed to the Chancellor and to Holstein, as well as to the Kaiser, absolutely necessary, since otherwise Germany's enemies could attack one of the allies and thereby involve her also in the war, while England remained free to consider that it was not a *casus fœderis*, since there had been no direct attack by two Powers.[2] Holstein remarked that Salisbury must not consider the bargain as a *marché du dupe*. But surely that contingency could have been precluded when formulating an Anglo-German treaty of alliance; and even if it did occur, an Anglo-German treaty in addition to the Triple Alliance would still always have had this advantage for Germany, that England would then have been bound not to take sides with Germany's enemies under any circumstances whatsoever.

In May 1901 Count Hatzfeldt, after a prolonged absence on sick-leave, had resumed the business of the embassy,

[1] Vol. xvii, p. 46.   Ibid. pp. 64 *seq.*

and Lord Salisbury, too, had returned from the Riviera, where he had been staying for his health. After one of his first interviews with Lord Lansdowne, the German Ambassador could definitely state that while the English Prime Minister was still prepared to conclude a treaty with Germany, he had objections to England's linking up with the Triple Alliance. Lord Salisbury had cherished an old disinclination to join forces with countries having Slavic or Latin populations and absolutely refused to take the roundabout road by way of Vienna in order to come to an agreement with Berlin. Lansdowne suggested that individual questions might be discussed first. He thought that all contingencies should be carefully scrutinized, as, for instance, the disruption of the Austrian Empire after the death of the Emperor Francis Joseph, or complications among the Mediterranean Powers on account of Morocco.[1] Holstein, however, stubbornly insisted on the bond—that Austria-Hungary should assume the rôle of mediator and that a discussion of details should only be entered into if England pledged herself to acknowledge that the *casus fœderis* had arisen, not only if Germany were attacked from two quarters, but likewise if Germany were obliged to hasten to the assistance of one of her allies.

On May 18th, Lansdowne proposed making a rough draft. In view of his instructions from Berlin, Hatzfeldt was loath to take the initiative in writing by giving Lansdowne the memorandum he desired, for he did not wish the English to be able to say that Germany had sought to obtain an alliance with England. On May 23rd, when Lansdowne was calling on him, Hatzfeldt summarized Germany's attitude as follows :

1. The German Empire must identify its interests with the continuance and integrity of the Austro-Hungarian monarchy, and can therefore only conclude an agreement if there is no doubt that England will consider it a *casus fœderis* if Germany comes to the assistance of the Austrian Empire in case it is attacked by two Powers.

[1] Vol. xvii, p. 59.

2. A storm of indignation would stir the Reichstag and public opinion in Germany if we were to conclude a treaty permitting England in such a case to remain a passive spectator.

3. Nothing stands between Germany and Russia but Austrian interests ; if we had been willing to abandon these we could have brought about the closest relations with Russia years ago.

Lord Lansdowne was courteous enough to express his thanks for this elucidation, but he pointed out that he would still have many difficulties—especially of a parliamentary kind—to overcome with the Prime Minister.

After this Holstein persisted in denying that there were any serious intentions on England's part and in counselling against anything in writing being given to Lansdowne. It must be conceded that Salisbury was just as distrustful and cautious as Holstein.   In a private audience of Hatzfeldt with King Edward on June 15th, the latter admitted that while Lord Lansdowne was very favourably disposed the Prime Minister was "quite exceptionally distrustful." Chancellor Bülow, too, had his share of suspicions and hesitations.   In this connection a marginal note in the long report of Count Metternich, dealing with all possible contingencies, is significant.   At that time Count Metternich was still Minister at Hamburg, but already he was slated to succeed Hatzfeldt at the embassy in London, for the latter was seriously ill.   In the report, among other things, it was stated : In case the United States should ever evince a desire to swallow up Canada, and Russia should wish to come to a reckoning with the English in Asia, an English treaty with the Triple Alliance would constitute a great obstacle to Russian plans, and probably the Russians would then concentrate all their hatred on Germany.   To this Bülow added the note : "That is the major objection to any understanding with England ; the Russians (Court and public opinion) would vent all their disappointment and rage on us, and the English would make use of this, in spite of the treaty, to get in well with Russia and to snub us in colonial matters.[1]

[1] Vol. xvii, pp. 63–82.

KING EDWARD'S RETURN FROM PARIS
"I think we have them in our pocket, dear Joe!"
(Jeanniot in *Le Rire*, May 1903.)

It was wellnigh impossible in such an atmosphere of brooding hesitation and suspicion for the ideas of an alliance to take root and grow.

On July 9, 1901, the Chargé d'Affaires, Baron von Eckardstein, reported that he had learned through the English Ambassador to Germany, Sir Frank Lascelles, while in England, that Lord Salisbury saw no need for the present to take up again the Alliance Question. Sir Frank Lascelles had added that the Kaiser had learned of the conversations concerning an alliance and wished to see the plan carried out. It appears from the German documents that no papers had been submitted to the Kaiser by the Foreign Office with the exception of a few which afforded no adequate insight. Consequently the customary marginal notes of the Kaiser are also lacking. Obviously the Chancellor, Count Bülow, kept the Kaiser informed regularly or occasionally by verbal reports on the progress of the alliance negotiations, and also occasionally advised him in writing. During King Edward's visit to Wilhelmshöhe on August 25th, the Kaiser had declared to his guest, when the question of an alliance was touched upon, that he would have nothing to do with it except under two conditions, ratification by Parliament and the inclusion of his allies. Evidently the Kaiser was in general well informed concerning the Chancellor's policy.

At Christmas-time 1901 Lord Lansdowne once more returned to the idea of an alliance. He believed that the mutual public feeling was a hurdle which it was almost impossible to take. But he thought there were important individual questions over which they could come to an understanding. As a matter of fact, there was a problem dating from Chamberlain's attempts at rapprochement, and the future showed that it was the most important of all—Morocco. At the end of the documents dealing with the offer of alliance there stands as the epilogue Lord Salisbury's proud remark to Count Metternich : " England's security depends not so much on alliances as on her chalk cliffs and her Navy." [1]

[1] Vol. xvii, p. 115.

Chamberlain himself, the author of the alliance idea, had been responsible through his Edinburgh speech of October 25th for the complete revelation of the wide gulf between the feelings of the two nations. In order to parry the attacks of a great part of the continental Press concerning British atrocities in the Boer War, Chamberlain asserted that the alleged barbarities did not compare with what other nations had done in Poland, in the Caucasus, in Bosnia, in Tongking, and during the war of 1870. While in the other countries referred to, Russia, Austria-Hungary, and France, this comparison was disposed of with more or less heated protests, in Germany it aroused tremendous indignation that lasted for months and awakened an arrogant echo in the English Press. It was to be foreseen that the resentment over the Edinburgh speech would be discussed in the Reichstag too. Bülow was urged in conversations and in letters not merely to protest against Chamberlain's unfortunate comparison, but at the same time to take a strong stand against the excesses of the Anglophobiacs. In fact, both before and after the Edinburgh speech, Pan-German newspapers were full of reckless aspersions on the British Army. The Ambassador, Count Metternich, urgently counselled against administering a sharp rebuke to Chamberlain, as it would exercise an enduringly unfavourable influence upon the Cabinet and the people in England. The Chancellor, irritated by reproaches levelled at him from various quarters for being too accommodating to other States, did not follow the advice. He contented himself with an effective quotation of words used by Frederick the Great in reference to a calumniator of the Prussian Army : " Let him alone, and don't excite yourself ; he is biting granite." A few days after the " granite " speech, Balfour publicly stated that the English refused to consider the disgusting floods of calumnies that were unceasingly poured out by the Press of the Continent. They refused, he said, out of a certain distaste and a certain indifference. He shared this distaste, he added, but not the indifference ; on the contrary, he considered it a serious matter.

Anyone who lived through those stirring times, or indeed anyone who merely realizes what it means when leading statesmen, driven by the indignation in their respective countries, make speeches of this sort against each other, will acknowledge that only a man of superior will-power, like Bismarck, might perhaps have been able to handle the violently antipathetic public opinion in the two countries. Such a man was not to be found. Count Bülow had only just entered upon the post of Chancellor. Internal rather than foreign affairs claimed his powers and skill. The bitter feeling in the ranks of labour against the personal regime had to be allayed ; the loud complaints of all those interested in agriculture against Caprivi's tariff policy had to be stilled. In order to win a majority in the Reichstag for a swing of the foreign policy over to the side of England, the Chancellor would have had to contend against the legacy of Bismarck as that period interpreted it, and at the same time against the eternally restless temperament of the Kaiser. He did not feel strong enough for such a task in the first year of his Chancellorship.

But this does not explain why the existing willingness of the English Government to settle serious individual questions was not turned to account. Had it not been for the restricted interpretation of the Yang-tse Treaty it would have been possible for Japan to make common cause not only with England but also with Germany. An *entente* concerning Morocco had been proposed on three different occasions, not counting the first feeler put out by Salisbury in 1897. An understanding in regard to the Bagdad Railway could, no doubt, have been reached just as well before the beginning of England's policy of encircle-ment as when its violent termination was at hand. The time needed for the re-establishment of friendlier feelings between the two peoples could not have been used to better purpose than by coming to an understanding in regard to individual questions of practical import.

After Germany had embarked on World Politics her " historico-political " destiny—placed in the centre of

Europe as she was—made it even more imperative than at the time when Bismarck directed the affairs of State to exercise the greatest circumspection in order to prevent England from settling her quarrels with France and Russia without the co-operation of the German Empire, or, worse yet, in a spirit hostile to Germany. The new political alinement was responsible for the fact that it was England and not Germany that saw herself driven to make a final choice. That this choice was an alliance with Germany made the old German " policy of the two irons " obsolete and called for new ways and means. The Germans, however, serenely continued their old course and were completely unconscious of the hidden reef. Granting that the time was not ripe for the idea of an alliance, at all events efforts should have been made to prevent England from going over to France, and ultimately to Russia. The best means to this end would have been the understanding offered in regard to Morocco.

Part of the responsibility for these lost opportunities must be placed to the account of Bülow's favourite theory that England always made other nations pull the chestnuts out of the fire for her, and part to Holstein's academic policy and to his dogma that the antagonism of England and Russia was an immutable fact. He also considered it impossible that Morocco, of all countries whose coasts the Greater Britain of Chamberlain's ambition, the mistress of the sea, was so zealously guarding, could ever form the bridge for an *entente cordiale* between England and France. Just as Bismarck in the Egyptian Question saw to it that the dispute with France should remain unsettled, so it would have been a sound policy not to refuse to co-operate with England in the north-west corner of Africa, that storm-centre in World Politics. If such had been the case, German statesmen would probably not have had to go to Algeciras and face the dilemma of a war or a diplomatic defeat.

CHAPTER III

THE SYSTEM OF COUNTER-BALANCES

AFTER the peace of Pekin, by which the most valuable booty, the peninsula of Liao-tung with Port Arthur, was again wrested from the victor of the Chino-Japanese War, Japan's next aim was to bring Korea completely under her dominion. Although for the time being she had to contend with serious economic difficulties, she did not fail to increase her military strength in order to be prepared to oppose the advance of her Russian rival in Manchuria and Korea. She went to work about this with great caution and with as little noise as possible. The first favourable opportunity for Japan to assert her equality with the other Great Powers was afforded by the Boxer riots in the Chinese province of Tschili, which produced exactly the same concern in all the countries having commercial or business interests in China. Japan's help was needed to save the lives of the menaced Europeans and Americans because she could most quickly bring pressure to bear on those regions where the persecution of foreigners was most violent. The leading statesmen in Tokio were clever enough not to thrust themselves forward. They foresaw that Russia would seek to exploit the difficulties in the co-operation of the Powers and the weakness of the Chinese Government in order to acquire new special privileges in Manchuria.

There were two groups of influential politicians in Tokio. One, headed by the Prime Minister, Marquis Ito, thought that an armed conflict with Russia over Korea should be avoided, if possible, on account of its economic and financial consequences. The other group, to which Viscount Katsura and Count Komura belonged, thought it out of the question that Russian arrogance would condescend to a treaty with Japan, and they considered that war was inevitable sooner or later, since it was the only solution. This opinion was shared by Baron Hayaschi, the Japanese Ambassador at London. Since both groups agreed that an isolated Japan was in no position to obtain the sovereignty over Korea, and that this end could only be attained in conjunction with a Great Power, the Minister-President, Marquis Ito, although favouring a policy of understanding with Russia, gave his consent to Baron Hayaschi to enter into confidential conversations in London. In June 1901 the Ito Ministry resigned, and was followed by the Katsura Ministry, in which Komura held the portfolio for Foreign Affairs.

During the negotiations over England's offer of an alliance with Germany, the idea emerged, not only of linking the entire Triple Alliance to an Anglo-German defensive alliance, but also of creating at the same time a Five-Power Group by interesting Japan in the plan. It is not absolutely certain who was the father of this idea. On April 15, 1901, at the close of the first period of the negotiations concerning an Anglo-German Alliance, the German Chargé d'Affaires in Tokio, Count Botho Wedel, reported that he had learned from a private Japanese source that, according to a telegram from the Japanese Minister in London, Baron Hayaschi, Germany's London representative, Baron von Eckardstein, had dropped hints of pending Anglo-German negotiations, and that he intended to invite Japan's co-operation. In his memoirs, which appeared in London in 1915, Baron Hayaschi writes that Lord Lansdowne had said to him in May 1901 that it was expedient not to limit the treaty concerning Eastern Asia, for which Tokio was working, to Japan and England, but to include a third Power, Germany. As a matter of fact, Hayaschi was instructed by his Government to sound London as to whether concurrent action with England might be possible for the solution of the Chinese Question, and, if so, by what methods. From his conversations with Lord Lansdowne he received the impression that England would not enter into any binding agreement concerning China unless Germany were a party to it. Nothing more, however, was said about this. The whole business of the so-called Five-Power Group was in abeyance during Lord Salisbury's absence on the Riviera from April to May 10, 1901. It is difficult to give an exact account of the events leading to the Anglo-Japanese Alliance, because the statements in the respective memoirs of Eckardstein and Hayaschi are at variance, and do not entirely agree with the German documents either. At all events, after the English Prime Minister had rejected the idea of linking the Triple Alliance with an Anglo-German Treaty,[1] the question of a " Group of Five " had necessarily to be dropped. Consequently the English Foreign Office also from thenceforth treated the Japanese suggestion of an agreement with England concerning Eastern Asia as a question by itself, quite apart from the negotiations dealing with the Anglo-German Alliance project, especially as the conversations concerning the treaty with Germany had in the meantime come to an impasse.

The negotiations concerning the Anglo-Japanese Treaty got under way in the summer of 1901. At the beginning of November, Baron Hayaschi received from Lord Lansdowne the first draft of the treaty. On January 30, 1902, the treaty was signed.

On February 3, 1902, the German Ambassador, Count Metternich, reported to his Foreign Office that Lord Lansdowne had handed to him the text of the Anglo-Japanese Treaty for the private information of the German Government, with the following observations : The Imperial German Government, he said, was the only one that had received this information so far. He added that he wanted to keep up the custom of frank discussion, quite in agreement with a wish expressed some time previously by the Kaiser to Sir Frank Lascelles, that the British Government might keep in touch with the German Government in regard to their plans in the Far East. How was this step

[1] *Vide supra*, p. 111.

to be interpreted? Under the influence of Holstein it had become the habit with the official circles in Berlin, when proposals or communications were made by other Governments, not to examine them simply and straightforwardly, but to let their minds run in devious paths searching for every sort of deep design. Thus Lord Lansdowne's friendly communication and his confidential transmission, of the text of the treaty to the German Ambassador were made the basis for the suspicion that the two contracting parties hoped Germany would commit an indiscretion, so that it would appear as though Germany were also a party to the treaty. It would be easy, then, to play this against Germany in Russia.[1]

The Anglo-Japanese Treaty was concluded at first for five years. Article I stated as its cardinal principle the independence of China and Korea, and affirmed that neither of the signatories harboured aggressive designs in either of these two countries. England was described as chiefly interested in China, whereas Japan, in addition to her interests in China, had also exceptionally important interests —political, commercial, and industrial—in Korea. If these interests should be threatened either by the aggression of another Power or by disturbances in China or Korea, either party to the compact would be free to take protective measures or to resort to intervention. The two succeeding Articles provided that if either Power became involved in warlike complications with a third Power, the other should remain neutral ; but should hasten to the assistance of the ally in case the latter's enemy were joined by a fourth Power.

History knows of few treaties of alliance that have proved so remunerative for both partners as the Anglo-Japanese. Great Britain acquired a companion in arms whose real strength she had been the first to recognize and who could aid her against the Power that had threatened her Asiatic possessions. Japan was no longer isolated, as in 1895. This alliance with England raised her to the position of a

[1] Vol. xvii, pp. 135–52.

Great Power, qualified henceforth to participate in World Politics. With redoubled zeal she proceeded with her armaments on land and on sea in order to achieve the defeat of her Russian rival in Korea and in Manchuria.

In St. Petersburg the Anglo-Japanese Treaty was received with great ill-humour. The Minister for Foreign Affairs, Count Lamsdorv, appeared completely astonished when the Japanese Minister showed him the treaty on February 20, 1902. He at once got the impression that the treaty was directed against Russia, and therefore must be taken " very seriously." He especially expressed his surprise that the two partners, England and Japan, should have envisaged in their agreement the possibilities of warlike complications. The Minister, therefore, proposed that Germany and Russia should give renewed expression to their hand-in-hand policy in the Far East, possibly by a declaration reserving common action in the event of the violation of their rights and interests in China. In this way a close co-operation of all the continental Powers was to be achieved, if possible. The Chancellor, Count Bülow, rejected this idea, which amounted to a renewal of the earlier East Asiatic Triple Alliance, giving excellent reasons and displaying such unwonted firmness that the Ambassador, Count Alvensleben, actually expressed apprehensions. With great pertinacity, Count Lamsdorv strove for a whole month to get Germany to rescind the refusal, but Bülow remained firm. Aside from the fact that the economic interests of Germany were already protected by the Yang-tse Treaty with England, he especially pointed out that Germany's participation in the Russian declaration might imperil the Triple Alliance, since under no consideration would Italy aline herself with England's enemies.

As a result of the German Government's refusal, the step proposed by Lamsdorv against the Anglo-Japanese Treaty was taken only by the Powers of the Dual Alliance. The declaration was presented to Berlin, March 19, 1902, in the form of a joint Franco-Russian note.

This diplomatic counter-move on the part of Russia

against the Anglo-Japanese Treaty proclaimed that the solidarity of Russia and France, allies in Europe, applied also to the *status quo* in the Far East. Among the German public the impression was created that this went far to confirm Bülow's words in the Reichstag on January 8, 1902. In the session of that day, in order to allay apprehension concerning the renewal of the Triple Alliance, Count Bülow had drawn a comparison between the present and the time when the alliance with Austria-Hungary was concluded, 1879, and had said in that connection : " At that time we were concerned only with European politics. The political combinations did not extend beyond the Mediterranean basin. To-day the policies of all Great Powers encompass the entire terrestrial globe. In the entire course of history there has probably never been a period in which so many mighty empires were in existence simultaneously as there are to-day. This gives rise to a system of counter-balances, if I may so express it, which naturally tends to preserve the peace of the world even without a special agreement. For there is no Power that would not have to ask herself, if she wanted to wage war in one quarter in Europe, ' What will happen in my rear ? ' For, after all, you cannot have your eyes everywhere."

And indeed, after the conclusion of the Anglo-Japanese Treaty and the subsequent statement that France and Russia would stand together in Eastern Asia too, did it not look as though the continual continental frictions were more and more to give way to a system of counter-balances which even without special contrivances was automatically keeping the pendulum of the great clock of the world oscillating regularly and quietly ? However, the Franco-Russian statement was only a blind. Shortly after its publication Delcassé made it plain in the Chamber of Deputies that there was no intention of extending the Dual Alliance to East Asiatic affairs. " What was the sense, then, of this joint declaration ? " quite rightly inquired Tardieu at a later time. " It misled public opinion in Russia, leading her to depend upon possible support

from France.   It irritated the Japanese, and accustomed
the entire world to the idea of a war by ranging the Powers
in two opposite groups—Japan and England in one, France
and Russia in the other." [1]

Tardieu, the former Secretary to the Embassy, later, in
the World War, the Special High Commissioner to the
United States and delegate to the Versailles Peace Conference, was still writing for the *Figaro* in 1902 under the
name of Villiers.   In an interview granted by Bülow, he
inquired what would be Germany's attitude if there were
a clash between the two East Asiatic Alliances.   The
Chancellor replied that Germany could not bind herself in
advance.   She was, he said, territorially far less interested
in Eastern Asia than were the other Powers, and could
afford to decide as each case arose whether to remain neutral
or to join the party that seemed most likely to champion
peace and the Open Door.   Time alone could prove whether
this policy of the Free Hand could usefully be continued
for long.   No doubt it was an enticing idea to be able
to play the part of *tertius gaudens* between alliances
with mutually antagonistic aspirations.   As far as England
was concerned, the pact with Japan was the first decisive
action with the object of restoring her predominance in
World Politics.   Germany, on the other hand, was threatened
with the rôle of *tertius patiens* the moment that England
should choose to change the system of counter-balances in
Europe by joining France.

Shortly after the Franco-Russian Declaration, on April 12,
1902, a new agreement with China regarding Manchuria
was published in St. Petersburg, providing for the restora-
tion of Chinese sovereignty and the withdrawal of Russian
troops.   The *Official Gazette* added, however, that if China
for any reason whatsoever should fail to fulfil her obligations,
Russia would no longer consider herself bound by the
terms of the treaty.   Then followed a revival of activity
in the great forest enterprises on the Yalu, in which
aristocratic and influential circles in St. Petersburg were

[1] André Tardieu, *La France et les Alliances*, Paris, 1909, p. 22.

interested, and the establishment of the Government of the Far East.

The treaty with Japan was principally the work of Lord Lansdowne. Shortly after it was concluded, in July 1902, Salisbury, on account of his age, voluntarily relinquished the direction of English politics. With him disappeared from English political life the man who for a whole generation had exercised the greatest influence on England's position in the world, and who for seven years had wielded such power that he was popularly styled "His Majesty Salisbury." He belonged to the ancient family of the Cecils that since the days of Queen Elizabeth had given many dignitaries to the State. With increasing years he displayed the immovability of a rock that remained unmoved in sunshine and in storm. To his strong pride of family he joined an unshakeable faith in the greatness of the British Empire. His spirit seemed reflected in the words used by his son, Lord Cranborne, shortly before his father's retirement : "England does not solicit alliances, she only grants them." This was not the language of the time when Chamberlain was endeavouring to reach an understanding with Germany. We have already seen that Salisbury himself had once replied to Count Hatzfeldt's successor at the London Embassy that England relied only on her Navy and her chalk cliffs.[1]

So far, England had not as yet changed her relation to the two groups of Powers on the Continent, the Triple Alliance and the Dual Alliance. So far, the Anglo-French differences had not yet been adjusted, and consequently the renewal of the Triple Alliance could be consummated without direct opposition from England. But what had been changed in the last years, and changed to the detriment of the inner coherence of the Triple Alliance, was Italy's relation to France, and also the benevolence that England had hitherto displayed towards Italy's union with the Central Bloc. About the same time that England,

[1] *Vide supra*, p. 113.

out of concern for her predominance in World Politics, came out of her isolation and secured Japan's support against Russia in Asia, the German Government had to deal with a crisis in the Triple Alliance under conditions that were far more unfavourable than those at the time of its twelve-year extension in May 1891.

At that time, a year after Bismarck's retirement and the conclusion of the so-called Heligoland Treaty, England co-operated materially to keep Italy in the Triple Alliance. During the negotiations concerning the Heligoland Treaty she had received the assurance that Germany would not assist Russia in pursuing her goal in Asia, which was to reach "the Indian Seas."[1] Ten years later England and Germany had been alienated by the hostility of the two peoples both before and after the Boer War and by the fruitless attempts of the two Cabinets to reach a rapproche-ment. In 1891 Italy still looked upon France as her enemy from the point of view both of politics and of economics, while Germany was pursuing a commercial policy which promised to make up to Italy for her loss of the French markets by facilitating the disposal of Italian goods in Germany. But in 1901 Germany was preparing a new tariff with increased duties, while Italy had not only made her economic peace with France by her Commercial Treaty of 1898, but had also reached a political agreement with France in December 1900 by which Italy's claim to Tripoli was recognized in return for her recognition of French precedence in Morocco. This great change in Italy's position had gradually come about after her disaster in the war against King Menelek of Abyssinia. The defeat at Adowa brought in its train the fall of Crispi, and made the Italians again susceptible to the allurements of their "Latin sister nation." Delcassé and his helper, Barrère, the Ambassador in Rome, were only too successful in fanning irredentist and republican agitations, in enlisting the Italian freemasons on the side of France, and in drawing the gaze of the statesmen on the Roman Piazza away from

[1] *Vide* Julius von Eckardt's *Berlin-Wien-Rom*, p. 93.

Tunis and Morocco and in directing it towards the Adria against their ally, Austria.

But perhaps the severest blow to the Triple Alliance was the assassination of King Humbert by an anarchist on July 29, 1900. " It is all over now with the Triple Alliance," St. Petersburg exulted.[1] The murdered King had been a convinced and stanch adherent of the Triple Alliance, while his successor, the young King Victor Emmanuel, was under the influence of his wife, the Montenegrin Princess Helena, who had strong Slavic leanings, and would have liked nothing better than to see her father, the Prince of the Black Mountains, raised to the rank of king after his country had been enlarged.

In his speech of January 8, 1902, which contained the expression " a system of counter-balances," Count Bülow dealt also with the Franco-Italian Mediterranean Agreement, which recognized Italy's claim to Tripoli and its Hinterland, and with the renewal of the Triple Alliance. He compared the Triple Alliance to a happy marriage in which the husband does not have to fly into a rage if his wife once in a way has an innocent extra dance with someone else. The extra dance with France can hardly be regarded as so harmless as all this, if the consequences are taken into consideration ; for barely ten years later it turned suddenly into an Italian war-dance with Turkey over the question of Tripoli. To his witty comparison Bülow added the solemn warning that although the Triple Alliance had proved to be an excellent guarantee of peace, nevertheless it was no longer absolutely necessary to Germany. By this remark he meant to remind the Italian statesmen who were enthusiastically advocating a Latin alliance that France would never have entered upon such friendly relations with Italy but for her rank as a Great Power, which she would never have attained if it had not been for her association with the Central European Alliance brought about under Crispi.

In Rome, since February 1901, a Ministry of the Left

[1] Vol. xviii, p. 501.

under Zanardelli had been in power with Giolitti as Minister of the Interior and Prinetti as Minister for Foreign Affairs. The Consulta had not had so Francophile a leader as Prinetti in twenty years. Nevertheless, during the discussions over the alliance with the German Ambassador, Count Karl Wedel, which began in 1902, he shared the King's views, and he had no intention of dropping the Triple Alliance. One of the difficulties lay in Prinetti's wish that the new German-Italian Commercial Treaty might be consummated at the same time as the political alliance. It was impossible to satisfy this wish, because the time before the expiration of the Triple Alliance in May was too short in which to finish the new German tariff, since work on it had only recently begun. In this matter Prinetti contented himself with Germany's promise to conclude a new commercial treaty forthwith. Another and more important request of the Italian Government was that several alterations should be made in the text of the Triple Alliance Treaty. The most objectionable proposal amounted to a guarantee of the *status quo* in the Balkans. This proposal Count Bülow flatly rejected. In the instructions to the Ambassador, February 26, 1902, he said as follows: " We may take it for granted that the plan of interposing the Triple Alliance as a barrier between Russia and the Bosphorus has not been adopted by Prinetti without the knowledge of his adviser, Barrère, if it did not altogether originate with the latter. If the French Government were able to say: ' France would not object to Russia's coming into possession of the Straits, but the Triple Alliance is unalterably opposed to it,' this would mean a tremendous success for France's policy, and the idea of *la revanche* would have come a good deal nearer its realization. French diplomacy will have to forgo this success, for already the Viennese Government have refused to discuss further this guarantee project as being absolutely futile."

During his interview with Prinetti in Vienna on March 28, 1902, the Chancellor, Count Bülow, succeeded in obtaining a renewal of the Triple Alliance with no changes whatsoever.

This effectually dissipated all apprehension lest changes in the text of the treaty might further the ends of anti-German agitation in Paris. Likewise in the Tripoli Question, concerning which Prinetti wished to see a statement of *désintéressement* inserted in the text, the Italian Premier finally was satisfied with the verbal promise that Germany would put no obstacles in the way of Italy's aspiration to Tripoli.[1]

Nowhere was the outcome of the negotiations over the Triple Alliance in 1902 awaited with such tense interest as in the Nationalist Press of the French capital. Although the earlier hope of Italy's defection had had to be abandoned, still papers like the *Gaulois* remained convinced that a new wording would be agreed upon, with the omission of all provisions for protection against a French war of aggression. From Germany's standpoint that would have deprived the treaty of any value. Delcassé was in a great hurry to express his views in the Chamber of Deputies concerning the renewal of the treaty, and did this in a way that was calculated to strengthen the belief that the treaty would be weakened so as to allow Italy more extra dances. A few days after the signing of the renewal of the treaty, on June 28, 1902, Delcassé stated in the Chamber of Deputies : " Italy's policy is not aimed against France, either directly or indirectly, in consequence of her alliances. In no case and in no way can it become a menace to us, either through the channels of diplomacy or through protocols and military conventions. In no case and in no way can Italy become the tool or the accessory to an attack on our country." The simple fact that the Triple Alliance neither was at that time, nor ever had been, an offensive but always and exclusively a defensive alliance, really did not call for such a redundance of categorical statements. Obviously they were for the purpose of creating the impression that a weakening in the compact had been achieved, and the reference to concurrent military conventions lent colour to the supposition that Italy henceforth was not bound

[1] Vol. xviii, pp. 501-90.

to render any military assistance in the event of war if the *casus fœderis* arose.

The alliance in no way and at no time set limits to Italy's freedom to determine for herself the peace strength of her army, nor consequently the amount of her financial burdens. The agreements between the General Staffs, however, which were concurrent with the Triple Alliance, did provide that Italy, in the event of a French attack, would under certain circumstances send a definite number of troops across the Alps for use on the western frontier of Germany. According to an agreement reached in 1888, Italy had, in case of a Franco-German war, to transport the Third Army of five corps to the Upper Rhine for employment on the German left wing. This stipulation was again incorporated in the military conversations at the renewal of the Triple Alliance in 1902. It was entirely on Italy's initiative that an agreement had been reached concerning the transportation of Italian troops. It was also at the suggestion and instigation of the Italian General Staff that a conference of both General Staffs took place in Berlin in the autumn of 1900, which resulted in a formal agreement on December 5, 1900. No text of this is to be found in the German archives.

The most troublesome question was, by which route the five Italian corps were to be transported with the greatest dispatch and safety to the Upper Rhine. The coast railroad, the Rome-Pisa-Genoa route, had to be regarded as impracticable from the outset, because the trains would be exposed to firing from the sea. The King, Victor Emmanuel, was interested in the transportation problem. In an audience granted to the German Military Attaché, von Chelius, the King said it was anything but a pleasure for Italy to send five of her best corps together with two cavalry divisions out of the country. He added that he had heard from one of his wife's relations residing in France that they knew in France exactly the time required for the transportation and the choice of detraining stations south of Strassburg. Subsequently the Chief of the General

I

Staff, Count Schieffen, reported to the Imperial Chancellor
that the King consented to send a great part of his army out
of the country. This certainly was deserving of recognition,
he said, but unfortunately the French had blocked all the
Alpine passes with fortifications from the neutral zone of
Savoy to the Mediterranean. The original Italian plan
of taking the army across the mountains in order to join
forces with the German left wing by marching in a north-
westerly direction had also been frustrated by a carefully
planned system of fortifications. The next idea of attempting a union with the German Army by crossing neutral
Switzerland, even if this involved a show of force, had to be
abandoned after Switzerland had first fortified the pass of
St. Gothard and then had barred the roads in the Rhine
valley by the fortifications at St. Moritz. In the records
of the German Foreign Office there is not a single document
that shows that the violation of the neutrality of Switzerland
might have been contemplated or sanctioned.

In view of all these difficulties, and out of consideration
for the wish of the Italian King to be relieved of a binding
obligation to send troops out of the country, the German
Military Attaché, von Chelius, was instructed to state to
the Chief of the Italian General Staff, Saletta, on behalf of
Count von Schlieffen, that Germany waived her claim to
the co-operation of Italian troops on the Upper Rhine.
However, the German official documents are not entirely
clear in this matter. General Saletta, it is expressly stated,
had not taken official cognizance of the German renunciation,
and had, in spite of it, discussed anew the sending of an
auxiliary corps. It would appear that the waiving of the
claim was a temporary expedient, mutually agreed upon,
to ease Prinetti's position in the Chamber of Deputies.
The Left wanted to ask questions concerning Italy's military
obligations. It was to be feared that the anti-German
sentiment of the people, which had been deeply stirred by
newspaper articles inspired by the French Ambassador,
Barrère, would find vent in violent protests against the idea
of sending Italian soldiers out of the country and lead to

disturbances, especially in Northern Italy. Exactly as the Ambassador, Count Wedel, had from the first been sceptical about Italian help, Count Schlieffen stated in a report to the Chancellor on December 14, 1902, that not only could the German Army not reckon on the Third Italian Army, but must be prepared to deal on the Alpine border with the entire French Army.[1]

The French Yellow Book,[2] *Les Accords franco-italiens de 1900-1902*, shows that on June 4, 1902, a few weeks before the renewal of the Triple Alliance, Prinetti, after conversations with Ambassador Barrère, caused a formal statement to be transmitted to Delcassé containing substantially what Delcassé later announced in the Chamber of Deputies. This one-sided declaration was followed in the beginning of November 1902 by an exchange of notes in Rome. These notes provided for an amplification of the Mediterranean Agreement of December 1900, and in addition a neutrality clause regarding the general relations of the two countries. In respect to Morocco and Tripoli, both parties henceforth were to be entirely free to develop their spheres of influence. As to their general relations, it was agreed that either party was to observe strict neutrality in the event of a direct or an indirect attack upon the other party by one or more Powers, even though the party attacked might perhaps feel compelled to take the initiative in declaring war in order to defend his honour or security. This provision, to which Delcassé attached the greatest weight, was limited only by the stipulation that the intention of declaring war was to be communicated in advance to the other party, in order that the latter might judge whether a provocation did in point of fact exist. French diplomacy appeared to be guided by the idea that Germany could misuse the Triple Alliance *sous des dehors défensifs* for an aggressive war; they thought it would be much easier for Italy to preserve her neutrality if it were stipulated that even a declaration of war by France was not necessarily to be regarded as proof positive that France was the aggressor.

[1] Vol. xviii, pp. 683–708.   [2] Paris, 1920.

The counterpart of this compact is to be found in the provisions of the Franco-Russian Military Convention of August 17, 1892. This stipulated that if the Triple Alliance, or even if only one of its members, should mobilize, France and Russia were immediately to mobilize their entire armies, and to engage them without delay in decisive combat in order to oblige Germany to fight a war on two fronts.[1] Just as in the Franco-Russian Military Convention the beginning of hostilities was to be quite independent of a declaration of war, so the terms of the Franco-Italian Treaty of Neutrality of November 1902 deprived any declaration of war of all significance as to the aggressive or defensive character of the conflict.

According to a report of Ambassador Barrère on March 10, 1912 (also published in the Yellow Book), concerning the Agreements of 1900–1902, the exchange of notes on November 1902 was not in the nature of a *contre-traité*, but of a *contre-partie de la Triplice*. Even if, all this notwithstanding, we wish to be lenient in our judgment of the agreements arrived at by Prinetti and Delcassé in 1902, certainly as far as Italy's treaty allegiance towards her Central European Allies was concerned, the worst feature of this counter-play was the fact that the Governments in Berlin and in Vienna were kept completely in the dark. Not until several years later, when the Marquis di San Giuliano, belonging to Crispi's school, was Minister for Foreign Affairs, did reports reach Berlin that during Prinetti's time there had been secret goings on with France scarcely consistent with Italy's treaty obligations towards the Central Powers.

In Germany at large the conclusion of the negotiations with Italy, reached with so much difficulty, did not seem to warrant any anxiety as to Germany's security and position in Europe. A rapid survey shows that to all appearances the system of counter-balances was still working well and without friction.

The internal affairs of France were still coloured by the long-drawn-out Dreyfus scandal and the so-called *fiches* (the

[1] Cf. the Yellow Book of 1919.

lists that had been found). The Waldeck-Rousseau Ministry had been engaged since 1899 in fighting the monastic orders and in keeping clerical and nationalistic influences out of the Army. After the voluntary retirement of Waldeck-Rousseau there followed Combes's Ministry, whose radical and anti-clerical character was even more pronounced. The humiliation of Fashoda still rankling in the people's minds and the anti-English feeling rampant during the Boer War helped to make popular an exchange of courtesies between Germany and France : on the death of President Faure ; after the earthquake in Martinique ; on the Kaiser's visit to a French training-ship in Norwegian waters ; on the occasion of General Bonnal's visit to Berlin ; so that one might speak of a period of rapprochement. In France the Socialist leader, Jaurès, urged his countrymen in speeches and in articles to banish *la revanche* from their hearts and minds. In Germany the repeal of the dictatorship for Alsace-Lorraine had been repeatedly passed in the Reichstag, and came into effect in June 1902. This showed that the German Government had become convinced that the passing of one generation had sufficed to reconcile the population of the Imperial Province to the new order.

A glance in the eastern direction revealed an equally pleasing prospect. The meeting of the Emperors at Reval, August 1902, which Count Bülow and the Russian Minister for Foreign Affairs, Count Lamsdorv, attended, served to show the world that the wire between Berlin and St. Petersburg was again in good working order. The Anglo-Japanese Treaty, pointed unmistakably against Russia, had again brought home the value of the German friendship. In token of a fraternization of historic import the two rulers exchanged their *aiguilleten* (hanging cords of the admiral's uniform) ; the Tsar presented the Kaiser with a Bojar helmet about thirty inches in height, of chased silver and ornamented with Russian jewels ; in return he received the gift of a gold inkstand. Shortly afterwards, in two addresses made in Posen in the presence of the Governor-General of Warsaw, General Tschertkov, the Kaiser extolled

the loyal friendship of the two rulers and the companion-
ship in arms of their forces, announcing at the same time
the repeal of the radius law for the ancient fortress town.
A French authority described the Franco-Russian Alliance
as *faussée et dévoyée* because *sans action* in Europe.

With the new World Power in North America the German
Empire was on good terms.   Prince Henry's visit to the
United States was in every respect a success.   In acknow-
ledgment of the friendly reception accorded to his brother,
the Kaiser announced his intention of presenting Washing-
ton with a bronze statue of Frederick the Great ; and President Roosevelt closed his reply with these words : " It is
a good augury for the whole human race that at the opening
of this century the American and German nations are co-
operating in sincere friendship."

Only from England a chilly wind was blowing.   After
three years' war in South Africa, England was gathering
new strength.   Clemency and generosity towards the
defeated Boers gave promise to the British Empire of a
large increase of power within the widened boundaries of
Cape Colony.   The King's visits to the Courts of Lisbon
and Rome were followed in May 1903 by a magnificent
entry into Paris.   At a hint from the police the old anti-
English pamphlets and caricatures disappeared from book-
shops and news-stands ; the Royal guest was joyfully
welcomed.   Of course, his account was burdened neither
with the Fashoda Incident nor the tribulations of the
Boers.   The Russo-Japanese War was looming in sight.
King Edward strongly advised the French Government
not to participate in this conflict as an ally of Russia, for
then the *casus fœderis* towards Japan would arise for
England.   In February 1904 the East Asiatic war did
actually break out, and shortly afterwards the close bond
of friendship was formed between England and France.

This was how things looked in the world outside.   But
even within the Alliance of the Central Powers there was
another weak spot besides that of Italy's reawakened
love for France.   It escaped the attention of the Germans

because the chance remark dropped in the previous century, that the Austrian Empire would have to be invented if it did not exist, had become a dogma to which they blindly adhered. Others, however, had better sight, and discerned the weak spot : such as Lord Salisbury, when he objected to entering into an alliance with a State containing strong Slavic units in its population ; and also Lord Lansdowne, when, in considering all future contingencies in the event of an Anglo-German Alliance, he also referred to the disintegration of the Austrian Empire. It is a long time ago that Austria's virile poet, Grillparzer, writing of the progressive spirit of the age, said : " The entire world will gain fresh vigour by this new order of things ; [1] Austria alone will fall to pieces as a result of it. The fault lies with the abominable Machiavellianism of her leaders, who furthered and fostered the mutual aversion of the various nationalities in the provinces in order that the dynasty should constitute the only bond of political unity. The Hungarian hates the Bohemian, who hates the German, and the Italian hates them all. Like unwilling horses lashed together, they will disperse in all directions if the advancing spirit of the age weakens or breaks the power of the constraining yoke." To be sure, such historical processes are only slowly consummated ; their progress is reckoned not by years but by generations, and for the time being reverence for the venerable old gentleman in the Hofburg still kept the ill-mated team harnessed to the common Coach of State. But the task grew increasingly difficult every year. In Bohemia there was no end to the conflict between nationalities. Kramarsch, the leader of the Young Czechs, who during the era of Badeni was second President of the Austrian Chamber of Deputies, compared the Triple Alliance to a costly but old piano that was still too ornamental to be relegated to the lumber-room, but too worn-out to play upon any more. In Hungary, where the Magyar dominion over the Rumanian, German and Croatian elements had been established with great

[1] Grillparzer referred to the July Revolution of 1830 in France.

energy and not without harshness, fanatical enthusiasts for independence were striving to loosen and to undo the most effective clamp at the King-Emperor's disposal. This clamp was the joint Army of the Empire of Austria-Hungary. The Italian Irredentists pushed their claims to the heights of the "Brennero" and clamoured for a university of their own. All these disruptive movements were accorded open sympathy and secret support in Paris.

Thus, while the world was listening in astonishment as the Kaiser expounded again and again to his Germans high-sounding ideas of a world-dominion of the German spirit, of the trident being in our fist, and of the German arm reaching to the uttermost parts of the earth, gradually the hidden reef emerged.

BOOK IV

THE ENCIRCLEMENT OF GERMANY

CHAPTER I

THE ENTENTE CORDIALE AND THE TANGIER INCIDENT

THE chasm that had appeared during the Boer War between the two cognate peoples, the English and the German, remained open in the years following and made it difficult for the two Governments to re-establish their old relations of mutual confidence. They had for the time being to be satisfied with avoiding everything that could arouse new outbursts of passion. During the visits of the Boer generals—Botha, Delarey, and De Wet—to London, Amsterdam, and Berlin, the old anti-English feeling of enthusiasm for the Boers flamed up again in Pan-German newspapers, while the German Government observed a calm, correct attitude. Something similar occurred in England in the winter of 1902-3, when the anti-German sentiment led to a revolt of public opinion against the Government because they had been induced by the similarity of their claims to join Germany and Italy in taking concerted action against the arbitrary rule of President Castor in Venezuela.[1] At the end of an address in Liverpool in February 1903, Balfour exhorted all those who had any influence on public opinion to reflect how deeply accountable everyone would be who lent himself to the easy business of embittering the relations of the two peoples. This same idea the German Chancellor had expressed shortly before, during the debate in the Reichstag on the refusal to receive the Boer generals, reversing the words of Horace about the delirium of kings and the defeated Greeks.

[1] Vol. xvii, p. 241.

The growing estrangement between England and Germany and the keen antagonism between Russia and Japan suggested to the Russian Government the idea of inquiring in Berlin in February 1902 whether the German Government would be inclined to renew in some other form the East Asiatic Triple Alliance of 1895 between Russia, France, and Germany.   Count Bülow, contrary to his former willingness to do Russia a favour, definitely, although mildly, refused the suggestion of St. Petersburg, because it would make England openly the enemy of Germany.   It was not even certain whether France would not be compelled, on account of her alliance obligations, to fight on the side of Russia in the impending Russo-Japanese War.   As a matter of fact, France remained neutral when the war came. Russia had already received ample favour in that the Kaiser had promised the Tsar to protect his rear in case Russia became involved in war in Eastern Asia.

The idea of an alliance of Germany, Russia, and France had already loomed up in the conversations during the Tsar's visit to Danzig, September 11, 1901.   Count Lamsdorv told the Kaiser that they ought to strive for a real alliance between the continental Powers in order to ensure world peace.   The Tsar enthusiastically concurred, and promised that he would do all in his power to realize this "great idea."   All the exalted personages, monarchs, and ministers apparently bothered themselves very little as to what the third in the proposed alliance might say to the anti-English plan.   But the French Foreign Minister, Delcassé, was already at work arranging a substantial bargain with Spain over Morocco and establishing an intimate understanding with England.

In the face of the ever-approaching danger of such an understanding between England and France, what was the attitude of the men who were directing Germany's policy ? During his visit to England in November 1902, the Kaiser remarked to Balfour that the Navy was a necessity for Germany ; he was not concerned about a few palm-trees, more or less, in the tropics, but the Navy strengthened tremendously the idea of unity in that mosaic structure, the German Empire ; if there were good will on both sides it would be easy to settle colonial disputes. (As though favourable opportunities for this had not been missed !) When afterwards all sorts of reports appeared in the newspapers that negotiations about Morocco were going on between England and France, Bülow never wavered in his policy of marking time ; he said that one could not be phlegmatic enough about the matter. Holstein insisted that an understanding between the Western Powers was a mere phantom of the imagination ; that it was impossible of realization unless France renounced the idea of *la revanche*.

As early as the beginning of 1903 articles had appeared in Paris journals suggesting, in case the affairs of Morocco should necessitate European intervention, that France would claim recognition as the paramount Power, and in return would recognize similar claims of other Powers elsewhere. The return visit of President Loubet to London, the beginning of July 1903, the first time within fifty years that the head of the French State had visited England, made it impossible any longer to doubt that a permanent rapprochement was under way between the two countries, implying the peaceful settlement of all disputes. The watchword of the cordial understanding (Entente Cordiale) came into circulation on both sides of the Channel. Nine months later, on April 8, 1907, the Anglo-French Treaty regarding Egypt, Morocco, etc., was signed in London.[1]

The rectification of frontiers in West Africa in favour of France, the French renunciation of ancient fishing rights in Newfoundland, the declaration regarding Siam and the New Hebrides, did not concern Germany. Her entire attention was concentrated on the cardinal provisions of the agreement : the simultaneous settlement of the Egyptian and the Moroccan Questions. France promised " not to hamper England's actions in Egypt," while England renounced " political influence in Morocco," and conceded

[1] Vol. xx, Chap. 141.

to France the right " to watch over the peace of Morocco
and to render the Sultan's Government any necessary
assistance for administrative, financial, or military reforms."
A clearer proof of the actual existence of a cordial understanding could not have been given.   France was renouncing
definitively the carrying out of an idea that had originated
in the mind of the German philosopher, Leibniz, the founder
of differential calculus, and which Napoleon a century later
attempted to realize.   This was the plan of obtaining the
key to world dominion by occupying the Isthmus of Suez
and the Nile Country.   England promised in return to
give France a free road for her advance in Morocco, with
the stipulation, however, that the African coast opposite
Gibraltar was not to be fortified ; in other words, that
the watch at the entrance to the Mediterranean Sea was
to remain under the control of England alone.   There was
no mistaking the fact that a French protectorate as implied
in the English declaration must have an important bearing
on the freedom of commerce guaranteed by the Madrid
Treaty of 1880, and also on the economic equality of any
third Power.

In the German Reichstag the Anglo-French Colonial
Agreement was referred to by various members as early
as April 12th and 14th, 1904.   The National Liberal deputy,
Sattler, spoke of a rearrangement in European politics ;
the Socialist leader, Bebel, saw in the agreement a measure
of civilization in which Germany had been too little considered, which seemed to indicate increasing isolation ;
the anti-Semitic member, Count Reventlow, a brother of
the well-known author, deplored the humiliating fact that
other Powers were securing for themselves greater influence
in Morocco than was Germany.   Faced by these objections
and apprehensions, Count Bülow tried to make the best of
a bad business.   He insisted that Germany's interests in
Morocco were purely economic, and that there was no
reason to fear that any Power would disregard her.   He
scouted the idea of isolation in view of the fact that the
German Empire had a definite alliance with two Great

Powers while enjoying friendly relations with five others. The relations with France, he added, were calm and peaceful, and would remain so as far as it depended upon Germany. In order to acquire a piece of Morocco, Germany might have had to draw the sword, and to embark on a policy of adventure would be sheer recklessness. Impatient critics who were asking what had become of the Kaiser's World Politics when other States could settle old disputes in utter disregard of Germany's interests were the very ones who had done their best to smother all conciliatory feeling in England by their insane anti-English agitation.

As a matter of fact, circumstances—the war in Eastern Asia and England's going over from the Triple Alliance to the side of France—imposed an attitude of reserve upon Germany. Under official influence, public opinion in Germany was altogether in accord with the Chancellor's statements in the Reichstag that it would be sheer recklessness to plunge the country into war on account of Morocco. Germany's relations with the French Republic were so little disturbed that as late as the end of April 1904 serious-minded people were to be found in Paris and in Berlin who believed that a meeting between the Kaiser and President Loubet in Italian waters was within the range of possibility.

Many rumours about this incident were afloat at the time in official circles, and subsequently in the Press also. When the idea of a meeting came to nothing, some journals attempted to represent the failure as due to the cool stoicism of the President, which had wrecked the Kaiser's attempt at rapprochement. The history of the affair is as follows : There was a prospect that the Kaiser would be on a cruise in the Mediterranean in April 1904. In the same month the President of France wished to return the visit the King of Italy had made in Paris the previous summer, when the " happily concluded rapprochement " between Italy and France had been celebrated. The idea of utilizing the favourable opportunity for a meeting of the heads of the French and the German States in Italian waters originated in the mind of the Prince of Monaco, who on account of his fondness for deep-sea research and aquatic sports was in the Kaiser's good graces, and who at the same time kept up various connections with eminent persons in Paris. In inviting President Loubet to Monaco, the Prince spoke of the Kaiser's approaching journey to the south, the end of which, he said, would about coincide with the President's visit to Italy. The President in reply manifested the desire to make the acquaintance of the Kaiser, but at the same time expressed his doubts as to whether the Nationalists and the Clericals in France would quietly submit to such a step.

Nevertheless, the President throughout February repeatedly inquired in chance conversations with the German Ambassador, Prince Rodolin, about the programme of the Kaiser's journey. With the exception of the arrival in Naples on March 24th and the welcome by King Victor Emmanuel, no definite plan had been arranged for the stay in the Mediterranean, which was to include visits to Calabria, Sicily, and Apulia. There was, however, the likelihood that the Kaiser would still be in Italian waters at the time of Loubet's visit to Rome and Naples. As early as the beginning of April a report appeared in Italian and in French newspapers that a meeting between the Kaiser and the President, at which the King of Italy, too, might perhaps be present, was imminent. As a matter of fact, Tittoni, the Minister for Foreign Affairs, had joyfully welcomed the possibility of such a meeting of the three, but a formal suggestion could be made by Italy only after sounding the Paris Government. No Franco-Italian proposal providing a basis for the German Government to proceed further with the project was made ; obviously because Delcassé and the Ambassador, Barrère, opposed it for fear of vehement opposition in Nationalist and Clerical circles in France

President Loubet's visit to Rome promised to pass off as brilliantly as possible. But that which especially aroused enthusiasm among the Italian Radicals, the failure of the head of Most Christian France, of France the guardian

of the States of the Church, to pay a visit to the Pope in
the Vatican, greatly scandalized the French Clericals ; and
if a meeting with the Kaiser had been added to this, there
certainly would have been no lack of violent counter-
demonstrations in Paris. In order to avoid even an acci-
dental meeting between the Kaiser's yacht and the French
squadron with the President on board, the Kaiser was
induced by the Chancellor to make the return trip from
Sicily by the way of the Adriatic, and to land at Venice
instead of at Genoa, as he had intended. When Loubet
was taking leave of Victor Emmanuel in Naples on April 28th,
the Kaiser, but just returned via Venice, was making an
address to the Chief Burgomaster of Karlsruhe, in which
he expressed his hope that peace would be preserved in
Europe and at the same time his confidence in the courage
and unity of the German people if it should become necessary
to intervene in World Politics. Thus on both sides, on
that of the Kaiser as well as that of the President, the disposition existed to make the acquaintance of the other
and to strengthen the hopes of peace in their respective
countries through a dramatic meeting at sea. But " they
were not able to reach each other, the water was much too
deep." [1]   But in England too they did not wish the Colonial
Agreement with France to appear as evidence of unfriendliness towards Germany. On the contrary, during the discussion of the treaty in Parliament, several members of
the Opposition, Sir Edward Grey among them, recommended, with most complete concurrence from Lord
Lansdowne, that this treaty should be used as a practical
model in other cases of disputes between rival nations, and
the Prime Minister, Balfour, expressly controverted the
idea that the Anglo-French Entente was incompatible with
an amicable Anglo-German agreement. These assurances
were certainly not entirely candid, at least not inasmuch as
certain secret clauses in the treaty with France had at the
same time to be concealed, clauses which, as we shall see
later, were directed against German interests in Morocco.

[1] Vol. xx, Chap. 142, Appendix.

K

Shortly after this King Edward, at the Kaiser's invitation, took part in the regatta at Kiel. The old personal discord between uncle and nephew seemed to have disappeared. The Kiel banquet to all appearances passed off most harmoniously. The Kaiser in his first toast spoke frankly of the German Navy and its peaceful objects. The King responded as honorary German admiral with the words : " May our two flags float beside one another to the most distant time as they float to-day, for the maintenance of peace and the well-being not only of our countries, but of all other nations." At a farewell banquet given by Prince Henry, and seasoned with sanguine naval speeches, the King asserted that he was returning to England with the most agreeable impressions. There was no inkling here as yet of an English policy of encirclement towards Germany. But neither courtesies exchanged between the two monarchs nor smooth and alluring Parliamentary speeches could gloss over the fact that as far as Germany herself was concerned only disadvantageous results could be expected from the Entente Cordiale. It reduced the value of the old Anglo-German friendship; it weakened the Triple Alliance, and strengthened French hopes of the abrogation of the Treaty of Frankfort.

During the summer of 1904 France and Spain continued their unconcluded negotiations concerning the partition of Morocco. It is true that both Powers had already agreed in November 1902 to a plan which accorded to Spain a larger sphere of influence than that which she later obtained, and which provided that Spain could lease a harbour to Germany on the Atlantic coast, either Casablanca or Rabat. But after the fall of the Silvela Ministry on July 20, 1903, strong pressure from London prevented the Queen Regent, Marie Christine, from putting her name to the treaty. The result of the fresh Franco-Spanish negotiations appeared in a " Declaration " of both Powers published on October 5, 1904, in which it was stated that an agreement had been reached concerning the extent of their rights and the guarantees of their interests in Morocco. Moreover, both parties gave assurances that they would unalterably adhere to the principles of the integrity of Morocco and of the sovereignty of the Sultan. The agreement referred to was kept secret, and not until much later did the public know of its contents. In complete contradiction to the public statement about the integrity of Morocco and the suzerainty of the Sultan, the secret treaty in a number of subsidiary clauses granted to Spain the right of action if the *status quo* should not be maintainable, just as the Anglo-French Treaty of April 8, 1904, had awarded France the right of watching over peace and order in Morocco. This right of action was nothing more nor less than a deceptive circumlocution of the actual partition of the Moroccan Empire.

In addition there was another special provision in the Franco-Spanish Secret Treaty aiming at the exclusion of Germany from every share in the territory. This point a Paris newspaper, the *Journal des Débats*, indicated clearly enough in the following sentences : " We had to avoid an estrangement between ourselves and our neighbour on the south-west on account of Morocco, such as Tunis had occasioned between France and Italy. After we had deprived the Triple Alliance of its early disquieting character by means of the recent Franco-Italian rapprochement, it would have been exceedingly unwise to jeopardize anew the regained ground by making an enemy for ourselves on another border. We would then have had to fear a double danger : that Spain might turn to Germany, and that she might cede to her as a coaling station one of her present presidios, one, for instance, in the neighbourhood of Algeria." As matter of fact, Spain had had to bind herself in the secret treaty under no circumstances to demand help of a foreign Power. Even more precisely was it stated in the secret agreement of the Anglo-French Treaty of April 8, 1904, unknown to the public until 1911, that Spain, France's partner in the partition, must pledge herself not to allow any of her spheres of influence in Morocco to pass into other hands.[1]

[1] Vol. xx, Chap. 144.

With such preparations as these for the parcelling out of Morocco, what was left of the international arrangement for the independence of the Sultanate, of economic equality, or of the Open Door on the coast ? The moment was approaching when the German Government would have to decide either to put up with the concealments and the contradiction between appearance and reality, or to abandon the Chancellor's declared policy of calm reserve. Whether to yield or whether to trump, that was the question !

While Germany was still maintaining a temporizing policy, until far into the winter of 1904–5, Delcassé, immediately after the conclusion of the negotiations with Spain, proceeded to place the Sultan under French supervision, at least as far as the greater part of his empire was concerned. Around the New Year of 1905, the French representative in Tangier, Saint-René Taillandier, was sent on a special mission to Fez, to lay before the Sultan a military programme and a list of rigorous demands dealing with the service of the loan, tariff control, concessions for public works, etc. In executing this commission, the envoy was to refer to the fact that France had received a mandate from the European Powers to organize the military and civil government in Morocco. The Sultan affirmed before the Imperial German Consul Vassel, in Fez, that this had been done ; the French envoy denied it. In Germany people believed the Sultan, while in France, naturally, they believed the envoy. At any rate, Delcassé laboured under the belief that he need not expect further protest from Germany, and that France could carry out the rôle of political protector according to the treaties with England and Spain without considering the economic interests of foreign countries, which the Madrid Convention of 1880 had protected. Papers devoted to him, like the *Journal des Débats*, frankly declared that Morocco was to be the companion picture to Tunis. That meant practically that all non-French candidates would be excluded when Government commissions and when economic concessions were bestowed, and especially that they would be crowded out of commercial life in Morocco.

The German counter-action now set in. Germany stepped to the front in the most impressive manner, assuming the posture of an old trooper, his legs wide apart, his sword between them, and his hands on its hilt. Upon the advice of his Chancellor, who himself had been advised by Holstein, the Kaiser allowed himself to be persuaded against his better judgment to touch at Tangier during his Mediterranean cruise, which had begun with a visit to the King of Portugal in Lisbon. Even in the roadstead of Tangier, with a heavy sea running, the Kaiser hesitated about landing, until the Secretary of the Embassy, von Kühlmann, came aboard with dispatches from Berlin and informed the Kaiser of the preparations for his reception on land. The two hours' visit went off in dignified fashion. The Germans, Moors, and Spaniards were in raptures ; even the English colony had erected a triumphal arch ; the French element maintained a courteous and correct attitude. In reply to the address of the Sultan's uncle, Muley Abdelmalek, the Kaiser said : The visit was to the Sultan as an independent sovereign ; he hoped that a free Morocco, without monopolies or annexations, would continue to be open to the friendly competition of all nations ; he would do all in his power to protect effectively German interests in Morocco.

The Kaiser's visit and his demeanour in Tangier made a great sensation throughout the world. Everyone was asking what was its object. Was it intended as a preparatory note for the tumult of war in the midst of Europe at the very moment when the Russo-Japanese War was coming to an end ? At the opening of the year 1905 the Japanese had taken Port Arthur ; by the end of February the decisive battle of Mukden had begun, which lasted fourteen days, and in which the Russians were completely defeated. Or did Berlin wish to take advantage of the moment when France's ally was thus powerless, and threatened besides with internal troubles, in order to bring strong pressure to bear upon Delcassé and the French Nationalists with their unceasing aspirations for the reconquest of Alsace-

Lorraine, and so to force them formally to renounce *la revanche*? As a matter of fact, nobody in Berlin thought of a war with France. In spite of the tense situation, there is not a trace of a desire for war discoverable in the German State Papers. They wanted only to make an *acte de présence*, to make a demonstration against the continued ignoring of German interests and against the impetuous action of the French Minister in Morocco, and perhaps, if possible, to obtain guarantees for equality of rights in Morocco.

William II, who did not set a high value on Morocco any way, had the right feeling when, in spite of his liking for magnificent gestures, he showed a certain repugnance to the "theatrical Tangier journey." It was altogether too serious a matter to interpose the person of the Emperor for a mere demonstration, which after all was not without its danger, particularly since it was at the same time directed against England. On April 6, 1905, Lord Lansdowne explained to the German Ambassador that England would go even further than her treaty obligations to support France in conflicts arising over Morocco.

The real object of the Tangier visit was for the public at large shrouded in mystery, and this naturally gave rise to all sorts of absurd rumours, and the German Chancellor himself contributed to these by his instruction to the Foreign Office on March 24, 1905, to give out no explanation whatsoever to foreign diplomats, should they make inquiries, but to play the Sphinx.[1]

To the great mass of the German people Morocco was as Hecuba; and as for the question of national prestige resulting from Delcassé's disregard of Germany's economic rights, it would have been difficult, if it had come to war, to arouse the necessary universal enthusiasm. The Social Democratic Workers' Party was in close touch with the French Socialists, whose leader was Jaurès, and they bluntly refused to think of a war over Morocco. By their invitation Jaurès was to come to Berlin and speak at a

[1] Vol. xx, Chap. 146.

public meeting on the programme of the proletariat in the preservation of the peace of the world. Germany's foreign policy could have profited by the appearance in Berlin of this bitter opponent of Delcassé's Morocco policy and true friend of a Franco-German rapprochement. The Chancellor wavered as to whether he ought to permit or hinder Jaurès' coming until the scale was turned by the internal conflict against the Social Democrats. Jaurès did not allow the refusal to divert him from his efforts to establish peace, nor from his exhortations to his countrymen to beware of insidious hostility against Germany.

On March 31st, the very day on which the Kaiser appeared at Tangier, Delcassé made a speech in the Chamber which was both conciliatory and apologetic. He did not refer to the Kaiser's journey, but he acknowledged that foreign nations could claim the right of protecting their commercial interests in Morocco. He was already confronted by an Opposition that reproached him with having unnecessarily and dangerously wounded Germany's legitimate pride. The Socialists under Jaurès demanded more light on the subject, and urged Delcassé to make a second speech. In this he protested that France had intended only to make propositions to the Sultan of Morocco; that she wanted to injure nobody, and was willing to enter into discussions with other Powers concerning possible misunderstandings. But the Kaiser's speech in Tangier had already settled that the international character of the Morocco Question was to be the basis of the German policy, and Holstein exerted all his influence to prevent any deviation from the legal point of view, according to which all parties to the Madrid Convention should have a voice in the matter, preferably in a conference to be suggested by the Sultan.

Germany's claim that, as one of the Powers that had drawn up the Madrid Convention, she should be consulted about the "Tunification of Morocco" planned by France was, according to international law, indisputable. For Germany silently to surrender her interests in Morocco would not have done, for then, as the Chancellor stressed in an order to the Ambassador in London, other Powers observing this would be encouraged to show similar disregard of German interests in other questions of perhaps greater importance. The very objectionable secret clauses in the treaties with England and Spain were at that time not yet known ; if they had been, the visit to Tangier would not have seemed so much like a challenge.

Any attempt to clear up the whole history of events preceding and following the Tangier visit brings to light various contradictions and whimsicalities. The chief motive, to be sure, stands out quite clearly : to make good in as unmistakable a way as possible the loss of prestige occasioned by Delcassé's disregard of Germany in the settlement of a question affecting World Politics. But Holstein stuck obstinately to his idea that the Morocco Question could be solved only by an international conference called by the Sultan, and he characterized any deviation from this line as a defeat equivalent to that of Olmütz and Fashoda.[1]

After the Sultan of Morocco, on May 28, 1905, had invited the Powers that had been signatories to the Madrid Convention to a conference at Algeciras, the French Minister-President, Rouvier, informed the German Government that he was ready to bring about the dismissal of Delcassé from the Ministry, expecting that Germany would then cultivate friendly relations with his successor. Instead of graciously accepting this strong proof of good will, Count Bülow, urged on by Holstein, clung to his standpoint that first and foremost they should make it plain beyond any doubt that there could be no alteration in the economic equality of all nations without the consent of all the signatories to the Madrid Convention.

During April and May in 1905 public opinion was still excited in both countries, and the Governments considered it desirable that first of all there should be a period of tranquillity. Accordingly Delcassé retired into the background for a while and left the handling of the Morocco

[1] April 1905.

Question with the German Embassy to the Minister-President, Rouvier. The latter, together with distinguished Members of Parliament such as Jean Dupuy, owner of the *Petit Parisien*, gave repeated evidence of a spirit of fairness and conciliation. On April 28th Rouvier informed Prince Rodolin that the idea of a conference was distasteful to him ; a French circular note to all the signatory Powers seemed to him to serve the purpose better, if such a step were acceptable to Berlin. If the majority of the Powers concerned should not show themselves inclined to French action in Morocco, then France would certainly not go to Morocco. He also took pains again and again to learn what concessions Germany wanted for relinquishing her demand for a conference, and showed himself even ready to enter into a general agreement concerning disputed colonial questions.

In April the German Ambassador had reported that Rouvier disapproved of Delcassé's conduct in the Morocco Question, and was inclined shortly to get rid of him. In reference to this report, the First Secretary of the Embassy, von Miquel, was instructed on May 30, 1905, as a mark of confidence, to call the French Premier's attention to the excited frame of mind due to Delcassé's continuation in office, and at the same time to give him a list of Delcassé's blunders and unfriendly acts. For " reasons of etiquette," and in the interest of the Ambassador's personal position, this catalogue of sins that covered five incidents in Delcassé's seven years of office should be presented to Rouvier, not by the Ambassador, but by the Secretary of the Embassy. It is also indicative of Rouvier's honest endeavours to bring about a real reconciliation that directly after Delcassé had retired and Rouvier himself had taken over the Ministry for Foreign Affairs, he begged Prince Rodolin to induce the Berlin Government to announce that they intended to pursue an amicable policy towards him.[1]

Now that Rouvier had overthrown Delcassé, and had thus made compensation for the diminution in Germany's

[1] Vol. xx, Chap. 149.

prestige caused by Delcassé's disregard of German interests, it might have been expected that Berlin would have sought to make Rouvier's difficult position easier. Count Bülow nevertheless instructed the Ambassador, Prince Rodolin, to declare in Paris that only by agreeing unconditionally to a conference could France make compensation for her challenge. The Ambassador even added the threat that Germany's entire force was behind the Sultan. In a conversation with Bihourd, the French Ambassador at Berlin, Count Bülow uttered the grave warning against keeping any longer to a course that might lead to precipices and abysses. Whereupon Rouvier agreed to a conference.[1] After the conclusion of the preliminary discussions concerning the programme of the conference at the end of September, Rouvier took his revenge for this rough treatment ; for when Prince Rodolin expressed the willingness of his Government to come to an agreement at this time on other colonial questions too, such as the boundaries of Cameroon and the Bagdad Railway, as earlier suggested by Rouvier, the latter returned the cool answer that he had, as a matter of fact, proposed this under the supposition that the conference would not take place, and that Germany and France between themselves would amicably settle the Morocco Question. Now, since he had agreed to a conference, he preferred to await its results.

Thus Rouvier was correct in his conviction that the conference would turn out favourably for France, whereas Holstein, with his stubborn insistence on a conference, cherished the illusion that the indisputable legality of the German point of view would finally triumph at Algeciras, perhaps through the assistance of President Roosevelt, an adherent of the policy of the Open Door. The conference could not end favourably for Germany·after a considerable concession had already been made to France during the preliminary negotiations of the summer of 1905. The Protocol of July 8, 1905, recognized not only the independ-

[1] Vol. xxi, Chap. 151.

ence of the Sultan and the integrity of his territory, and
economic freedom and the advantage of reforms, but also
the special interest that France had in the supervision within
the Shereefian Empire on account of the extensive con-
tiguity of her frontiers.   Thus Rouvier had already gained
a valuable priority for France.[1]

Before Delcassé's fall English papers had done their best
to induce the Minister who was so valuable for England
to stay at his post.   Some English papers went so far as to
hold out the prospect of military assistance in case of a
Franco-German war. After Delcassé's retirement, the
Paris *Temps* admitted that all sensible Frenchmen had
become uneasy over England's war agitation, and that a
great nation like France ought not to engage in a war " in
order to look after the affairs of another Power."   This
was in the spring.

But neither Delcassé's arrogant action in Morocco nor
Rouvier's yielding attitude in the face of his rough treatment by Berlin was fully disclosed until the revelations in
the *Gaulois* in July 1905, and later in the *Matin* in October
1905, made by the Minister, who had been attacked from
all sides after his fall, and who was a much embittered
man.   From these it appears that in the decisive Council
of Ministers on June 4, 1905, he referred to the assurance
of armed assistance from England, and relying upon pledges
received, he was willing to run the risk of a war with
Germany over the question of a conference.   At first there
was dispute as to what he had stated concerning the proposed armed assistance of England (blockade of the mouth
of the Elbe, occupation of Schleswig with 100,000 men).
" This is not our understanding of the agreement with
England," wrote Jaurès.   " Delcassé has produced the impression on the English Government of being ready for
anything, and the English Government has played the
rôle of tempter to his vanity."   From the official documents
discovered in Berlin we know that in January 1906 the
British Military Attaché, Barnardiston, informed the Belgian

[1] Vol. xx, Chap. 148.

General, Ducarme, that England had provided for the
landing of 100,000 men in Calais and Dunkirk in the event
of a German attack upon Belgium. We may assume
that these were the same 100,000 men to whom Delcassé
referred in his revelations. Probably an original landing
plan directed against the Baltic Canal was later changed at
France's desire in favour of one for the coast of Flanders.

While the greater number of Frenchmen were in a serious
and thoughtful mood after the visit to Tangier, and later
under the influence of Rouvier and Jaurès, gradually the
old hostile feeling came again to the surface during the
protracted diplomatic negotiations and owing to Germany's
blunders in psychology. The military friendship with
England, to whose existence Delcassé testified, contributed
no doubt in no small degree to this revulsion of feeling.
The younger generation, born after 1870, turned their back
on the pacifism of their elders and on the Pro-German
efforts of the so-called humanists of the preceding period.
Men like Léon Daudet and Barrès, who fired anew the
militaristic disposition of the French and their pride in
their alleged cultural superiority over the German " bar-
barians," took the place of those who admired the German
mind, such as Renan, Taine, and Monod. In his studies
of Germany's intellectual life in the last century, Renan felt
as though he were treading on holy ground.

One of the strongest incentives to this new spirit in
France was Holstein's " Hostage Theory." It appeared
first in an article by Theodor Schiemann in the *Kreuzzeitung*,
and ran as follows : " Germany was agreed that if a conflict with England should occur France would be responsible
for it ; therefore Germany would wage such a war nowhere
but in France." The Paris Press took up the threat of the
Kreuzzeitung, which came to the same thing as Holstein's
" Hostage Theory," and condemned most vehemently the
" Schiemannism " of Germany's policy. As a matter of
fact, there was scarcely anything that could irritate the
French more. Its result was the direct opposite of what
Bülow was striving for : that was to bring about a better

understanding between the two peoples. Even Jaurès could not help being deeply stirred over this "Hostage Theory." He became less ardent in his struggle against *la revanche*, and as late as 1909 he made an indignant speech about the threat that France would be the first to suffer in an Anglo-German war. This shows how even on the eve of Algeciras the general sentiment in France was against Germany, and that the inner process was beginning which culminated in the belief, shared even by understanding writers like Romain Rolland, that German Imperialism was outrageously arrogant.

CHAPTER II

THE NAVAL SPECTRE. THE BJÖRKÖ TREATY. ALGECIRAS

THE outbreak of the Russo-Japanese War brought great relief to Germany in her European policy, inasmuch as the disturber of the peace in the Near East was for some time completely occupied in the Far East. Germany had no treaty obligations of any sort towards either of the belligerents ; she could preserve neutrality towards both. England, too, could at the outset declare her neutrality, for according to the Anglo-Japanese Treaty of Alliance of January 30, 1902, the *casus fœderis* was not to arise unless one of the allies should become involved in war with a third Power.[1] Nevertheless, in the course of the East Asiatic War there were situations in which Germany, through her benevolent neutrality towards Russia, could have come into conflict not only with belligerent Japan, but also with neutral England. A good example of this was the sailing of Russia's Baltic Squadron for the theatre of the East Asiatic War. The squadron, which was to prevent the occupation of Port Arthur by the Japanese Navy, set out in October 1904 under the command of Admiral Roschdesvenski. The incident off the Dogger Bank, not far from Hull, when the Russian Admiral fired on some English fishing-boats in the belief that they were Japanese, gave rise to the suspicion that Germany was mixed up in the affair. There was great difficulty in providing the squadron with coal on its long voyage. Early in December 1904 the London papers raised an outcry over the fact that

[1] *Vide supra*, p. 120.

the Hamburg-American Line had undertaken the coaling of the vessels. The English Government threatened to prohibit German coal barges from clearing from English ports, on the grounds that it was contrary to England's treaty obligations towards Japan that Germany should be provisioning Russia with coal from English ports. In a letter of December 7, 1904, to " Nicky," the Kaiser stated that in the face of such a danger as a war with England and Japan he must demand absolutely positive guarantees from the Tsar, otherwise he would prevent German ship-owners from providing the Baltic Squadron with coal.

A second case in which there was a question of the correctness of Germany's neutral attitude occurred after the Baltic Squadron had reached East Asiatic waters. After Japan's naval victory off Port Arthur three Russian vessels had taken refuge in the German port of Tsin-tau. In a quite unofficial conversation Lord Lansdowne expressed himself as very anxious over the fact that a conflict could arise between Germany and Japan about the treatment of the fugitive vessels, and that Japan could then plead the *casus fœderis* to England. He was much gratified when Count Metternich told him immediately that the Russian ships had been dismantled according to international rules and that the crews would be interned.

As to the absolute guarantees which the Kaiser demanded in his letter of December 7, 1904, to the Tsar, the matter is as follows :

On October 27, 1904, the Kaiser, with the knowledge and consent of Count Bülow, wrote to the Tsar that in consideration of the danger of a conflict with England over the coaling of the vessels, it might be well to remind France of the obligations she had assumed in the Dual Alliance. Although Delcassé was an enthusiastic partisan of England, he would nevertheless understand that the British Navy was quite unable to defend Paris. This idea was almost identical with the above-mentioned " Hostage Theory " of Holstein. In this way a powerful group would be formed by the three strongest continental Powers. By

October 24th, Holstein had already discussed with the Russian Ambassador, Count Osten-Sacken,[1] the proposition of a continental alliance that differed in the last analysis very little from the new East Asiatic Triple Alliance which Bülow had rejected in 1902. On October 30th, a treaty draft which the Tsar had requested was sent to St. Petersburg. According to this draft both parties were, in the event of an attack by a European Power, to assist each other with all their land and sea forces, and were jointly to remind France of the obligations she had assumed in the Franco-Russian Dual Alliance. The treaty draft was accompanied by a long letter from the Kaiser, dated October 30th, which Count Bülow had composed in German. In order to avoid every indiscretion, Bülow begged the Kaiser to make the English translation himself. There is a marginal note of the following day by the Kaiser : " I have worked seven hours, till a quarter past one at night, when, more dead than alive, I finished laying the foundation of this hoped-for new phase in Germany's World Policy."

The pointed anti-English intention in the outlined treaty was obvious. France was not to be taken into their confidence and asked to join until the two Courts had bound themselves to an agreement ; until then absolute silence was to be observed towards France, Russia's ally. The Tsar and his Ministers had misgivings about this stipulation, as we can easily understand. Count Lamsdorv attempted to get the Kaiser and Count Bülow to agree at least to acquainting Delcassé in a quite general way with the two Emperors' plan, but Berlin, with good reason, refused. Thereupon the Tsar drew back hastily, or, in the

[1] As Admiral von Tirpitz states in his *Erinnerungen*, a conference was held at the Chancellor's on October 31, 1904, at which were present, besides the Admiral, the Chief of the General Staff (Count Schlieffen), the Secretary of State (Baron von Richthofen), and von Holstein. Von Tirpitz and von Richthofen considered Holstein's psychology wrong when he expressed the opinion that military pressure by a united Germany and Russia would lead France to join those Powers.

ENGLISH AND GERMAN WATER-COLOURS, OR THE GIFTED PUPIL.

THE ENGLISH AND GERMAN NAVAL PROGRAMMES

The Uncle : " Willie, your little marine sketch is very nice ! But to speak frankly I should let it remain just a sketch ! "

(Kladderadatsch, 1908, No. 38.)

language of the Kaiser, he got " cold feet " and became
" flabby." Further negotiations came to nothing.

This was the first act of the wonderful drama of the two
Kaisers. A second act did not follow until a half-year
later, and was played on an island in the Eastern Baltic.
Between the two acts there was a dangerous interlude
which took place in London, and which had a certain
connection with the plan for a continental alliance against
England.

Directly after the opening of negotiations between Berlin
and St. Petersburg an explosion of anti-German feeling
occurred in England. We cannot but ask ourselves: " Had
Delcassé after all got wind of those secret transactions
between Berlin and St. Petersburg, or had a warning
reached London in another way ? " Spring-Rice, the First
Secretary of the English Embassy in St. Petersburg, told
Count Metternich, in a chance meeting in Berlin, that no
one could have any idea how indiscreetly Russia was
behaving in regard to Germany ; every minute one heard
that the Kaiser had given Russia this or that information
or advice, although from the nature of these statements
one could conclude that they had not been intended for
any but Russian ears. As a matter of fact, the abruptness
of the violent outbreak of hostility towards Germany was
evidence in itself that dark rumours from St. Petersburg
about a plot against England had given rise to the absurd
notion of a German plan for a naval " raid " on England,
and this in turn brought about the so-called " Navy Scare."
At first the Society paper, *Vanity Fair*, which had a large
circulation, sounded the alarm in several articles, and
preached a preventive war against Germany.[1] It was a
more serious matter when, later, the *Army and Navy Gazette*
expressed similar views. Finally, even Lee, the Civil Lord
of the Admiralty, early in 1905 sounded a loud réveille
against the German danger, and later the retired Admiral,
Fitzgerald, demanded the immediate annihilation of the
German Navy. The main idea in this excitement in English

[1] November 1904.

L

naval circles was obviously that : If we wait any longer, and inactively watch the German Navy growing stronger, we shall lose too many ships in the next naval war. On the other hand, the Navy spectre seems at first to have exercised very little influence on the Foreign Office in London. King Edward expressed to the German Naval Attaché, Captain Coerper, his great indignation at the idle talk of silly newspapers that England wanted to wage an offensive war against Germany. According to Count Metternich's report of January 11th, Lord Lansdowne explained that *Vanity Fair* was a gossipy paper that no one took seriously, and as for the *Army and Navy Gazette*, although it was true that retired officers contributed articles to it, it was not in any sense the mouthpiece of the Admiralty. The Ambassador himself was of the opinion that no rational being was thinking of a war against Germany.

Even though Lee's advice that a sudden raid be made on Germany's coasts—a brutal plan which occupied the thoughts of Lord Fisher, too, the First Sea Lord—was not adopted, still, after the spring of 1905, the English Government proceeded to take certain measures, such as the augmenting of the fleet in home waters, the strengthening of the naval base at Rosyth on the coast of Scotland, and the sending of a strong squadron to the Baltic. No English squadron had been seen there since the Crimean War, and its appearance could not fail to give the impression of aggressive preparations against Germany.

The expansion of the German Navy was in no way in the beginning connected in English public opinion with the notion of approaching danger. For years after the period of the New Course it was considered perfectly natural on the other side of the Channel that Germany should ensure the protection of her coasts by strengthening her Navy, and by building cruisers both large and small to protect her extensive interests overseas. England did not begin to be disturbed in her unconcern until Germany, in order to make an impression abroad, began to build boats that were larger than those in her coastal and overseas service and also fit for other uses.

But even then Britain remained as phlegmatic as ever. It was a display of the lively feeling of immense superiority among the English when, in reference to the noisy propaganda for more warships carried on by his nephew the Kaiser, the Prince of Wales uttered the watchword : " Let him play with his fleet." This Goliath attitude towards the German David was maintained even when, after the Naval Law of 1900, a German fleet of warships was built on a programme allowing for further expansion, and which Tirpitz, its author, declared in the Reichstag it would be risky for even a very strong naval Power to attack.

This conception of risk, whose basis was the idea of warding off an attack, was in itself free from objection. The obnoxiousness for England lay in the rapidity with which the organizing genius of Admiral Tirpitz understood how to create a Navy that commanded respect, and in the noisy agitators in the Navy League and among the Pan-Germans, who did not know what calmness and restraint meant, and privately more than publicly acted on the watchword, " To down England." The Naval Law of 1898 provided for 17 battleships, 8 ironclad coasting vessels, 9 large and 26 small cruisers. The law of 1900 doubled the number of ships. There was again a prospect of a supplementary law for 1906 that was to contain provision for building a large type of vessel. This meant not only a greater risk for any assailant, but for England, in addition, on account of her established principle of the two-Power standard (double the strength of the next strongest naval Power), a much heavier financial burden, and this contributed materially to the increasing ill-will towards Germany.

In the first half of the year 1905 the political situation in Europe had fundamentally altered. Russia was powerless as a result of her crushing defeats in Eastern Asia and because of the internal troubles with which she was threatened. The French people, after getting over the first shock of the Tangier visit, were looking forward to the

Algeciras Conference over Morocco in capital anti-German spirits, relying on the Entente Cordiale. In England the public, with threats and execrations, had opened a furious campaign against Germany's naval programme. The Kaiser considered this moment of general unrest a suitable one for resuming the negotiations with the Tsar for a continental alliance of Germany, Russia, and France against England, which had been broken off in January. Upon his return from his customary northern trip, he suggested by telegraph a secret, private meeting with the Tsar. The Tsar acquiesced willingly, and the island of Björkö, off the coast of Finland, was agreed upon as the meeting-place. On the second day of the meeting, July 24, 1905, during a conversation on politics in general, the Kaiser casually inquired what was the real reason that the discussions of the preceding year had come to a standstill. The Tsar, in reply, said that France had not wanted to enter into the treaty on account of her strained relations with Germany. The Kaiser rejoined that this obstacle no longer existed, since they both had come to an agreement about Morocco. He meant by this the Protocol of July 8, 1905, according to which Rouvier, under certain stipulations, had agreed to the conference. As the Tsar did not recollect exactly the text oft he tentative draft of the autumn of 1904, the Kaiser produced a copy and gave it to the Tsar. Behind closed doors, with the Kaiser watching in great suspense, the Tsar carefully read the text through several times, and then said that he gladly agreed to all its points.

The " Treaty of Björkö" bears the date of July 24, 1905, and the personal signatures of the two Emperors. It was countersigned by the German Ambassador, von Tschirschky, who had accompanied the Kaiser, and by the Russian Minister of the Navy, Admiral Birilev. The text tallied with that of the draft of the autumn of 1904, except for two words which the Kaiser had added to paragraph 1. According to the earlier draft, if one of the signatories to the proposed treaty were attacked by another Power, his allies were to hasten with all their forces to his assistance.

This obligation to render assistance was, through the words added by the Kaiser, to apply only in Europe.

The Chancellor, Prince Bülow, who was on the *Semmering*, had probably been informed beforehand of the improvised meeting of the two Emperors, likewise of the Kaiser's intention of returning to the subject of the treaty at the meeting, but not of the Kaiser's interpolation of " in Europe." Consequently the Chancellor felt himself slighted and passed over. He raised an objection to the Kaiser's addition, for which he refused to accept the responsibility, and he finally placed his offices at the Kaiser's disposal. The Kaiser, who thought he had accomplished an act of historic significance, an act that was to be the introduction to a chapter of peace and good will among the Great Powers, felt most deeply hurt, and thought it would be the greatest disaster if Bülow deserted him. He reminded the Chancellor that he had made him a prince quite recently, and that he had yielded, in spite of his disapproval, to the Chancellor's Morocco policy. " Do not forget that you involved me in the Tangier affair against my will in order to succeed in your Morocco policy." These effusions of the Kaiser were absolutely genuine, and came from his inmost being. All his real self was not contained in his boastful phrases and threatening gestures, as foreign critics believe ; but, instead, he was under the delusion of being the instrument of Providence, a saviour of the whole world. Only after a long verbal discussion did Prince Bülow withdraw his resignation.[1]

The official documents do not throw complete light on the reasons for Bülow's attitude. On the other hand, in many places Holstein's strong influence on Bülow is clearly seen in the entire affair. The Chancellor saw, as did Holstein, that the only possibility for Russia to render effective assistance in the event of a continental war against England would be by rushing her troops in Persia to the Indian frontier, although the Chief of the German General Staff declared that such an undertaking was impracticable. At

[1] Chap. 138.

the same time, however, the Chancellor believed that the Björkö Treaty was decidedly advantageous for Germany, in spite of the fact that the obligation to render military assistance was limited to Europe as a result of the Kaiser's interpolation. It seems very probable that Bülow's real motive in tendering his resignation was to teach the Kaiser a lesson, and to strengthen the position of the Chancellor against autocratic velleities on the part of William II.[1]

The subject of the Björkö Treaty was never again mentioned in the correspondence of the two monarchs, nor did it play any further rôle in the political considerations of the leading statesmen.   We merely find in the official documents the following final memorandum for the Kaiser : " We consider the Russo-German Defensive Alliance signed by both exalted sovereigns at Björkö on July 24, 1905, as being in force. His Majesty the Kaiser did not agree to the additional declaration respecting France, later desired by His Majesty the Emperor of Russia, since, according to the Tsar's explanation, the Franco-Russian Alliance has a merely defensive character, therefore does not come into collision with the Russo-German Defensive Alliance. Russia was reconciled to this."

The Tsar had the same experience with his Ministers in St. Petersburg as the Kaiser with his Chancellor. They recommended a supplement to the treaty explaining that in case of a Franco-German conflict, Russia's obligation of support was not to obtain. The Franco-Russian Alliance was, of course, the explanation of this, but it was entirely inconsistent with the purpose of the Treaty of Björkö, which was to curb French Chauvinism (*la queue de Delcassé*) with Russia's help, and to guarantee a peaceful Franco-German neighbourhood. Witte, too, was decidedly opposed to the treaty. The continental alliance for which he was working was to be an economic agreement to facilitate the interchange of commodities, but was not to serve military or political ends. The official negotiations came to a standstill after this, and all that was produced in this

[1] Cf. Erich Brandenburg, *Von Bismarck zum Weltkrieg*, p. 202.

curious unreal world of phantasy, where it was believed the fate of nations could be guided by means of secret treaties between rulers, was merely something that was stuck away in the pigeon-hole of a discrete archive.

The error in the attempt to influence decisively Russia's policy by means of dynastic relations lay largely in an underestimation of the Tsar's personal weakness. The close friendship assumed between the Houses of Hohenzollern and Romanov had in reality ceased to exist since the death of Alexander II. Nicholas II did not have it in him to carry on a brotherly friendship with another dynasty like those of earlier times. Whereas under Alexander III the Russian Minister for Foreign Affairs, von Giers, was glad to conceal himself behind the broad back of *Sa Majesté l'Empereur*, his son's slender form disappeared behind the stalwart figures that took into their own hands, both in St. Petersburg and in Paris, the furthering of Russian Imperialism. England had more than Germany to offer defeated Russia, especially after the extension of her treaty with Japan on August 2, 1905, for ten years more had provided increased protection on her Indian frontiers. At the very time that the Tsar's Ministers were busy invalidating the Treaty of Björkö, the first conversations were already under way in London concerning an Anglo-Russian agreement in Central Asia. This agreement was realized two years later by the division of Persia into spheres of influence, and was preliminary to Russia's return to Europe by the side of England.

The Treaty of Björkö was not, therefore, as William II thought, a new page in world history that was to form the introduction to a chapter of peace and good will among the Great Powers, but a courtly interlude without any practical result. It did not even bring about a friendlier relation between Germany and Russia. This was clearly shown as early as the International Conference at Algeciras, which followed shortly.

The opening of the conference in Algeciras was fixed for January 16th. In a speech in the Chamber on December 10, 1905, the Prime Minister, Rouvier, struck rather a firm note. The summer of discontent had given way to a winter of enhanced feeling of strength. Rouvier laid great stress on the fact that Germany had already in the Protocol of July 8th recognized France's exclusive competence to preserve order in the Moroccan regions along her extensive Algerian frontier. He showed that as a result of the Franco-German negotiations, even if France's rights were not all recognized, they were at any rate all reserved. But the tone of the speech was due not so much to these remarks as to the unavowed certainty that France was going to the conference more of one mind, and diplomatically much better equipped, than Germany. A Paris newspaper summed up in a brief sentence the tenor of the reverberations of the speech throughout France : " We are ready ! Half a year ago we were not, but now we are ! " The effect of the speech was intensified further by a Yellow Book of 368 documents showing the course of Morocco policy since 1901, and containing a certain justification for Delcassé's resistance to the conference forced upon France by Germany. In the spring of 1905 he had been reproached chiefly because he had neglected to apprise the German Government officially of the Treaty of April 8, 1904, with England. But, according to the Yellow Book, as early as March 23, 1904, fourteen days before the conclusion of the treaty, he communicated all essential points of the agreement to the German Ambassador, Prince Rodolin, in a confidential conversation ; moreover, he had sent a report of this conversation to Bihourd, the Ambassador at Berlin, for his use in the Foreign Office. The verbal apprisals were intentionally ignored by the German Government because, as it was put in an order to Rodolin, the official written form, " consecrated by diplomatic usage," was required in communications of such importance. After the disclosures in the Yellow Book, people in France felt that this strict distinction was due to the inflexibility of pettifoggers, especially since the concluded treaty had been immediately published. At any rate, they generally felt there were extenuating circumstances connected with the fallen Minister's action.

The negotiations at Algeciras dragged during the first six weeks. There is to-day no longer any value in discussing in detail the subjects of contention. In general the Press correspondents at Algeciras held the evil intentions of Germany responsible for every untoward event. Public opinion in France was growing more and more distrustful of Germany's policy. The situation became critical ac the beginning of March. Except for her second, Austria, Germany was almost completely isolated. The Entente Cordiale had grown enormously stronger during the conference. England stood manfully by the side of France.[1] Russia, in spite of Björkö, supported France where it was possible. The instructions of the Russian plenipotentiary were identical with those of his English colleague, and on the soil of Algeciras Russia took the first discernible step towards attaching herself to England.[2] Italy, despite the best of intentions, could not do much to help her northern ally ; like Spain, she was bound by treaties. As for the Americans, the bones of contention were more or less *non valeurs*, and French sympathy worth at least as much as German. In Germany the prospect that the conference which had been brought about by such vigorous methods was going to break up without achieving anything was depressing. The chief thing was to get gracefully out of the blind alley of Algeciras.

[1] E. van Grootven, the Belgian representative in London, reported to Brussels, January 14, 1906 : "Recently Sir Edward Grey (Minister for Foreign Affairs in the new Liberal Cabinet) has said again and again to the various accredited ambassadors in London that Great Britain has assumed obligations towards France that she will fulfil to the last letter, even in the event of a Franco-Prussian war, and at all hazards."—Belgian Documents, p. 18.

[2] Cf. Prince Trubetzkoi, *Russland als Grossmacht*, 1917, p. 93 : " It was evident from the friendly agreement displayed by the representatives of the two Powers that the Governments in London and St. Petersburg desired only to be guided by their consciousness of changed conditions and of existing mutual interests, and that they wished completely to forget the earlier discords."

Therefore Prince Bülow determined to take over the handling of the conference. To put an end to Holstein's policy of resorting to subterfuges and keeping things uselessly stirred up,[1] everything that came in now had to be submitted to the Chancellor, and all orders had to pass through his hands. He took up again an earlier proposal of the Austro-Hungarian delegate without the additions with which Holstein had loaded it. After the proposal had been universally approved as a suitable basis for a settlement, the conference came rapidly to a peaceful end. The material results were small in comparison to the large apparatus that had been set up. The principle of the Open Door was recognized on paper ; the guarantees to ensure its remaining open were insufficient. The longest dispute was concerning the organization of the police in the ports. The most natural arrangement would have been to set up an international police force. Instead of which, they were content with a neutral inspector-general with insufficient authority, who was to supervise the partly French, partly Spanish police in the ports. Obviously, similar or even more effective concessions might have been obtained by direct agreement between Paris and Berlin, the method proposed by Rouvier after Delcassé's fall. The general impression was that the Kaiser's policy, in spite of its high tone in the spring of 1905, had had nevertheless finally to give way.

The success of the French Morocco policy inflamed the new spirit in France to a quite extraordinary degree. Retired Ministers for War and generals in active service made speeches in the following year in which they announced frankly that war was imminent, and that the lost provinces would speedily return to France. The *France militaire* and its readers were enraptured with the idea that the French Army both in tactics and in artillery was far superior to the German Army. It was hardly necessary for them to court the Tsar's favour any longer. They began to watch more sharply, to make sure that the fresh French billions also were actually applied to the construction of

[1] Cf. O. Hammann, *Zur Vorgeschichte des Weltkrieges*, Berlin, 1918, pp. 229 *seq.*   [2] Chaps. 151-2.

military roads in Western Russia. Pacifism was dead, the War of Revenge was in sight.

On April 5th, the very day of the Morocco debate in the Reichstag and of the Kaiser's acceptance of Holstein's oft-tendered resignation, the Chancellor was seized with a serious fainting fit in the Reichstag. The decision to part officially with his old friend and collaborator had not been easy for Prince Bülow. But he was too clear-headed to be in any doubt about the fact that Holstein's attitude during the Morocco complications, and indeed from the time of Chamberlain's first offer of an understanding, and especially in the last period beginning with the Tangier visit, was an attempt at a Bismarckian policy without Bismarck's judgment of men and of things. It is very significant that the following passage occurs in the first important speech [1] which Prince Bülow made after his complete recovery : " As to the frequent references to Prince Bismarck, careful study of the speeches and actions of this incomparable statesman will convince anyone that his greatness did not consist in the clinking of spurs, or in the wearing of cuirassiers' boots, or in rattling the sword, but in a true judgment of men and of things. Making dogmas out of Prince Bismarck's words has become not only a mania with us but almost a calamity. We are suffering from Prince Bismarck the Misunderstood." [2]

Bülow did not fail to make use of Holstein's experience in European policy after he had resumed personal relations with him. But Holstein had lost his power to issue instructions which were due to his incalculable moods and his propensity to manage things by devious methods and by personal intrigues. Holstein's passionate exertions for the welfare of the Empire and his personal disinterestedness were beyond doubt. But he had the suspicious and inquisitive mind of a detective. Like the Kaiser, who often seemed to him a spoilsport, he had the radical fault of treating the foreign relations of a great nation as a wrestling-ground for personal wills.

[1] November 14, 1906.
[2] " *Wir laborieren an dem missverstandnen Fürsten Bismarck.*" This sentence provided the title for the first edition of this work. *Cf. supra*, p. 7.—TRANSLATOR'S NOTE.

CHAPTER III

THE ENTENTE NET. THE SECOND HAGUE CONFERENCE

BALFOUR'S Unionist Ministry had resigned the beginning of December 1905, having suffered a defeat in the House of Commons as far back as July. After the retirement of Chamberlain in 1903, who thenceforth devoted himself to working for his tariff reform for Greater Britain, the Government's majority gradually became precarious. During the first half of the decade that the Unionists were in power, England had sought Germany's friendship; during the second half of this period the good will gradually changed, until finally unconcealed distrust took its place. This was apparent in after-dinner speeches made by its two most important members just before the Cabinet's resignation. Lansdowne said that England had been hampered from time to time by the fact that she was confronted in various parts of the world with rivalries which could be advantageous to no one except to a monarch who understood how to utilize them. Balfour said he did not believe in a coming war if peoples or Governments did not bring it about because of their conviction that they could only realize their schemes for national expansion by trampling upon the rights of their neighbours. Thus we see that quite nine years before the World War William II had the reputation of being a crafty promoter of war. For this he was certainly somewhat to blame, but nevertheless, if the peculiar character of his mind be carefully considered, the reputation was unjust.

These speeches show clearly how much mistrust and hostility were at work in England against Germany. Lansdowne and Balfour had for years held important posts in the British Empire ; both passed everywhere for highly cultivated, prudent, and moderate statesmen. They had together honestly striven at the turn of the century to foster and strengthen the traditional friendship with Germany. Were juster views and a more friendly disposition to be expected from the Liberal Cabinet ? With regard to their relations with Germany, for a long time no essential differences had been perceptible in the attitude of the two great English parties. The Pan-German enthusiasm over the Boers, the Navy Scare, and the Kaiser's attempt to form an anti-English Continental Alliance had generated a uniform mood bordering on hatred against the leading Power of the Central Bloc. Both in Liberal and in Conservative camps the fundamental inclination was to keep Germany down and to hem her in.

The diplomatic legacy from Balfour's Ministry contains two documents of exceptional value : the Entente Cordiale with France and the ten-year renewal of the alliance with Japan, which, besides recognizing the integrity of China and the policy of the Open Door in China, guaranteed the territorial rights of Great Britain in India, and all Britain's measures for the protection of the Indian frontier. Moreover, Campbell-Bannerman's Liberal Cabinet, appointed on December 11, 1905, found negotiations which had been entered into with Russia, the defeated opponent of England's ally, Japan, immediately after the Portsmouth Treaty of Peace.

In Campbell-Bannerman's Cabinet Asquith was Chancellor of the Exchequer, Sir Edward Grey was at the Foreign Office, Lord Haldane was at the War Department, John Morley was Secretary of State for India, and Lloyd George was President of the Board of Trade. Any fundamental change in the foreign policy (the Entente Cordiale with France, the alliance with Japan, the reconciliation with Russia) was naturally not to be thought of. Asquith had urged in a speech as early as 1898, at the time of the first attempt to abandon splendid isolation, that England come to an understanding with Russia. On October 20,

1905, before he had taken the portfolio for foreign affairs, Sir Edward Grey had specified the friendship with the United States, the alliance with Japan, and the agreement with France as the three chief features of England's foreign policy, and had added : " In these three things no change is desired, I believe, by either party or by the people of this country. It is urgently desirable that Russia's position and influence should be re-established in the councils of Europe. I cannot mention Russia without saying a word about Germany. It must be, in my opinion, a condition of any improvement in the public relations between Germany and ourselves that the relations of Germany with France should be fair and good also." [1] This programme left nothing to be desired in the way of brevity and clarity—whether it was just to refer to fairness in regard to Germany is another question.

The business of the settlement with Russia dragged on a long time. In the meanwhile there was further eager weaving on other portions of the net of *ententes*. During King Edward's visit to Madrid a Mediterranean agreement was reached between England and Spain, which bound the contracting parties in critical situations to confer with each other and to reach an accord. With this agreement the old friendship between Germany and Spain came to an end. Then followed, on July 30, 1907, under England's assistance, a Russo-Japanese convention.

There were now in existence the following telegraph wires : the lines between Paris and St. Petersburg (1891) ; between London and Tokio (1902) ; between London and Paris (1904) ; between Paris and Tokio (1907) ; between St. Petersburg and Tokio (1907). Only the last link in the system was now lacking, the line between London and St. Petersburg. On August 31st, the Anglo-Russian Entente dealing with Persia, Afghanistan, and Tibet was completed, " forming the last mesh in a matchless tissue of diplomacy." [2]

[1] The Author is indicating the programme and so does not indicate one or two unimportant omissions in and between these sentences to be found in *The Times'* report of the speech.—TRANSLATOR'S NOTE.

[2] Rudolf Kjellén, *Dreibund und Dreiverband*, München, 1920.

However wonderful may have been the cleverness with which the statesmen of the Isolation Policy excogitated and set going the system of *ententes*, still they were not clever enough to foresee the full magnitude of the disaster which the explosion would bring upon the whole world.

On November 14, 1906, at the time when the Anglo-Russian Entente was nearing its consummation, Prince Bülow made an important speech in the Reichstag in which, in the following impressive language, he gave warning of the imminent danger of a world war : " Unless the World Powers were friendly towards Germany, the Entente Cordiale would endanger the peace of Europe. A policy which aimed at encircling Germany, at creating a circle of Powers around Germany in order to isolate and cripple her, would be a policy hazardous for the peace of Europe. It is not possible to form such a ring without the use of certain pressure. Pressure begets counter-pressure, and finally explosions can result from pressure and counter-pressure."

Germany could advance no claims at the parcelling out of spheres of influence in the Far East. (Northern Persia, as far as the region of Ispahan for Russia, Southern Persia and Afghanistan for England, Tibet for China.) In Persia she had important commercial interests, but absolutely no political interests. According to the treaty the independence of Persia was to be respected. Although in the explanations exchanged concurrent with the treaty, the special interests of England on the Persian Gulf were recognized, still Sir Edward Grey at the same time protested that England harboured no desire to debar other Powers from legitimate commerce, i.e. the door was to remain open for commerce.[1]

In the negotiations England had displayed an accommodating spirit, inasmuch as Russia's share, estimated according to area, population, and revenue, was many times as large as England's. Compared with the programme of conquest which the Russian Ambassador had presented to Berlin on January 1, 1898, it was little enough.[2] These

[1] Chap. 183.   [2] *Vide supra*, pp. 62-3.

concessions to Russia were of no importance at all to England in the face of the extraordinary increase of the strength of her position in World Politics.

With the Anglo-Russian Entente the ring around Germany was complete. It is true that the first object of the English statesmen in this treaty was to protect further the Indian frontiers, an aim in itself comprehensible and legitimate. But undoubtedly they had besides the design of guiding Russia's ambition back to its old scene of action in the Near East, where the most dangerous firebrand in Europe was smouldering under the ashes. That they were conscious that the consequences were harmful to Germany could be inferred from the special eagerness with which King Edward sought to expedite the agreement with Russia. Just as Count Witte, Russia's representative at the Portsmouth Peace Conference, was about to return from America, he received an invitation through the Secretary of the Russian Embassy in London, Poklevski, a friend of King Edward and a notorious enemy of Germany, to return by the way of London ; enclosed was the rough draft of an Anglo-Russian Treaty dealing with Central Asia and approved by the King and the Foreign Office. Witte preferred to take the direct route home.[1] On the way he stopped first in Paris and then went to Berlin, where he was received by the Chancellor, with whom he discussed the renewal and amplification of the Anglo-Japanese Alliance as an indication that England had now acquired land forces for the protection of her Asiatic possessions, especially for India, and by relying upon the Japanese Navy could turn to European use a large part of her warships now stationed in Eastern Asia. The Kaiser invited Witte to Rominten and, having obtained the Tsar's consent, made him acquainted with the contents of the Treaty of Björkö. Witte, according to the Kaiser's report, wept for joy. This was not very likely, for Witte was an able business man, and was concerned above all about getting financial aid for his country, and also, as a matter of fact,

[1] E. J. Dillon, *The Eclipse of Russia*, London, 1918, p. 350.

he did not advocate the Björkö Treaty after his return to St. Petersburg.

It is also significant what great things Sir Edward Grey expected from a conciliated Russia. In reply to the treaty's critics in the House of Commons, who took exception especially to the settlements in Russia's favour in Northern Persia, he insisted vigorously that the friendship of the great Empire of Russia was worth much more than concessions in frontier regions in Central Asia. He felt sure that the Slavic expansion movement would now once more be turned in the direction of the Near East, in accordance with the desires of the Russian people, where it was less dangerous to Britain's world interests and where it could also more easily be made to serve England's continental policy. As a matter of fact, it was soon evident that Russia would return to Europe from Asia, not at the side of Austria, but arm-in-arm with England.

King Edward repeatedly combated the idea that the Entente policy was aimed against Germany, and explained that its purpose was purely to guarantee peace. It was a plausible argument to hear from English lips : " How can Germany feel herself threatened, when others are peaceably settling their disputes ? For had not Germany herself established the Triple Alliance ? " That looked good and sounded right too, but was not, however, real gold. That England was gathering about her as many Powers as possible was certainly her just right, so long as the peace of the world was not imperilled by any aggressive actions. By the Entente Cordiale England had concluded the closest possible alliance with an Empire that beyond a doubt was yearning for a war with Germany and was awaiting with impatience a favourable political alinement to make the attack.

The attempts of the King and his Ministers to give the English Entente policy a harmless and purely peaceful interpretation, and their professed inability to understand Germany's complaints about England's unfriendliness, were mere bluff. No impartial judge will concede that

M

the regular *conversations d'ordre militaire*, which had been
kept secret from Parliament, and instituted in accordance
with secret clauses in the Treaty of the Entente Cordiale
and verbal promises, were only for the purpose of settling
differences, and that they had no aggressive character.

Both in England and in France, Germany was considered
as an enemy. To close and envious observers Germany,
after her successful struggle for national unity in a generation and a half, had certainly become too big and too strong.

In the summer of 1906 the British Secretary for War, Lord
Haldane, came to Berlin on the Kaiser's invitation to
attend the christening of the eldest son of the Crown Prince
and to study the German military establishment. It was
not until the appearance of Lord Loreburn's book, *How the
War Came*, and Lord Haldane's article in the *Atlantic
Monthly* for October 1919, that general attention was called
to the fact that there was a very special motive behind this
study of Germany's military establishment beside a new
War Minister's need to obtain general information. At the
very time, in January 1906, that Sir Edward Grey told the
accredited Ambassadors in London that Great Britain
would fulfil to the last letter the obligations she had assumed
towards France, quite secretly and without consulting the
Cabinet—only the Prime Minister (Campbell-Bannerman),
the Chancellor of the Exchequer (Asquith), and the War
Minister (Haldane) were informed—he had approved a proposal of the French Ambassador, Paul Cambon, which gave
a new character to the Colonial Agreement of April 8, 1904.
It was agreed that there were to be conversations from
time to time between the Military and Naval Staffs of the
two countries to prepare for co-operation in case of war.
Grey himself revealed this in his war speech on August 3,
1914, but too little attention was paid to it during the
clamour of the first period of the war.

Lord Loreburn, in his book, does not question Grey's
honesty in protesting that this new arrangement with
Cambon had not affected Great Britain's freedom of decision
in case of war, but he sharply criticizes Grey for failing to

appreciate the real state of affairs, and for having actually given England's peace into the keeping of Russia. After these military understandings the question was no longer that of assisting France in the pursuit of her Moroccan claims, but that of England's policy ; for through these agreements she was bound, morally at least, to support France in the event of any war with Germany, for confidential intercourse of the Military and Naval Staffs of two Powers presupposed a political friendship of a lasting character. The secret arrangement, under the persistent influence of his partner, the very clever French Ambassador, could easily lead the British Secretary of State for Foreign Affairs farther than he himself had originally intended, until Wallenstein's soliloquy in Schiller's drama became a true picture of his predicament :

> Wär's möglich, Könnt' ich nicht mehr, wie ich wollte,
> Nicht mehr zurück, wie mir's beliebt ? Ich müsste
> Die Tat vollbringen, wie ich sie gedacht ?
> Nicht die Versuchung von mir wies ?

Lord Loreburn shows in detail the close connection between the secret alliance, which had been reaffirmed in November 1912 in letters recording the agreement, and the outbreak of the World War. French policy could absolutely rely on this " equivalent of an alliance," as Lord Loreburn calls it, to stand the test of all vicissitudes as long as Sir Edward Grey remained at the head of the Foreign Office in London. It would have been a miracle if men like Isvolsky, Sazonov, and Sukhomlinov had not also, sooner or later, obtained information of Grey's liabilities. The English people and their Parliament, on the other hand, not to speak of the German people, including the Kaiser and the Chancellor, had no inkling of them until the day war was declared against Germany. The question whether the crisis of July 1914 might have ended peacefully, or have taken a different course from what it did, if there had been no secret agreements between France and England, opens up a gloomy subject that haunts one's mind.

Lord Haldane perceived at once that there was a new
" Army problem " in the agreement of January 1906 with
the French Ambassador. The advice which he sought
from the Prussian Minister for War, von Einem, was to be
used to remedy the chief defect in English Army organization—slowness in mobilizing England's auxiliary troops
if there should be a continental war.

Lord Haldane received an invitation also to the German
manœuvres in the autumn of 1906. He has himself frankly
acknowledged how fruitful for him this study of Germany's
military organization was. He describes how only three
years later he could mobilize 160,000 men in the swiftest
manner possible, and within twelve days transport them
to the points on the French coast agreed upon by the French
and English Staffs. This assistance which Germany rendered the English Minister for War proves irrefutably how
completely unsuspicious the German statesmen and generals
were in regard to the anti-German policy of England at that
time. It would have been a piece of unparalleled stupidity
for the German Government to have behaved in this fashion
if they had really intended to resort to war to solve the
disputes with the Anglo-French Entente, or even if they
had only deemed such solution possible.

At the time when Lord Haldane had to give all his attention to his new Army problem, and Sir Edward Grey was
still occupied with concluding the negotiations with Russia
for an Asiatic Entente, a second Peace Conference was about
to be held at The Hague. The first suggestion of this had
been made by the President of the United States as early
as the end of 1904, and, indeed, this new conference was to
be chiefly devoted to the reform of the rules of naval warfare.
Russia, at whose express wish the calling of the conference
was postponed until the East Asiatic War was over, undertook to draw up a programme, and to issue the invitations
after the date of the conference was finally settled upon
for the summer of 1907 in deference to the Pan-American
Congress. At first the programme contained only legal
questions ; first and foremost, questions of naval law and

of perfecting the procedure of arbitration determined upon
at the First Hague Conference.   Drawn together by an
exchange of views, the English and American Governments
demanded that the question of universal disarmament, a
question, as we have seen, discussed at the First Hague
Conference, be made a subject for discussion.   England was
undoubtedly the prime mover in these proposals.   Through
them she wanted to try to preserve her strong numerical
superiority at sea for years to come without too great
further cost.   The English statesmen clearly perceived
that the existing ratio of strength was to be maintained
only at great financial sacrifice, in consequence of the
steady increase of the French, the Japanese, and, above
all, the German Navies.   So even before the convening
of the Peace Conference a lively dispute arose over the
formulating of the programme.   The German statesmen
from the Kaiser down were unanimously opposed to accepting the English proposal, chiefly because it might interfere
with the growth of the German Navy.

The German Ambassador, Count Metternich, to prevent
possible insinuations in the English Press, advised his
Government not to shun discussion of the critical question.
Prince Bülow, however, preferred to play " the part of the
honest man," and while referring to the differences in the
geographical, economic, military, and political circumstances
of States, he refused to participate in the discussion of
the question of disarmament.   In a debate in the Reichstag
on April 3, 1907, the speakers of all the bourgeois parties,
referring to the strained relations which had been brought
about by King Edward's " Policy of Encirclement "—he had
just recently had meetings in Cartagena and Gaeta with the
Kings of Spain and Italy—declared themselves in favour
of each country determining for itself what was to be the
strength of its armaments.   The Chancellor succeeded
in achieving an effect in England by a clever speech which
contained, among other things, a reference to the fact that
Lord Derby, at the Brussels Conference in 1874, had cate-
gorically refused to discuss the question of the right of

capture at sea.   While praising the speech, Unionist newspapers could at the same time get in a word of party criticism
of the Liberal Cabinet, whose disarmament proposal was
opposed as unpractical and contrary to England's unbroken
policy of naval armament.   But even the Liberal Press
called especial attention to the dignity and fairness of the
Reichstag debate.   Since Russia and Austria-Hungary
were likewise of the opinion that the disarmament question
was not sufficiently clarified, it was eliminated from the real
debates of the conference itself.   Nothing came of it but
a resolution, approved also by the German representative,
Baron von Marschall, which reaffirmed the *vœu* recorded
at the First Hague Conference, that the Governments would
look into the disarmament question.

The Second International Peace Conference, as already
mentioned, was convened for the working out of an
agreement about rules and practices in naval warfare.
The question of abolishing the right of capture at sea
was not expressly mentioned ; it was only stated on the
programme that even the treatment of the private property
of belligerents at sea was to be regulated.   Neither
at the Second Hague Peace Conference nor at the subsequent London Conference on the rules of naval warfare
in the winter of 1908–9 was there a systematic reorganiza-
tion of the question of right of capture at sea—only a
modification of the principle of the *voyage continu*, and the
establishment of an International Prize Court.   Still, in view
of the outcome of the World War, it is worth while to go
more into detail about the domestic discussions, characteristic of the Anglo-German relations of that time, which were
held before the session of the Hague Conference between the
military and civil officials in Berlin and in London on the
possibility that there might be an international unrolling of
this question.

With the existent political tension it was quite natural
that both sides based their discussions on the possibility
of a war between Germany and England, and made their
conclusion depend upon their opinion as to which of the

belligerents would gain the greater military advantage from the right of capture at sea. The opinion of the German Navy Board, in which the Admiralty, the War Office, and even the General Staff concurred, was as follows : England, even without the right of capture at sea, would be able to cripple importations by sea by means of blockade and a strict interpretation of the rules of contraband. For that reason only those shipowners in Germany would benefit by the abolition of the right of capture at sea who could employ a part of their steamers in trade between neutral ports.   On the other hand, there was the hope of threatening the very life of England before long by making use of this right of capture by sea, and so of shortening the war.   Quite at variance with these views was the standpoint of civil officials in Berlin : those in the Imperial Department of the Interior, the Board of Trade, and the Ministry for Public Works.   They cited the difference in size between the English and the German Merchant Marines, which in 1906 was in about the proportion of five to one ; and consequently they concluded that even with the greatest success possible from the exercise of the right of capture at sea, the German Marine would be able to do only an insignificant percentage of damage to the English Mercantile Marine, while the very existence of the German Mercantile Marine would be threatened.   Furthermore, since the destruction of Germany's Merchant Marine and sea trade might be almost the only war aim of England, the abolition of the right of capture at sea would furnish an effective guarantee for the continuation of peaceful relations between Germany and England.

In answer to this, the German Navy Board brought up the question of England's economic condition, which had radically changed since the time of the great naval conflicts for supremacy on the sea.   They contended that even at the time of the Declaration of Paris, dealing with naval law, England had been almost independent of the world as to her food supply ; that to-day only the assurance of uninterrupted importation would make it possible for England

to think of war.   This was the inference to be drawn from
the recommendations of the " Royal Commission on Supply
of Food in Times of War," for more than 85 per cent. of
England's food-stuffs, including meat and fodder, had to be
imported, whereas Germany was in the fortunate position
of being able to get her necessary provisions through neutral
countries.   In considering the abolition of the right of
capture at sea as an additional guarantee for peace, the
fact that there was likewise a guarantee for peace in the
fear felt by the English public for what might be a menace
to its imports should not be overlooked.   They held that the
abolition of the right of capture at sea was a one-sided
reform in England's favour ; only by restricting the right of
blockade at the same time could a really liberal, i.e. an
impartial, guarantee of the immunity of private property at
sea, and of maritime commerce, be secured.

The German Imperial Department of the Interior,
however, remained of the opinion that the continuance of
the right of capture at sea would under every circum-
stance result to the decided advantage of England.   The
State Secretary of that time, Delbrück, displayed true fore-
sight when he rejected the assumption that every loss of
an English merchant vessel reported in the City would
bring Germany nearer peace, and held that a ruthless war
on commerce would be much more likely only to aggravate
the animosity in London and cause England to use her
superior Navy relentlessly to destroy the German Merchant
Marine.

The scope of the discussion was still further widened
in a report of the German Ambassador in London.   The
most noteworthy passages are as follows : " The essential
cause of the political tension between England and Germany
lies of late years not in the commercial relations, but in the
increasing significance of our Navy, of which England is
afraid.   If war or peace depended upon the big merchants in
the City of London, we might be relieved of the fear of a
war with England.   These gentlemen tremble at the thought
of war.   But not perhaps chiefly because they fear that

the English cruisers (30 armoured cruisers, 83 protected cruisers) cannot protect England's imports from our cruisers (7 armoured cruisers, 27 protected cruisers), but because they know that all values decline in war, that English capital invested abroad, England's chief wealth, would suffer enormous losses, that the stability which is the basis of commercial relations would disappear, and that war swallows up sums of money which must afterwards be paid, and later appear in the form of national debts. . . . Every Englishman knows that if England's imports are cut off he will speedily be as hungry as a church mouse. But he also knows that it is for this reason that he wants a Navy that shall be at least twice as strong as that of the next strongest naval Power, and that is what he has. Above all, he has three times as many cruisers, and with these he can protect his own commerce and destroy that of his enemies. On the other hand, he fears our Navy, which is growing up not far from his coast, and which before long will exhibit numerically no such great difference to his own Navy. . . . If private property and commerce were to be immune from attacks, then an English war against Germany would certainly lose something of its importance ; but the guarantee for peace would rise in value. The task of the Navy would be restricted, but the Navy is not an end in itself, but only a means to an end." Count Metternich therefore advocated the abolition of the right of capture at sea, even if they were not successful in obtaining the necessary correlatives (the limitation of the blockade to naval ports, revision of the regulations concerning contraband of war, and free importation to and between neutral ports).

There was in London also a similar antagonism in the views held by military and civil officials. Exactly like Admiral von Tirpitz, the First Sea Lord (Admiral Sir John Fisher) recommended the retention of the right of capture at sea, except that he demanded that it should be unlimited. He was wholeheartedly supported by Sir Edward Grey, not only on account of England's military interests, but also because of the avowed purpose of keeping the fright-

fulness of war as a deterrent before the eyes of other nations
—a point of view whose root naturally was in the consciousness of England's naval supremacy. The principal opposition came from the highest official in the British judicial
system, the Lord Chancellor, Lord Loreburn, an old supporter
on humanitarian grounds of the abolition of the right of
capture at sea. The Prime Minister, too, Sir Henry
Campbell-Bannerman, had a leaning towards Loreburn's
view. In agreement with his natural disposition, he
favoured increasing the protection for private property
at sea and mitigating the rigours of warfare both on sea
and on land. So we see that both in London and in Berlin
imperialistic and pacifistic wills were at odds ; and at both
places the imperialistic tendency proved the stronger.

If we compare the general attitude of the other Great
Powers *in puncto* of the freedom of the seas even in war-
time, that of the United States of America resembled
Germany's most of all. The United States, too, together
with the kingdom of Prussia, were the first to set the shining
example of advocating the great ideals of mankind.
America's representative in Europe, Benjamin Franklin,
concluded that treaty of friendship with Frederick the
Great in 1785 in which for the first time two States recognized the principle of the sanctity of private property at
sea as against the practice of capture in war. We always
find American statesmen among the champions for humanity
and for the mitigation of war usages in all efforts towards
a further development of international law recorded in
the diplomatic history of the previous century. President
Monroe demanded that war should be exclusively a war
between States, not a war of private individuals, and he
laid down the principle : No warfare against private property. President Franklin Pierce refused to subscribe
to the Paris Declaration of 1856 on naval law solely because
it provided merely for the abolition of privateering and
not also for the abolition of the right of capture by Government vessels. His successor, Mr. Buchanan, went a step
further. He held that to prohibit privateering without

at the same time abolishing the right to blockade open ports would only deprive the weaker naval Powers of a means of fighting the stronger ones.

These reminiscences could not but inspire Berlin with the idea of working for a new agreement between the United States and the German Empire along the lines of the old Prussian-American Treaty, in case, as was probable, effective international machinery to assure the freedom of the seas in time of war should not be set up at The Hague. For had not the occupant of the White House at that time, Theodore Roosevelt, himself, in two messages to the American people, regretted there was no world organization for the prevention of wrong-doing ? And, as a matter of fact, the outline of a memorial in the Berlin Foreign Office contained the sentence : " Our agreement with the humane principle of the United States' policy, many times manifested, and our conviction that the actual condition of the two lands and peoples gives promise of lasting peace and sincere friendship, justify the proposal that the two Governments adopt a common attitude towards the question of naval law, and plan to arrive at an understanding for the abolition of capture at sea and of blockading open ports."

The radical differences of opinion held in official circles in Berlin in regard to this question resulted in putting a check on the energy necessary for the execution of the proposed scheme. Whoever would have dreamt at that time that at some future day, on account of a conflict over questions of maritime law, the United States would intervene as the decisive factor in a World War against Germany ? To-day there can be no dispute as to the falseness of the hope that by making use of the right of capture at sea Germany, with a vastly inferior number of cruisers, could have achieved in a war against England what she was not able to accomplish with a superior number of hastily built submarines employed [1] in ruthlessly destructive warfare

[1] Chap. 172.

BOOK V

THE YEARS OF CRISES, 1908–1912

CHAPTER I

REVAL AND FRIEDRICHSHOF

IMMEDIATELY after Russia's return from the Far East the old continent was seized with fresh anxiety. Even at Algeciras it was clear to see that in spite of the Treaty of Björkö, Russia was going to abandon her old friendship with Germany and to seek her salvation in a union with the closely allied Western Powers. The questions of the Near East that had been quiescent during the Russo-Japanese War were again coming more and more into the foreground.

The change in relations demanded new men. At St. Petersburg, in May 1906, Count Lamsdorv's place at the Foreign Office was taken by von Isvolsky, formerly Minister at Copenhagen, and one of the most cunning and insincere diplomats of his age, who afterwards, as we shall see later, ascribed to himself a large share of the responsibility for the World War. It was not long before Berlin knew what to expect of him, in spite of his repeated assurances of friendliness to Germany. Early in June 1907 the German Ambassador at St. Petersburg, von Schön, had to say to Isvolsky on behalf of the German Government that they could well understand it if Russia should come to a settlement with England about controverted points, but they could not comprehend it if Russia should form a coalition with two other States which, no matter how loudly it might be labelled purely defensive, was nevertheless aimed directly at Germany. Russia's connection with such a coalition was, he said, incompatible with the continuance of the existing relations with Germany.

A month later, in Vienna too there was a change in the

foreign policy. Count Goluchovski was succeeded by the former Ambassador at St. Petersburg, Baron Aehrenthal, an intimate friend of the Archduke Francis Ferdinand, the Heir to the Throne of Austria-Hungary. Baron Aehrenthal, who had been for many years Ambassador at St. Petersburg, was in no way antagonistic to Russia ; on the contrary, he cherished the idea of reviving, if possible, the old Three Emperors' League. Especially did he understand that his most difficult task would be that of binding the quarrelsome Slavic elements in Austria-Hungary more closely to the Monarchy, which presupposed that Russia would continue to exercise moderation in Balkan Questions. But it shortly appeared that the purpose of Russia's policy was, with the help of the Western Powers, to strengthen her position against the Monarchy of the Danube. As early as June 1907 a rumour was afloat that Russia was planning to transfer what was left of her Navy to the Black Sea. This meant the unrolling of the question of the Straits. With Count Lamsdorv in St. Petersburg and Count Goluchovski in Vienna, a defensive Balkan policy had been pursued by their respective Governments. Under Isvolsky and Baron Aehrenthal, the Balkan policy assumed an offensive character. Hitherto it had been a question of friendly adjustment between competitors ; now it became a struggle, both covert and open, for predominant influence.

This decided change in Russia's policy appeared very clearly in the protocol of a conference held on February 25, 1908. Instigated by Isvolsky, the conference was presided over by Stolypin, the Minister-President, and Kokovzev (Minister of Finance), Dikov (Minister of the Navy), Palitzyn (Chief of the General Staff), Polivanov (Acting-Minister for War), and Subastov (Acting-Minister for Foreign Affairs) took part in it. In his speech outlining his programme, Isvolsky said : " Count Lamsdorv endeavoured to restrain Bulgaria and at the same time to obtain an understanding with Austria. Such a policy is purely negative in character. It cannot lead to any solution of the Balkan Question which can be considered favourable from the point of view

THE SIGNIFICANCE OF THE ENGLISH VISIT

"What have you there in your pocket, dear Uncle?
"Europe, dear Nephew!"

(G. Brandt in *Kladderadatsch*, February 7, 1909.)

of Russia's historic interests. On the other hand, it has
the one merit of hastening the shelving of the question.
At any rate, that is not the policy that will lead to real
success, towards the ends we have been pursuing." He said
that it was difficult to count on France and Italy ; that
on the other hand a close rapprochement with England
could lead to splendid results and bring about the unrolling
of the whole Turkish Question ; he said that the English
Ambassador in St. Petersburg had already hinted to him
about such a combination when referring to the common
interests of their respective countries in the Near East.
Stolypin, in the conference, proved to be bitterly opposed to
Isvolsky. He held that a fresh mobilization would intensify
the Revolution from which Russia was only just beginning
to extricate herself ; he declared that any other than a
strongly defensive policy for the present would be the
hallucination of an erratic Government, and that it might
endanger the dynasty.

Thus we see that, on one hand, there was the desire that
there should be a rapprochement with England and then
a war ; while, on the other hand, there was fear of a fresh
revolution and the fall of the dynasty. But the main
point at issue was only the question of time, not the policy
itself. According to Stolypin, Russia had urgent need of
a " breathing spell " before she could again carry on an
energetic policy as a Great Power.[1]

In his speech at the Conference of Ministers, Isvolsky
had also referred to Aehrenthal's statements in the Delegations announcing the plan to extend the Bosnian railroad
from Uvatz to Mitrovitsa through the Sanjak of Novi-
bazar, by which direct connections would be established
between Vienna and Salonika by way of Agram, Sarajevo,
Mitrovitsa, and Uskub. Although in doing this Aehrenthal
was able to refer to the right reserved to Austria-Hungary
by the Berlin Treaty of 1878, still a great clamour was set
up against it, especially in the Russian and in the English
Press. There was no gainsaying the right to construct

[1] Professor M. Pokrovski, *Drei Konferenzen*, Berlin, 1920.

N

the railroad nor the economic importance of such a through line. But the Russian and English opponents of the plan objected on the ground that it constituted an infringement of the spirit of international co-operation, and that the economic advantage would very soon be transformed into political ascendancy for the Danubian Monarchy. The Serbs, of course, were boiling with rage ; but even in Italy there was uneasiness on account of Adriatic trade and intercourse with the Levant.

Baron Aehrenthal had surprised the whole world by his announcement about the Sanjak railroad. Even Isvolsky had received no previous notice. He severed his friendship with the Baron, and announced that Russia could not permit an Austro-Hungarian *pénétration pacifique* of the Balkans *à la* Morocco. He was not disturbed until he heard that Aehrenthal had not, as he believed, promised the Sultan his veto for Macedonian reforms.

The first great success of Isvolsky's active Balkan policy was won as a result of the meeting of the monarchs at Reval. The significance of King Edward's visit to Reval was at once revealed by the fact that besides Hardinge, the Under-Secretary of State for Foreign Affairs, Admiral Fisher and General French were also in his suite, and that the Tsar had brought with him not only the Foreign Minister, von Isvolsky, but also the Minister-President, Stolypin. In the after-dinner speeches there it was acknowledged that the object of the meeting was " to bring the two countries more closely together " and to reach a friendly adjustment of " certain important questions." What was meant in general by this was stated frankly by the Northcliffe Press when it recalled King Edward's epoch-making visit to Paris in 1903, and when it expressed its satisfaction that now the Franco-Russian Alliance and the Anglo-French Entente Cordiale would be supplemented by an Anglo-Russian understanding in Europe.

Among the important questions which were discussed at Reval by the two rulers and by Hardinge and Isvolsky, the foremost was that of the programme of Macedonian

reform, which amounted to a new international control of
the province of Macedonia. This territory was inhabited
by Turks, Bulgars, Serbs, and Greeks, and was in a state
of confusion owing to continual conflicts among the various
nationalities. However, no new written agreement was
made at Reval. England only agreed in general to assist
Russia in looking after her interests in the Near East.[1]

The special political significance of the meeting at Reval
may be clearly seen from Isvolsky's official memorandum
to the Russian Ambassador, Count Benkendorv, on
June 5–18, 1908. Among other things he states there :
" The general impression in respect to politics is extremely
favourable ; King Edward has frankly expressed his satisfaction, and sees in the meeting a confirmation and
strengthening of the Anglo-Russian Agreement (the reference is to the Asiatic Agreement of August 31, 1907), and
also a pledge of the further solidarity of the two Governments. . . . Summing up Hardinge's various statements,
I must emphasize the fact that there has been no attempt
on his part to go beyond concrete agreements—the one
in existence and that under consideration—nor to draw
us into a general political combination. Sir Charles stated
that the English Cabinet was entirely of his opinion in
believing that the interview at Reval need not cause other
States any anxiety ; as for Germany in particular, the
English Government sincerely desires to maintain the very
best of relations with that country, and does not believe
that these relations will become more acute from any cause
in the immediate future. ' *Nevertheless*,' said Sir Charles,
' *no discerning person can shut his eyes to the fact that a very
disquieting and tense situation can arise in Europe in seven
or eight years if Germany continues her naval preparations
at the same accelerated pace ; in that case Russia will undoubtedly be the arbiter of the situation ; and for this reason,
in the interests of peace and of the preservation of the balance,
we desire that Russia shall be as strong as possible both on
land and on sea.*' Sir Charles repeated these ideas several

[1] Chaps. 189, 190.

times, obviously because he wished to intimate that he was expressing not his own personal opinion, but the definite political conviction of the English Cabinet."

The importance of this document is obvious. Hardinge's hypothetical prophecy, which is not among the German but the Russian official documents,[1] was wrong only by a year. The World War broke out not in 1915 or 1916, but as early as 1914, and Russia, in truth, played the part not of arbiter but, relying upon England's assistance, that of aggressor.

There was a certain inner connection between Hardinge's political explanations and the fact that the interview at Reval was followed by one at Friedrichshof, near Kronberg. In England there was no silencing the voices that clamoured that the German naval programmes were fraught with peril for England's naval supremacy. Anti-German politicians made use of incorrect figures and combinations, and understood how to create an atmosphere which must in the long run endanger the good relations of the two Powers. Above all, the legend that Germany was secretly laying down many more ships than were provided for in the Budget was not to be dispelled. The Press was full of articles of this sort, but both Houses of Parliament, too, had thoroughly discussed the German and the English naval policies in March 1908. In order to furnish influential Anglo-Saxon circles with the real facts in these matters, Albert Ballin, Director of the Hamburg-American Line and friend of the German Emperor, a man endowed with unusual political instinct, took pains to have a conversation in the spring with Sir Edward Cassel, an intimate friend of King Edward. The conversation took place at the end of June 1908.

According to the detailed report of the conversation, published by Huldermann,[2] the English King was fully convinced that the rapid growth of the German Navy threatened England's naval position. It was true, he said, that the King recognized that his nephew would never

[1] Siebert, *Diplomatische Aktenstücke*, Berlin and Leipzig, 1921.
[2] *Albert Ballin*, Oldenburg, 1922.

recklessly enter into a quarrel, and that war with its horrors was repugnant to his inmost nature. . . . It was the anxiety over the German peril that was the driving-power of the whole Entente policy—a policy which did allay this anxiety. In reply to Cassel's intimation that some day the Triple Entente might ask Germany whether she intended to halt in the increasing of her naval armaments, Ballin said that such a question would mean war, for Germany would resist such a Fashoda with all her might. In a letter in conjunction with their first conversation, Ballin suggested that the King should not fail to arrange to see the Kaiser when he went to Marienbad. Cassel replied that according to what he had heard, it was already arranged that on his way to Marienbad His Majesty was to have a meeting with the Kaiser.

During the meeting of the monarchs at Friedrichshof there was also a long and energetic discussion between the Kaiser and Sir Charles Hardinge, information about which is given in two detailed telegrams of the Kaiser to Bülow. The King had originally intended to discuss the naval question himself with the Kaiser, but foreseeing the negative result, he left the discussion of the matter to Sir Charles. The latter talked first to the Kaiser about military systems, but soon passed to the Navy Question. Hardinge termed the German naval programme, which would shortly make the German Navy the equal of the English, an object of grave apprehension in all English circles, particularly since the German Navy was always concentrated in home waters, therefore just opposite England. The Kaiser then explained it was exactly from considerations of foreign policy that they wanted to avoid displaying the German Navy too much abroad. At first Hardinge received this explanation sceptically, and then advised that this principle be abandoned completely, since in England it had brought about just the contrary of the effect intended. It was difficult for the Kaiser to convince Hardinge of the real limits of our naval programme. He sent for the *Nauticus*, which was unknown to Sir Charles, and pointed out to him graphic tables printed there. According to the *Nauticus* for 1908 the relative strength of the two Navies was as follows : Of ships of the line of over 10,000 tons, England possessed 52, Germany 22. As to armoured cruisers of over 5,000 tons, England had 34 as against Germany's 8. By 1911 England would possess 56 ships of the line and 39 armoured cruisers, while Germany would only have 25 ships of the line and 10 armoured cruisers. According to this estimate, therefore, England had a vast superiority. The trouble was that people in England doubted the truth of the statements about Germany's naval construction and believed that additional ships were being secretly built.

The conversation, in which both parties had displayed much sharpness and excitement, reached its point of culmination when Sir Charles made a direct demand of the Kaiser for a limitation of armament, saying, " You must stop or build slower," to which the Kaiser immediately replied with the thrust : " Then we shall fight, for it is a question of national honour and dignity." This sharp rejoinder, which showed the Englishman plainly that he had ventured too far, had, according to the Kaiser's account, an excellent result, for Hardinge apologized, and begged that his remark should be considered as unsaid.

The Kaiser was very satisfied with himself. He had told the British the unvarnished truth for once ; that is, he had characterized the English people's deep anxiety over the German Navy as "absolute nonsense," and yet he believed, in spite of his categorical refusal of a naval agreement, he had made a favourable impression on his guest.

What hopes the Cabinet at the Court of St. James had placed upon an understanding about naval construction may be seen from an interview which the Chancellor of the Exchequer, Lloyd George, granted to a representative of the *Neue Freie Presse* at the very time of the meeting of the two monarchs at Friedrichshof, and which was published in that paper on August 12, 1908. Speaking of such an Anglo-German understanding, Lloyd George said : " It is the only way in which to terminate the anxious suspense brooding over Europe ; there is really no occasion for strife between the two peoples ; this agreement must be directed exclusively towards the limitation of the building of new ships in the future." Besides, in this connection he called the reproach that England had conspired to bring about the isolation of Germany a " shocking suspicion." If we compare this interview with that noteworthy speech of July 29, 1908, by the same Lloyd George, in which he pointed out to his own countrymen the injustice of the Two-Power Standard, we must believe in the sincerity of his expressed opinion that it was only the question of naval construction that stood in the way of a real political understanding between the two nations. The following sentences appeared in the speech [1] : " Germany's distrust of England is much easier to understand than England's distrust of Germany (1). We had an overwhelming preponderance at sea, but we were not satisfied. We said : ' Let there be Dreadnoughts.' What for ? We did not require them. Look at the unfairness of our so-called Two-Power Standard (2). Look at the position of Germany. Her Army is to her what our Navy is to us—her sole defence against invasion. Yet she has not a Two-Power Standard, although she is between two Great Powers which in combination could pour in a vastly greater number of troops than she has." Sir Edward Grey, too, in the summer had combated with stronger emphasis than usual the notion that England's policy was to isolate Germany ; and Churchill, the President of the Board of Trade, declared that it was a " diabolical crime " that the Press and the clubs were unleashing the dogs of war by snapping and snarling at Germany. All this compels us to conclude that the English

[1] As the author states, he is quoting sentences from the speech, and he does not indicate omissions that exist between some of these sentences. There is something omitted after the words " require them " and something before " but she is between." I do not find in *The Times* report of the speech the sentences which I have marked (1) and (2) respectively, although there are words that convey the gist of sentence (2).—TRANSLATOR'S NOTE.

Cabinet stood behind the proposal of Hardinge, and was taking pains to prepare for its friendly reception by the Kaiser.

After the Kaiser's refusal of a naval agreement at Friedrichshof, neither Lloyd George nor any other English statesman ever again made so Pro-German a speech. Against the better judgment of the Chancellor, the Kaiser, who was of one mind with the Grand Admiral von Tirpitz, wished that under no circumstances should there be any interruption in the building of big battleships, no matter how often the German Ambassador at London, Count Metternich, might say in his reports : " What is the object ? If we build one ship the English will build two. There is no end to it."

The Kaiser was probably conscious that the Anglo-German antagonism would become more acute as a result of his unfavourable reply to the English proposal, but he underestimated, however, the dangerousness of the situation. About the time of the meeting at Friedrichshof a Frenchman, General Prudhomme, writing in the *France militaire*, called for war against Germany. " Never," so he wrote, " will a better opportunity offer for us to recover our place in the world, thanks to the unexpected double support of Russia and of England, who is striving to destroy Germany's Navy and commerce." From the Belgian official documents we know that the Belgian representatives in Berlin, Paris, and London, in striking accord, reported again and again during the years 1906–8 that the object of England's policy was to create enemies for Germany.

The diplomatic encirclement of Germany was accomplished ; the danger lay in the probability that the circle would be transformed into a ring of iron. In contradistinction to the Triple Alliance, whose peaceful character had been proven for more than a generation, the Dual Alliance was a non-peaceful creation from the day of its birth ; each of its signatories was pursuing a goal which could not be attained without violent changes in the *status quo* in Europe. As long as England remained neutral the military strength of the Triple Alliance sufficed for its protection. On the other hand, if England joined the Dual Alliance, entering into military obligations, secret or open, then, as Bismarck clearly foresaw, any active support of her allies on Italy's part in case of war would be delusive, and thus the ratio of military strength would shift to the advantage of the Dual Alliance.

But the venerable seer in the Sachsenwald had not only clearly understood that the effect on Italy would be unfavourable if England turned away from the Triple Alliance, but he had an uncanny presentment also that the German Imperial Navy would produce this fateful change in English policy. Immediately after the first announcement of more intensive naval construction, his mistrust of " parade ships " and " phantastic plans " was awakened, and when there was talk of protection against attack on the high seas he declared : " I should like to know of what assailant they are thinking ; not, it is to be hoped, of someone who could become such if an un-German passion for prestige and hurried naval armament, which could be interpreted as a sign of hostility, should drive him into a coalition erected against Germany." [1] What Bismarck had a presentiment of in 1898 was by 1908 already a half-accomplished fact.

From Friedrichshof King Edward went to Ischl to visit Emperor Francis Joseph. Ever since 1903 he had interested himself in fostering in every way the relations between the Government of England and the Hofburg in Vienna. In 1904, Prince George, the present King of England, and his wife Mary, whose brother, the Duke of Teck, was playing an important social rôle at the Austrian Court as Military Attaché at the British Embassy, paid a visit to the Hofburg. This was followed up the next year by the King's very intimate visit to Ischl. In 1906, Eugénie, the ex-Empress of the French, who was treated with chivalrous attention by the Emperor, was busy there too, with reminiscences of the time when for the Germans

[1] *Vide Zukunft*, April 24, 1915.

there existed only an Austrian Emperor. The object
was to alienate the Emperor from Prussian Germany, and
in consequence she was considered an envoy of the King
of England. The first unequivocal attempt to make the
Emperor swerve in his treaty loyalty is said to have been
made by King Edward during his visit to Ischl in 1908.
It is certain that the King had confidential talks with the
Emperor Francis Joseph, and that the leave-taking was
somewhat chilly.   According to the testimony of a personage
very close to the Emperor Francis Joseph, Hardinge made
the highly significant remark at the departure of the King :
" A grand old man in every respect, the Emperor ; a capital
fellow, though perhaps he missed just now one of the best
opportunities of his long life." [1]   Prince Bülow, too, says in
his book, *Deutschland unter Kaiser Wilhelm II* [2] : " Similar
attempts in regard to Austria-Hungary on the occasion of
the meeting of the monarchs at Ischl failed because of the
steadfast treaty loyalty of the grey-haired Emperor Francis
Joseph." [3]

[1] Danzers, *Armeezeitung*, January 13, 1919.
[2] Berlin, 1914, vol. i, p. 27.   [3] Chap. 177.

CHAPTER II

THE BOSNIAN CRISIS

SHORTLY after the meeting at Reval an event occurred
which was one of the consequences of the new Anglo-
Russian Balkan Entente and its plan, which threatened
Turkish control in Macedonia, the execution of which was
bound to influence greatly the international situation in
Europe. This event was the revolt of the Young Turks
in the Army in June 1908.

The Sultan and his Government were at that time under
the dominating influence of the two Central Powers. The
German Ambassador, Baron von Marschall, was held in
especially high esteem by the Porte. Pasha von der
Goltz, too, the former reorganizer of the Turkish Army,
was once more in Constantinople. But a new age seemed
dawning for Turkey when the Young Turk rebellion in
the Army in June 1908 spread with astonishing rapidity
from Monastir to the shores of the Levant, and a liberal constitution was extorted in Constantinople on July 11, 1908.
When the old system tottered, so did its props ; the influence
of the Central Powers seemed paralysed for the time being,
and to have given place to leanings towards France and
England. Meanwhile it was soon evident that the driving-
power of the movement was a strong Turkish nationalism,
which was opposed to any interference in Turkey's internal
affairs by the foreign Powers. Under these circumstances it
was advisable to put aside for the time being the programme
for Macedonian reforms agreed upon at Reval. As early
as August 8th, Russia proposed in a note to all the Powers
to postpone action in Macedonian reform for the present,
owing to the revolution in Constantinople.[1]

[1] Chap. 191.

204 THE WORLD POLICY OF GERMANY

While Russian policy was retreating a step, the after-effect of the Anglo-Russian Balkan Entente, prepared at Reval, was so potent in Vienna that that Government determined on more stringent action against the continuous Great Serbia agitations in Bosnia, Herzegovina, and the Banat.

The construction of a railroad in the Sanjak of Novibazar no longer sufficed for Baron Aehrenthal, who was the personification of the feudal arrogance of old Austrian times. Austria's well-founded rights were to be established still more firmly by means of the formal annexation of Bosnia and Herzegovina, which the Berlin Treaty had only given to Austria to occupy and to administer. In order to attain this large ambition more easily, Aehrenthal retroceded the Sanjak to the Young Turks and relinquished all claim to build a railroad there. In this connection we should remember that as far back as Reichstadt, and later, in 1881, in the Secret Agreement of the three Empires, Russia had consented to the formal annexation of the two former Turkish provinces into the Danubian Empire. Nor can there be any contesting of the fact that Austria's action was one of self-defence. There are too many proofs that after Peter Karageorgevitsch had mounted the blood-stained throne of Serbia the South Slavic movement was systematically striving for the destruction of the Austrian Empire. Already in 1904, in a memorial drawn up at the instance of Paschitsch, it was urged that the most intense propaganda for union with Serbia be carried on among the Orthodox and the Mohammedan populations of Bosnia and Herzegovina. The danger to Austria's existence became all the more threatening the more the Government and the Duma in St. Petersburg made it their business to poke the Serbian fire.

The preparations in Vienna for the new move were kept secret as far as possible, so that the announcement of the annexation manifesto on October 5, 1908, made the greatest sensation on the public everywhere. Even her ally, Germany, was only informed of the approaching event on September

26th, by a personal letter of Baron Aehrenthal to Prince
Bülow. In this letter, Aehrenthal said also that he had
come to a definite agreement with Russia. This statement
was later contested by Isvolsky. A detailed exposition
of the previous diplomatic history of Aehrenthal's bold
and momentous step, which not only provoked Serbia but
aroused all the sleeping dogs in the Balkans, is rendered
more difficult because not all the diplomatic conversations
were reduced to writing, or else the records of them still
repose in the archives of Vienna and St. Petersburg.

This is particularly true of the important agreements
between Baron Aehrenthal and von Isvolsky in Buchlau.
It was Isvolsky who suggested a discussion in the Moravian
castle belonging to Count Berchtold, then Ambassador
from Austria-Hungary at St. Petersburg.

Prince Trubetzkoi, a lenient critic of Isvolsky, who was
at that time the chief of the division for the Near East
under Isvolsky, describes in his book, which appeared in
1917, the course of the conversations at Buchlau as follows :
In answer to Aehrenthal's question as to how a definitive
annexation of the two occupied provinces would be received,
Isvolsky replied that the annexation would be a violation
of the Treaty of Berlin, but that it would not bring about
a declaration of war ; Russia, on the revision of the Treaty
of Berlin, would demand the abrogation of Austria's claims
in the Sanjak of Novi-bazar and the independence of
Bulgaria, economic advantages for Serbia, and finally the
opening of the Straits to Russian war-vessels. Prince
Trubetzkoi stresses repeatedly the academic character of
the exchange of views, and points out that Aehrenthal was
chiefly concerned in learning whether Russia would consider
the declaration of annexation as a *casus belli*. Since no
military complication with Russia was to be expected,
especially if the independence of the vassal State of Bulgaria were declared at the same time, Isvolsky, says
Trubetzkoi, suddenly found himself confronted in Paris,
where he was working for the revision of the Berlin
Treaty, with two accomplished facts : the announcement

of Bulgaria's independence and the annexation of Bosnia and Herzegovina.

This version, in which Isvolsky appears as an uncommonly guileless victim, is contradictory to Aehrenthal's statement which he sent to Berlin just before the appearance of the manifesto of October 5th, and which he later repeated, to the effect that there was a clear understanding between himself and Isvolsky about an early declaration of annexation. Isvolsky himself had called on Schön, the Secretary of State, on September 25th–26th in Berchtesgaden, and in conversation with him had mentioned the annexation not as a question to be solved at some later time but as an event very near at hand, thus substantiating the truth of Aehrenthal's statement.

But there remains still another point that is not clear. The Moscow Professor, M. Pokrovski, stated in his revelations published in February 1919 that a written agreement had been drawn up at Buchlau which contained Aehrenthal's promise on the question of the Straits as compensation for the annexation of Bosnia-Herzegovina. Then, he said, Isvolsky got into a violent quarrel with Aehrenthal which outlasted the Bosnian crisis ; the latter threatened to publish the agreement, and thereby forced Isvolsky to exchange his ministerial post in St. Petersburg for that of Ambassador at Paris.

According to the German documents it is quite certain that Aehrenthal promised, if Russia raised no objection to the planned annexation, to renounce all expansion for Austria in the direction of Salonika, and also not to oppose Russia's wish for free passage through the Straits to warships of States bordering on the Black Sea. In the official papers, documents are frequently mentioned which bring into serious question Isvolsky's veracity : firstly, on the occasion of the meeting of the German Emperor and Francis Ferdinand at Eckartsau early in November 1908. In the course of the conversation Francis Ferdinand remarked : " If Isvolsky goes on lying in this fashion his written agreement to the annexation, which is in the Vienna archives, will be published." In the second place, from reports of the German Ambassador in St. Petersburg, Count Pourtalès, it appears that Isvolsky was greatly disturbed by Vienna's threat of submitting officially, or even of publishing his former promises, which he had concealed from the Tsar and the Minister-President, Stolypin.

The Austrian Manifesto placed Monsieur Isvolsky in a very painful position. He was reproached by society and the Press in St. Petersburg with having allowed himself to be taken unawares by Aehrenthal, and of having helped to create a situation that was entirely repugnant to Russia in her rôle of protector of the Slavs in the Balkans. Visiting London, Paris, and Berlin, Isvolsky sought with redoubled zeal to bring about a conference which should sit in judgment on the Bosnian Question and regulate anew the question of the Straits. It was clear that none of the Great Powers who were signatories to the Treaty of Berlin could put themselves in the position of seeming to refuse off-hand the proposal for a conference; Austria's action constituted a violation of the treaty to the detriment of Turkey in the first place, and the treaty could only be safeguarded by means of the *consensus omnium*. But every attempt to draw up a programme led to the collision of a multitude of intersecting interests. After the annexation was a *fait accompli*, it could no longer be made the subject of discussion without humiliating the Great Power on the Danube.

Nor did Isvolsky on his visits meet with any success in his endeavours in regard to the opening of the Straits. In Paris and especially in London he received many expressions of friendliness but not the wished-for promise. England, who was the party chiefly interested in closing the Straits, was just then busy in getting the Sultan to strengthen the fortifications on the Bosphorus, an effort which was successful. The English Cabinet, therefore, explained that the moment was inopportune for recommending Isvolsky's proposal of a conference.

The Kaiser was beside himself when he learned, through Bülow's report of October 5th, of Aehrenthal's procedure in the matter of the annexation. He called Austria's declaration of annexation " highway robbery " perpetrated against Turkey. He was strengthened in this frame of mind by reports from Baron von Marschall, who was gloomy about the future on account of the serious conflict which was inevitable between Austria and Russia. Prince Bülow, on the other hand, remained faithful to the Holstein thesis, that we must unconditionally support Austria's policy in the Orient.

The greatest peril to peace threatened from the quarter of Pan-Slavic agitations in Serbia, a State which had no grounds of complaint over the violation of an international obligation. The dream of a Great Serbia that should embrace the greater part of Bosnia and Herzegovina seemed to be destroyed for ever by this formal linking-up with Austria-Hungary. At the same time, in addition, the Serbs had to look on while their old adversaries, the Bulgars, transformed their land, together with that which they occupied, the former Turkish Eastern Rumelia, into an independent kingdom.

In Russia the opposition to Isvolsky'a policy grew wider and more intense. The party of the Cadets was the chief support of the radical Pan-Slavic activities. They were joined after Austria's declaration of the annexation by the Octobrists and a part of the Right. As early as the end of October 1908, a moderate member of the Duma, Count Bobrinski, asked the Government to refuse to recognize the annexation unless compensations for Serbia and Montenegro were agreed upon in a conference. The longer the delay over a decision about Russia's proposal for a conference the more violent became the behaviour of the Serbs, until they even began to arm. All through the following winter it was uncertain whether they would force their Government into a war in spite of the fact that big Russia from sheer necessity had refused military assistance.

How dangerous the situation had gradually become is seen very clearly from the fact that in the middle of March the Austrian General Staff demanded that the already augmented army corps on the Serbian border be still further strengthened, and that the opportunity be seized to inflict a crushing defeat on the Serbian Army and to destroy all Serbia's materials of war, and so to ensure peace for decades to come.   Even the Heir to the Throne favoured this plan as a means of procuring definitive peace ; for he thought the settlement was bound to come some time, and that it was a question whether the situation might not then have changed to the disadvantage of the Monarchy. A turn in the direction towards peace originated in Berlin. On March 21, 1909, Count Pourtalès was instructed in an order of the Imperial Chancellor, outlined by the Acting-Secretary of State, to make a " final proposal " to Isvolsky. This proposal began by pointing out that in the meanwhile not only had the Turko-Bulgarian dispute over the commutation of Eastern Rumelia's tribute and over the seizure of the Bulgarian section of the Oriental Railroad been adjusted, but also Turkey's recognition of the annexation of Bosnia had been brought about by means of a direct understanding between Vienna and the Porte, hence the conference for which Isvolsky had never ceased working had lost its object.   Germany's advice to Russia was to the effect that if the Vienna Government notified the signatories to the treaty that a conclusion had been reached in the negotiations with the Porte, and at the same time requested that the annexation of Bosnia be recognized, Russia should not refuse her sanction—in other words, she should renounce her demand for a conference.   This proposal afforded Isvolsky a bridge by which he could escape from the morass into which he had got.   He did avail himself of this bridge and so ceased to oppose Aehrenthal.   Russian and French newspapers spoke of " pressure " having been exerted on Russia ; as a matter of fact, the German warning took the form of a friendly discussion, as Isvolsky himself frankly acknowledged.   The only sharp expression in the order to St. Petersburg was the remark that if Russia did not follow this advice, Germany could do nothing more, and must let things take their course. Isvolsky alone would then be responsible for whatever might happen. This was certainly plain and pointed language, but was in no way a threat.

A collision between the groups of the Great Powers in the System of Counter-balances had therefore been avoided. The great danger of the future for the Empire of many nationalities on the Danube and for the peace of the world lay in two facts : that the intense embitterment of Serbia, who had open and secret support from Czechs, Slovenes, and Poles, survived the Bosnian Crisis, as did the deep irritation of Russian Pan-Slavic circles over the diplomatic defeat ; and, further, their readiness to make any sacrifice.

For Isvolsky, in his policy for Russia, the termination of the Bosnian Crisis did not mean the settlement of a difficult diplomatic complication, but rather the beginning of a warlike enterprise whose object was the destruction of the Monarchy of Austria-Hungary. Any doubt as to the truth of this disappears if we read the official documents in the appendix of the work *Kriegsursachen* (Zürich, 1919), by the former Serbian Chargé d'Affaires, Dr. Bogitschevitsch, as well as those documents in Professor M. Pokrovski's articles in the Moscow weekly *Pravda* for the month of February 1919 which have been inserted in the German White Book dealing with the question of responsibility for the World War.[1] From these it is very plain to see that the only reason why the World War did not break out in the winter of 1908-9 was because the " juncture of affairs," although diplomatically tolerably satisfactory, was not yet from the military point of view sufficiently favourable for those who were working for war in Russia at that time, and who later became war criminals. On October 25, 1908, three weeks after Austria's declaration of the annexation, the Minister Milovanovitsch, who had been sent to Berlin on a special mission, reported to Belgrade a conversation with Isvolsky, who was also in Berlin : " Isvolsky is incessantly condemning Austria-Hungary most bitterly, and says that she has entirely lost the trust

[1] Berlin, 1920.

of Russia and the Western Powers ; he expressed his conviction and his hope that Austria-Hungary would have to pay for this action with blood."

In making the annexation announcement, Aehrenthal had neither asked nor received Germany's advice. After it had taken place the German Chancellor, Prince Bülow, foreseeing the coming international crisis, and in spite of Russia's inevitable ill-humour, considered it proper not to allow Vienna and the general public to have any doubt about Germany's support of her ally. During the crisis Vienna and Berlin were in close touch, as was natural. The German Government's chief concern was to save Austria-Hungary from a humiliating diplomatic defeat. If Germany had been striving to render the situation more acute, the Kiderlen order of March 21, 1909, would not have been dispatched to St. Petersburg, and probably an ultimatum from Aehrenthal to Serbia about her war preparations would have ensued.

The support which Germany gave her ally was actually no greater than the backing the English Foreign Office accorded the St. Petersburg Government. The strong metaphor which Prince Bülow makes use of in his book, *Deutsche Politik*, when he speaks of having thrown the German sword into the scale of European decision, means no more than that in case of war Germany would have observed unconditionally her treaty obligations to Austria-Hungary, if the latter had been attacked by Serbia and Russia. It is quite probable that then England also would have come in before the war had been fought out. At all events, there is evidence for this opinion in a Paris note of April 5, 1909, found in the Belgian official documents, which states that, according to information from the best of sources in Paris and in London, engagements had been made to support Russia if war should break out.[1] This assertion seems highly plausible, judging from the report sent from St. Petersburg on the very same date, April 5, 1909, by the German Ambassador, Count Pourtalès, who said : " Nicolson

[1] *Zur europäischen Politik, 1897–1914*, vol. iii, p. 146.

(the English Ambassador at St. Petersburg) seriously
blamed the Foreign Minister, Isvolsky, for having accepted
Germany's proposal of mediation without previously communicating with France and England. Even Sir Edward
Grey, as my informant tells me, expressed his annoyance
before the Russian Chargé d'Affaires that Russia had been
so submissive in her policy, and characterized Isvolsky's
action as precipitate. The English Minister even went so
far as to discuss what attitude England would have taken
if it had come to a war between Russia and Austria and
Germany."

Isvolsky, as Minister, was doomed to a course of duplicity
both in word and action because of the necessity of not
openly proclaiming his programme of a war of Serbs against
Germans, and of having therefore at one time to admit,
and at another time to disavow, that he had such a
programme. Isvolsky as Ambassador, on the other hand,
during his time of service in Paris, where he could speak
unequivocally, laboured so successfully for his object,
that of war, that after the outbreak of the World War
he could in his satisfaction ejaculate, " *C'est ma guerre !* " [1]

On January 2, 1909, the Kaiser read to the commanding
generals, assembled to offer their New Year's greetings,
an article from the *Deutsche Revue* by the former Chief of
the General Staff, Count Schlieffen. On the basis of what
had been learned in the Japanese War, the author gave a
brief and thrilling description of modern large-scale warfare
in all its aspects and terribleness, and also an outline sketch
of the political situation in Europe at that time.

The main points were as follows :

" In the centre of Europe stand defenceless Germany
and Austria ; in a circle around them, behind rampart and
trenches, are the other Powers. The political corresponds

---

[1] Cf. *Der diplomatische Schriftwechsel Iswolskis, 1911–1914*, published by Friedrich Stieve by order of the Foreign Office. Also
Iswolski und der Weltkrieg, by F. Stieve. Both works adduce documentary evidence that from 1911 Isvolsky was consciously working
to bring about a World War.

to the military situation. Between the besieging and the besieged Powers exist antagonisms difficult to remove. . . . It is not certain that these passions and desires will be translated into actual violence. But there is, however, a zealous endeavour to bring all these Powers together for a joint attack on those in the centre. At the given moment the gates are to be opened, the drawbridges will be lowered, and armies millions strong will pour in across the Vosges Mountains, over the Meuse, the Könisgau, the Niemen, the Bug, and even over the Isonzo and across the Tirolian Alps, ravaging and destroying. The danger appears colossal."

This picture of dangers was not much altered by the outcome of the Bosnian conflict. There had been no essential change for the better in the real feelings of peoples towards one another as a result of the great diplomatic conflict. The successful localizing of the Bosnian-Serbian conflagration could on no account serve as a model precedent for the future. History never repeats itself as exactly as all that. Russia needed only to strengthen her Army and to construct strategic highways and railroads towards her western frontier with additional French billions, as she actually did, for the danger of a world conflagration to remain what it was—colossal.

* * * * *

A survery of the general European situation after the termination of the Bosnian Crisis shows that Germany's position between the Powers on her eastern and western wings had grown much more serious. England's need of a rapprochement with Germany, which was repeatedly shown during the New Course, and even in the first period of Bülow's official career in Berlin, a rapprochement that might have led to a junior partnership in international affairs, was satisfied by the Entente Cordiale with France and by Russia's transference of her policy from Eastern and Central Asia to the Balkans. In England's political system Germany was shifted into the fourth place, behind the Powers of the Dual Alliance. In the same way Germany had lost to England the second place with Russia, formerly reserved for her next to France. By her diplomacy Russia had obtained a claim on England's co-operation in the Near East. Italy was *immobil* in the Triple Alliance, and prepared by means of closer relations with Russia to carry out her claims against Turkey for Tripoli. As for Balkan affairs, Russia looked upon Germany as an adversary inseparably united with Austria-Hungary.[1]

The diplomatic success of the Central Alliance enhanced Germany's sense of power. Even before it had been achieved the Navy League and the Pan-Germans had made good use of the critical foreign situation, as they had done with every similar one before, in their demands for additional armament, especially naval. The effect of the success on other countries, however, all depended upon whether the defeated group of Powers would be spurred on by the lauded victory of the Nibelung loyalty to strengthen the net against the alliance of the Central Powers, or whether they would really succeed in checking the danger of a military explosion by dint of weakening the solidarity within the system of alinement of Powers. Now, as before, there was only one way of ensuring peace to Europe, that of an understanding between the strongest land Power and the strongest naval Power, between whom no such deep traditional hostility existed as that between Russia and Austria-Hungary and that between France and Germany. Prince Bülow himself, regardless of the laurels won in the Bosnian Crisis, to the very end of his Chancellorship wanted to follow that course. Likewise in England, statesmen were not

---

[1] Prince Sviatopolk-Mirski wrote early in 1910 in the *Peterburgskija Wjedomosti* : " Russia needs a war to freshen her moral atmosphere. France will have to provide the money for the war ; since she has already loaned enormous sums to Russia she would be interested in a Russian victory. It would be a pitiless conflict, waged until both the Central Empires lay in ruins. The Czechish Kingdom would receive Moravia, Denmark, and Schleswig-Holstein, while France, for her many billions, would again come into possession of Alsace-Lorraine." And this in 1910 !

wanting who sought to avert the disaster which was threatening. A substantial share in the frustration of these efforts was due to what Lord Northcliffe called in those critical days of July 1914 the " mechanism of the Ententes." By that he meant, in case of war, the automatic engagement of one Power in support of another, which must come into effect even if there were no reason for going to war, or even if a Power resorted to arms before exhausting all peaceful means for arriving at a settlement. As a matter of fact, it was such a mechanism as this, in which secret military agreements and naval conventions constituted its most powerful driving-forces, that finally proved to be stronger than the rational disposition for peace.[1]

[1] For the intimate relations between France and England, and the mutual progress of their military preparations, *vide* Hermann Oncken's *Deutschland und der Weltkrieg*, Leipzig, 1915, pp. 503 *seq.*, and Paul Rohrbach's *Deutschland unter den Weltvölkern*, Stuttgart, 1921, pp. 256 *seq.*

CHAPTER III

THE NEW CHANCELLOR. AGADIR AND TRIPOLI

THE origin of the change in Chancellors which occurred in July 1909 is traceable to 1908, that year of crises. The Kaiser's real reason for wishing to part with Prince Bülow was closely connected with the Chancellor's attitude in the November tempest that raged on November 10 and 11, 1908, after the publication of the Kaiser's Interview in the *Daily Telegraph*. The story of that unfortunate interview, whose publication almost led to a Kaiser Crisis, is as follows :

In 1907 the Kaiser and the Kaiserin, unattended by any Ministers, paid a visit to Windsor Castle. There were intimate after-dinner speeches and receptions for delegations during the visit, which passed off harmoniously. Sir Edward Grey publicly commended the friendly, conciliatory spirit. Afterwards, the Kaiser went alone to Highcliffe Castle, in the Isle of Wight, for a rest, and there spent several weeks in most agreeable company. The Kaiser was in the best of humours and charmed the guests by his simplicity, friendliness, and vivacity. This favourable impression led to the idea of publishing in an English paper observations the Kaiser had made to Englishmen. The journalist, Harold Spender, made an article out of some conversations of the Kaiser, and the owner of Highcliffe Castle, Stuart-Wortley, a retired General, sent the manuscript to Rominten for the Kaiser's approval. The latter had it forwarded to the Chancellor at Norderney to be more thoroughly examined. From the Chancellor it went to the Foreign Office, and from there, with its endorsement of *Placet*, it travelled back over the same route until it reached General Wortley.

The Kaiser had acted according to constitutional rule, but the official apparatus had failed to do its part ; the Foreign Office had only corrected a few actual errors in the manuscript, but had not weighed the question of the appropriateness of publishing the article. This is not the place to examine critically into the displays of negligence in the affair, nor to discuss in detail the question of the responsibility for them. There is no connection between this question and Germany's World Policy. What caused the November tempest was the *Daily Telegraph* article of October 28, 1908, on the Kaiser's Highcliffe conversations. The unfortunate impression was due to the following statements of the Kaiser :

(1) He said he had refused to receive the Boer envoys, who had been fêted in Holland and in France.

(2) He said that when the Boer War was at its height he had furthermore refused to humble England to the dust by intervening in the war along with Russia and France, also that he had informed the King of England of his refusal to do so.

(3) In the weeks that were dark ones for British arms in South Africa he had worked out a plan of campaign, he said, which, after its examination by the General Staff, he had sent to his Grandmother, and this plan very closely resembled Lord Roberts's successful plan.

(4) Lastly, he said that it was necessary for Germany to have a powerful Navy in order to join in the discussion of the solution of the question of the Pacific Ocean in future days that were perhaps not far distant.

Apart from the last opinion, which was only a pernicious tirade, there was some truth in every assertion, and yet everything, taken altogether, was distorted and overcoloured. The utterances were highly boastful, naïve, and impolitic. When they were published there was general indignation in every political party. All the annoyance, despondency, and resentment that had been accumulating during almost two decades, owing to the Kaiser's autocratic behaviour, was now let loose.

In the Reichstag sessions of November 10 and 11, 1908, there were questions about the *Daily Telegraph* disclosures on the day's agenda of almost every political party. Party wrangles ceased. The House was in a gloomy, resentful frame of mind. Speakers from the Left with more or less oratory put the Kaiser's remarks to the account of the personal rule and its concomitant phenomenon, Byzantianism. The Chancellor tried as far as possible to protect the Kaiser, but admitted that certain expressions in the article, especially that about the Pacific Ocean, were too strong, and he exhorted the Kaiser to observe more discretion even in private conversation. A Socialist member, Wolfgang Heine, put his finger on the essential point in the problem about the Kaiser when he stated the unvarnished truth : " No matter how much the Kaiser promises to exercise self-restraint, he cannot make himself different from what he is."

No resolution was drawn up nor was any address made to the Kaiser by the Reichstag. But the Chancellor succeeded during an audience in obtaining the Kaiser's consent to a notice in the *Reichsanzeiger* stating that " undisturbed by what he feels is the unjust, exaggerated criticism by the public, he sees his chief task is that of securing stability in the policy of the Empire, while at the same time strictly observing the Constitution."

The Kaiser continued to feel that he had been unfairly treated by the Reichstag and the Chancellor, and not sufficiently supported, although just in this case he had not acted on his own autocratic judgment. He had a nervous breakdown, and had to keep his bed for weeks. A feeling of ill-humour towards Prince Bülow survived which could be only temporarily dispelled.

Foreign Policy had nothing to do with Prince Bülow's resignation of the Chancellorship in July 1909 ; the ostensible reasons for the change in Chancellors were due to internal politics. Prince Bülow was not successful in overcoming entirely the Kaiser's ill-humour towards himself and in restoring the old relations of mutual confidence. The Conservatives, whose union with the Liberals in the last elections had made them uncomfortable, knew that the Kaiser would no longer keep Bülow under all circumstances. In the division on a finance bill containing a lineal inheritance tax, they changed sides from the Block forming the majority over to the Centre, thereby inflicting a parliamentary defeat on Bülow; whereupon he offered his resignation, and recommended as his successor von Bethmann-Hollweg, the Secretary of State for the Interior.[1]

The new Chancellor's personality was in certain respects the antipodes of his predecessor's. Without diplomatic experience, unpretentious in manner, averse to all clever tricks, he was impeded in coming to a decision by doubts and by a habit of self-criticism.

Prince Bülow bequeathed to his successor a completed Franco-German Agreement which had to do with the heated disputes over the Moroccan littoral, but it provided no definitive adjustment based upon principles for the regulation of Germany's relation to France in the Morocco tangle. Moreover, the new Chancellor found preparations towards an attempt to terminate the dangerous naval rivalry between Germany and England. Let us first consider Moroccan affairs.

In the years immediately following Algeciras one vexatious incident followed another. Firstly, the assassination of a French physician in Marakesh; then the attack by the Kabyles in the neighbourhood of Casablanca, and their plundering of the city; then a new dynastic struggle between the Sultan Abdul Aziz in Fez and his brother Abdul Mulay Hafid, who had revolted and was in Marakesh. Added to these various Moroccan incidents, which offered an equal number of opportunities for fresh frictions between Berlin and Paris, there was in the autumn of 1908 a sharp dispute between the commanding officer of the French

[1] Vol. xxiv, Chap. 178.

troops of occupation, General d'Amada, and the German consulate at Casablanca over a question of jurisdiction which might easily have resulted in serious tension between the respective Governments.

But the fact that the Bosnian Crisis began at that very time caused the Kaiser to instruct the Chancellor, Prince Bülow, as follows : " But in view of these circumstances, this miserable Morocco affair must be wound up, quickly and definitely. There is nothing to do about it ; France will surely have it. Therefore let us get out of the affair as well as we can, so that we can at last get rid of friction with France at a time when great questions are at stake." Faint reminiscences of Björkö played their part in this decision of the Kaiser—that is to say, he had the idea of diverting France from England, and of effecting a recon- ciliation between France and Germany. Besides, he wanted a speedy settlement with France because he did not want the impression to be created that King Edward, whose visit to Berlin was scheduled for February 9, 1909, had had a share in bringing about a decided change in Germany's Morocco policy to the advantage of France.

On the day the King and Queen of England arrived in Berlin the Casablanca Treaty, which had been drawn up two days before, was signed and immediately published.

In this agreement Germany expressly recognized that France had special political interests in Morocco, while France for her part repeated her recognition of the integrity and independence of the Shereefian Empire and of the principle of the Open Door for all nations. The Act of Algeciras remained formally in force. Whether the treaty of February 9, 1909, would prove to be a positive asset in the Bülow legacy all depended upon whether France's demeanour in Morocco would really conform to the reaffirmed principles of independence and economic equality.[1]

The very next year there began to be trouble in Morocco and fresh friction between Berlin and Paris. Germans besieged the Foreign Office in Berlin with complaints and

[1] Chaps. 179–82.

grievances about unjust treatment in the award of public commissions and concessions. The Mannesmann brothers wanted a protectorate over the Sus region, where they had acquired land containing ore deposits ; Spanish troops were pushing forward in Northern Morocco ; in the neighbourhood of Fez French posts had been established ; the occupation of Fez was imminent, and this would mean an indisputable violation of the independence of the Sultan— in short, there was a state of confusion that made a return to the Act of Algeciras impossible.

Von Kiderlen, who had become Secretary of State after Baron Schön had been transferred to Paris as Ambassador there, proposed in a note of May 3, 1911, that Paris be advised that in the event of a French occupation of Fez we should send a battleship to the harbour of Agadir, which we should hold in pledge until France offered satisfactory compensation to Germany for her renouncement of the Act of Algeciras. Informal suggestions from Paris, even from Caillaux, had encouraged Kiderlen to form this plan. The Chancellor agreed to it and persuaded the Kaiser also, who had thought that the whole miserable Morocco business had been disposed of by the agreement, to consent on principle to the sending of a battleship to Agadir. On May 21st Fez was occupied by the French. The French Minister, Cruppi, stated that Fez was to be evacuated as soon as order was restored. When the French Ambassador, Jules Cambon, gave Berlin officially to understand that Paris was prepared to give a part of the French Congo as compensation, Kiderlen replied : " It will have to be a very nice chunk." Kiderlen then expected that Cambon would make a definite offer. But nothing of the sort happened ; after his return from Paris, where he had gone for information, Cambon did not appear in the Foreign Office for days. Kiderlen now proceeded to carry out his plan. He went to Kiel, and there obtained the Kaiser's consent to sending to Agadir the small gunboat *Panther*, which happened to be not far from the coast of North Africa. The vessel reached the appointed place on July 1, 1911.

Simultaneously a German note was sent to the Great Powers explaining Germany's position in the matter and denying any intention of seizing Agadir. But even yet Cambon did not come out clearly about compensations, and not until a fortnight later did he enter into real parleys.

After tedious negotiations, the Congo Agreement was finally concluded on November 4, 1911, whereupon the *Panther* was recalled from Agadir, even before the debates in the French Chamber. In the meanwhile, public opinion in Germany had become more and more heated over the treaty. Pan-German circles had insisted stubbornly on the acquisition of the Sus territory with its ore deposits and supposed ideal conditions. The fantastic confusion of their minds is best shown by the fact that the chairman of the Pan-German League as early as the spring of 1911 wanted to publish a pamphlet which demanded nothing less than that Germany should appropriate the Rhône district as well as Morocco. Kiderlen quashed the publication of this "nonsense." [1] A conflict between him and von Lindquist, the Secretary of State for the Colonies, furnished fresh seeds of discontent. His long experience in the colonial service led the Colonial Secretary to want an extension of Dahomey instead of the enlargement of Cameroon by a strip of land from the French Congo. He persisted in his point of view, and offered his resignation even before the meeting of the Reichstag in November.

The November storm in the Reichstag in 1911 against the Franco-German Agreement almost equalled in intensity the November storm of 1908 against the Kaiser. It was directed against the Government, especially on account of their weakness in protecting German rights in Morocco. In the debates of November 10th and 11th, the leaders of the National Liberal and the Conservative Parties in more or less covert language joined in the Pan-German outcries of Shame! Olmütz! Jena!

What most contributed to bring about this storm of

[1] *Vide* Ernst Jäckh's *Alfred von Kiderlen-Wächter der Staatsmann und der Mensch*, Stuttgart, 1924, vol. ii, p. 122.

excitement was an after-dinner speech of Lloyd George on July 21, 1911, which sounded like a threat and an announcement of English intervention. In this speech he said : Britain could under no circumstances suffer herself to be treated as if she were of no account in the cabinet of nations. Peace at that price would be a humiliation, he declared. This warning or threat to Germany was not justified, since, as we have seen, the British Foreign Office, like the other Great Powers, had been notified in a circular note on July 1st of the sending of the *Panther* and of its peaceful object. During this whole time and up to the autumn session of the Reichstag, nothing was heard by the German public of an official German protest against Lloyd George's speech, so that the impression prevailed that the German Government had received a " box on the ear " from England without uttering a word. As a matter of fact, Kiderlen had instructed the Ambassador, Count Metternich, on July 24th, to lodge a strong protest with Sir Edward Grey against England's expressing her desires and admonitions in after-dinner speeches instead of by the customary diplomatic method. Kiderlen's order and Metternich's report on his " extremely animated " conversation with Grey were diplomatic masterpieces.

Erich Brandenburg has published the results of his study of the documents in the German Foreign Office in his *Von Bismarck zum Weltkrieg*. Although, as a rule, he weighs his statements very carefully, he expresses a very unfavourable opinion of Kiderlen and his acts when Secretary of State, especially those in connection with Agadir. He speaks of a very poorly considered policy, of a mad prank, and calls this and that step rash and unwise. Anyone who came into close contact with Kiderlen will not entirely agree with Brandenburg. It is true that when Kiderlen was called to direct Foreign Affairs he was not the man he was in the days of the *Kladderadatsch* attacks on the "Three men in the fiery furnace "—Holstein, Eulenburg, Kiderlen. He had formerly attended the Kaiser on his northern trips, but had fallen from favour on account of his

sarcastic remarks, which had been secretly reported to His
Majesty, and he had been " banished " for ten years to the
then very quiet post of Bucharest. This long set-back
in his official career had gradually embittered his former
good-humour. While he was at the Foreign Office his
unusual ability, especially his cleverness with his pen, was
highly prized by both Chancellors. In diplomatic circles,
even in foreign countries, he was held personally in high
esteem. This is evident from notices in great foreign
newspapers like *The Times* and the *Figaro* after his early
death. An understanding of the psychology of the people
was certainly not his strong point. If it had been he would
not have obstinately disdained to enlighten the German
public about his rebuff of Lloyd George. Bethmann-Hollweg,
who often groaned over Kiderlen's close reserve and wilful-
ness, once described him in these words : " A very uncomfortable colleague, but a fine fellow."

While the negotiations over Morocco were still going on,
Italy announced to the Powers that she was going to make
an attack on Turkish Tripoli (August 1911). The assertion
that she wanted to restore order there was only a pretext.
As a matter of fact, she was hastening to avail herself as
quickly as possible of the claim which had been conceded
by the Agreement with France in 1900, and of Bülow's
promise made on the occasion of the renewal of the Triple
Alliance in 1902.[1] In deciding on an extra dance [2] of a
military character in Tripoli, the Italian Foreign Office had
grounds for cherishing the hope that Russia would support
Italian interests in the Near East. The Russian Government, who were still harbouring a grudge against Baron
Aehrenthal after the termination of the Bosnian Crisis,
were striving energetically to strengthen their influence
among the Balkan States and to intensify the antagonisms
between Austria and Italy. This purpose was served when
the Tsar made a long detour in order to avoid passing through
Austrian territory on his way to meet the King of Italy

[1] *Vide supra*, p. 128.
[2] Ibid. p. 126.—TRANSLATOR'S NOTE.

A POLITICAL TOBACCO PARLIAMENT OF 1911

(A free adaptation of a well-known picture by A. Menzel.)

Kiderlen-Wächter has most horribly frightened a kind old gentleman with
his little tame panther.

(L. Stutz, in *Kladderadatsch*, July 16, 1911.)

in Racconigi in the autumn of 1909. Here a pact was concluded which provided that in the event of the disintegration of Turkey only the Balkan States were to receive something, whereas the Monarchy on the Danube was to go away empty-handed. This agreement was immediately brought to the attention of London and of Paris, and even of the Balkan States. Prince Trubetzkoi, whom we have already mentioned, says in speaking of this : " Russia gladly availed herself of the chance to use the Italian antidote against the Austro-German bacillus."

The Italian enterprise caused a good deal of embarrassment to the German policy, not unlike that after the announcement of Austria-Hungary's manifesto of the annexation of Bosnia and Herzegovina. In both cases Germany had to consent to the endangering of her own influence in Constantinople for the sake of an ally, only with this difference, that Italy had no need of active German assistance in her selfish move on the African coast. In the three years following the outbreak of the Bosnian Crisis and the deposition of the Sultan Abdul Hamid, the German Ambassador, Baron von Marschall, had succeeded in acquiring as complete an influence over the Young Turk regime as that which he had exercised under the rule of Abdul Hamid.

In order to force Turkey to recognize the annexation of Tripoli, which had been declared on November 5, 1911, the Italians occupied a number of islands in the Ægean Sea, among them Samos and Rhodes, in the spring of 1912, although Aehrenthal had previously protested against the extension of the war to the Ægean Sea. Since the Turks could not but fear that the Italian fleet might force an entry into the Sea of Marmora, they took measures for closing the Dardanelles. Then followed a remarkable diplomatic battle. The Russian Ambassador, von Tscharikov, presented himself to the Porte, and made far-reaching demands for free passage for Russian ships through the Dardanelles. The Porte, looking about for help, turned to the Ambassadors of Germany and Austria-Hungary. These both begged their respective Governments to authorize them to protest immediately against Russia's demand. Marschall feared that a passive attitude on their part towards Russia's demand would drive Turkey into the arms of the Triple Entente, and he threatened to resign if Berlin failed to approve his proposal. Kiderlen, however, did not relent, and held to his opinion that it would not be wise to rob the British Cabinet of the odium attaching to a refusal of Russia's proposals. As a matter of fact, in consequence of England's remonstrances to St. Petersburg, the Ambassador Tscharikov's action was disavowed by the Russian Government, and he was shortly afterwards recalled from Constantinople.

Another danger to the peace of Europe emanated from Vienna. Here a strong party had been formed which, under General Conrad von Hötzendorff, wanted a severe reckoning with Italy. The Emperor Francis Joseph, however, declared that as long as he lived he would make no war unless Italy attacked first. It was in connection with this idea of a preventive war, to which Aehrenthal also was opposed, that General Conrad was dismissed on December 2, 1911, but later, at the instigation of the Heir to the Throne, he took his place once more as Chief of the General Staff. What is strangest of all in the German official documents is the attitude of the Kaiser in the critical situation caused by the Tripoli adventure. He again bethought himself of his old panacea, a continental alliance with France against England. This complete misinterpretation of the ruling spirit in France could not have been more conclusively proved than it was by the other direct consequences of the Agadir conflict—the fall of the moderate Ministry of Caillaux, who was charged with being too pacific towards Germany—and by the calling of Poincaré, the most obstinate champion of *la revanche*, to head the new Government in February 1912.

A year after Racconigi, the Tsar accepted the Kaiser's invitation to visit Potsdam. Both parties wanted to bring about more friendliness in the Court and official relations, which had grown very cool as the result of the Bosnian Crisis.

Isvolsky had been replaced as Foreign Minister, the end of September 1909, by his former helpmate, Sazonov, son-in-law of the Minister-President, Stolypin.   Sazonov belonged to the Right and was therefore no Pan-Slavic hotspur. In conversations with the Chancellor, Bethmann-Hollweg, he explained that he would endeavour to maintain good relations with England, but that he would never enter into hostile combinations with England against Germany. He even suggested a written agreement.   However, when it came to drawing up the text, he evaded, and explained that he would only give his consent to the Chancellor's announcing in the Reichstag that it had been agreed in Potsdam that neither of the two Governments would enter into combinations that were pointed aggressively towards the other party (December 10, 1910).   Likewise, when the Kaiser made a return visit to the Tsar in Wolfs-garten on November 11, 1910, not much came of it.   Apart from a later agreement between St. Petersburg and Berlin about their mutual interests in Persia and about a branch line from Bagdad to Chanekin, the meetings of the two monarchs remained without any noticeable effects.

CHAPTER IV

GERMANY AND ENGLAND AT THE PARTING OF THE WAYS

AFTER Hardinge's conversation with the Kaiser about naval affairs at Friedrichshof, the Anglo-German relations were under the spell of a naval rivalry. The Chancellor, Prince Bülow, and the Foreign Office were firmly convinced that under no circumstances must they again irritate England by acceleration in naval construction. The German Ambassador in London, Count Metternich, felt this very strongly, too, and he never failed to insist constantly that the success of any attempt at reaching an understanding with England depended exclusively on Germany's willingness to make concessions in her naval programme.

Through various third parties, Prince Bülow had learned that England would consider an official statement from Germany to the effect that she would not exceed her naval programme as established by law as a sign of Germany's friendliness and as a basis for further conversations. After long opposition in naval circles the Chancellor was able to make the following involved explanation about our naval programme in the Reichstag on December 10, 1908 : " On the one hand, our geographical position, on account of which our security must always be dependent upon the strength of our Army, and, on the other hand, the measure of our economic and financial powers, already heavily taxed by our Army and by our social policy, which is far in advance of that of any country, absolutely preclude the possibility —and in this I am confident of the assent of our naval authorities—that our naval construction should exceed the

limit as determined by our need, and as accordingly fixed
by law." However, in order to give the English a visible
sign of our good will, Bülow, in a letter of December 25,
1908, to Tirpitz, attempted to get him to consent to a
retardation in the construction of the big ships, by proposing
stronger fortification of our coasts, and an increase in the
number of our mines and the creation of a strong flotilla
of submarines. He thus adopted again, to a certain degree,
Bismarck's old idea of developing our Navy chiefly for
purposes of defence. The reason that Bülow gave for
his proposal was his expectation that it would immediately
purify the general atmosphere, and that he hoped in this
way to get successfully through the especially perilous
year of 1911. He proposed, therefore, to reduce the number
of new ships to be built in the next three years from four
to three each year, and to make up for this reduction by
building three ships in those years for which only two ships
had been scheduled. We were, therefore, between the
years 1909–14, to lay down the keels of three large ships
a year, and between the years 1915–17 the keels of two,
which would mean no reduction in the total output. But
the Secretary of State for the Imperial Naval Board
remained impervious to Bülow's ideas, and rejected them
in a letter of January 4, 1909. This document is very
characteristic of the point of view of its author. It consists
mainly of a political lecture by the chief of a military
department to the statesman at the head of affairs.
Tirpitz says that the procedure suggested by the Chancellor
in his letter would appear both at home and abroad as a
backing down before England's threat, and in England
our compliance would be stamped as a humiliation for
Germany. All the English interested in the Navy who had
staged the Navy Scare would agitate still further. The
danger of war would be increased, not lessened. There
was sure to be a strong opposition in Germany to backing
down before England's threats. Furthermore, it would be
humiliating to reduce the annual output of big ships from
four to three. If that were to happen he should offer his

resignation. Tirpitz's attitude was due to the fact that he
was so blinded by patriotic ardour that he was unable
to see the real political situation, or to estimate objectively
England's motives in attempting to effect a reciprocal
limitation in the building of battleships. Not only in full
possession of the Kaiser's favour, but conscious also of being
able to count on the greater part of the Conservative-Liberal
Block and of the Centre, he had no need to fear a conflict
with the Chancellor.

Even in the latter part of his Chancellorship Bülow sought
to induce the Kaiser and the Grand Admiral, von Tirpitz,
to make such concessions as to the number of large battleships to be built as would be calculated to bring about an
agreement, and so to end this dangerous naval competition
with England. The Kaiser, however, swore by the opinion
of the Admiral, who felt and regarded every concession as
a "humiliation." Only in Venice, where Bülow met the
Kaiser on his way home from Corfu in April 1909, did he
succeed in getting William II's consent to the principle
of a naval agreement. Immediately afterwards, the clever
recorder for the English division in the Foreign Office,
von Stumm, who was well-acquainted with English
conditions—the Ambassador, Count Metternich, was absent
on leave—was sent to London on a special mission with
definite proposals for a defensive agreement. He was
received with outward cordiality, especially by Hardinge,
but the cause he represented met with so little encouragement that von Stumm preferred to go home without having
broached the concrete proposals. Sir Edward Grey said
that Europe was actually divided into two camps, and that
it would be difficult to bring all the Powers into one camp.
Obviously he feared to endanger the Entente Cordiale with
France by negotiations with Germany and to disturb the
good relations with Russia.

But Prince Bülow was not willing to rest here. On
April 13, 1909, he made an appeal to Tirpitz which ran as
follows : " I must in this event, that is to say if the Navy's
attitude renders impossible an understanding with England,

hold Your Excellency alone responsible before the Kaiser, before the country, and before the judgment of history." Since this appeal bore no fruit, Bülow then, on June 3, 1909, brought about a conference in which von Moltke (the Chief of the General Staff), von Tirpitz, von Müller (the Chief of the Naval Cabinet), von Schön and Bethmann-Hollweg (both Secretaries of State), and Count Metternich (Ambassador to England) took part. The Grand Admiral said that every retardation in construction would reduce the value of the entire naval law; at most, he could consent to an agreement which would fix the ratio of 3 : 4 for future construction. The Chief of the General Staff ranged himself absolutely on the Chancellor's side, since he held that Germany would be no match for the English in a naval war. Moreover, the two Secretaries of State and Count Metternich were of the same opinion. The latter very sharply opposed the Admiral's point of view. He thought the proposal of the ratio of 3 : 4 for large battleships was made with *reservatio mentalis*, since this ratio would be incompatible with the constant demand for the carrying out of the naval programme established by law for the period up to 1920. He considered it much to be regretted that Herr von Tirpitz had not made perfectly clear his plans of expansion before he, the Ambassador, had been instructed to state in London there was no thought of exceeding the former fixed limits. Metternich even went so far as to beg not to be instructed any more to make communications in London that only raised hopes which afterwards were not fulfilled.

The new Chancellor was even more deeply convinced than his predecessor of the necessity of establishing friendly relations with England by means of a naval truce. Indeed, he regarded this as his chief task in foreign politics, and an agreement about naval construction really was to him hardly more than a means to an end. What he had most at heart was a political understanding with England. He was confirmed in this opinion by two memorials sent him by Kiderlen-Wächter upon the latter's return to his post

as Ambassador at Bucharest after the termination of the
Bosnian Crisis. The first memorial of the end of September
1909 assumed that England, without actually coming to
hostilities, could in many secondary questions exact compliance that would appear like weakness, as in the case of
Fashoda. To lessen the possibility of such a danger must
be the main object of an understanding with England, and
for this, he felt, a purely naval agreement would not suffice.

As a matter of fact, in the course of the year 1910, at
Germany's instigation, negotiations for a political agreement, including a naval agreement, were started, but they
went no further than an agreement that the naval attachés
were to exchange information about the activities in the
shipyards of their respective countries. The real truth
of the matter was that again there was widespread suspicion
in England that Germany was secretly accelerating the official
tempo of her naval construction. The English statesmen,
unlike the German, treated a political agreement as a matter
of secondary importance. For them the chief question was
whether the building of German battleships could be limited.

During the excitement over the *Panther's* spring, Lloyd
George's speech, and the discussion over Morocco in the
Reichstag, diplomatic efforts towards establishing friendlier
relations with England were of necessity at a standstill.
On the other hand, the German Navy propagandists took
advantage of every single flurry of excitement to strengthen
both the German people in their anti-English feeling and
the Kaiser in his disinclination to make any concession in
regard to the Navy. The political authorities and the naval
authorities were working against each other, with this
difference, that only the Navy possessed the full confidence
of William II. What the Chancellor was hoping for, a
neutrality agreement together with a mutual limitation
of naval expenditure, was the very thing that the Grand
Admiral feared.

As early as the summer of 1911 the Kaiser had declared
that he agreed with the proposal of the Admiralty that, if
possible in the current session of the Legislature, a new

Supplementary Naval Law should be introduced which should increase the size of the Navy by adding three large ships in addition to those provided for by the existing naval law. The Kaiser's idea was : We can reach an understanding with England only by means of a still stronger Navy, of which the British will be afraid.

After the November storm of 1911 over the Congo Agreement, one could be pretty confident that the Blue-Black Block, the Centre and the Conservatives, would agree without ado to the three new ships. All that the Chancellor was, with difficulty, able to get the Kaiser to consent to was that the new naval concoction should be prepared over a slower fire, and not set before the Reichstag until after the new elections. Kiderlen wrote on November 26, 1911, to the official who had accompanied the Kaiser to Rominten, that the decision in regard to the Naval Question was very serious and fateful for our whole future. In the first draft of the letter there was even a request to the Kaiser not to listen to one-sided departmental interests, but rather to his qualified counsellors. For, he said, we are actually standing at the parting of the ways, and it is too serious a matter to decide far from the capital, without consultation with the advisers His Majesty himself has chosen. The Chancellor at bottom was of the same opinion as the furious hotspur Kiderlen.

The result of the lively electioneering of January 1912 was a Reichstag in which the membership—the Social Democrats had doubled theirs, 110 as against 55 before—showed a majority for the ideal " from Bassermann to Bebel." [1] This majority was not of one mind within itself, however, even on questions of armament, and so was not capable of taking action against the Blue-Black Block. Besides the Supplementary Naval Law the new Reichstag was to occupy itself with the question of strengthening the Army. The general political situation, the net of

[1] Naumann's idea. He wished that the Social Democrats under Bebel and the National Liberals under Bassermann should unite under the leadership of the latter.—TRANSLATOR'S NOTE.

ententes around Germany, and the notorious, uninterrupted
military preparations of France and Russia, entirely justified the Minister for War and the Chief of the General
Staff in their demand that the Army should no longer be
inferior to the Navy. The Speech from the Throne on the
opening of the new Reichstag referred in general terms
only to the bills for increased armaments and for meeting
the cost of the same which were still before the Bundesrat,
without giving particulars as to their contents.

Since repeated soundings had yielded no results, it was
now indeed high time for the Chancellor to come to some
understanding with England. The idea of trying to bring
this about by means of personal conversations originated
with Lord Haldane. Sir Ernest Cassel, who had kept in
close touch with Ballin since 1908, presented to the Kaiser,
the end of January, 1912, on behalf of Grey, Churchill (First
Lord of the Admiralty), and Lloyd George, a memorandum
stating that in return for Germany's recognition of England's
naval supremacy and Germany's renouncement of an expansion of her naval programme, England would promise to
further Germany's colonial aims and to enter into mutual
declarations of neutrality in the event of aggression on
the part of a third Power. The answer to this, in the form
of a confidential note, was to the effect that a spirit of
accommodation in regard to England's wishes in the Navy
Question was possible, if guarantees could be given as to
the friendly orientation of England's policy. The hope
was also expressed in the note that an English Minister
might come to Berlin for a confidential interchange of ideas.

On behalf of the English Cabinet Lord Haldane came
to Berlin for a frank discussion. He was not authorized
to conclude a binding agreement. On February 8th and
10th he had conversations with the Chancellor, and on
February 9th an audience with the Kaiser, at which the
Grand Admiral, but not the Chancellor, was present. In his
Betrachtungen zum Weltkrieg, vol. i, p. 54,[1] Bethmann-

---

[1] English translation under the title *Reflections on the World War*.
—TRANSLATOR'S NOTE.

Hollweg describes his conversations with Lord Haldane as follows : " Haldane admitted to me without reservation that we had to bring in a Supplementary Naval Law, and that we had to have the third squadron. The formation of this squadron would certainly oblige England to maintain a large North Sea Fleet ; but that was a matter of indifference to England. He laid chief stress on the fact that England should not be compelled to reply to an increase in the number of German dreadnoughts by having to build double that number. He acknowledged that the retardation in the construction of the three dreadnoughts which the Supplementary Law was to provide for would meet England's wishes if the construction years were fixed at 1913, 1916, and 1919. I did not enter into a discussion of these technical questions, and stressed, on my side, that in so far as it involved a question of politics, the scope of the political agreement was of decisive significance."

We may have our doubts as to the wisdom of separating technical and political questions in discussing the matter with the English envoy. It is also extraordinary that neither the Chancellor nor the Secretary of State for Foreign Affairs, von Kiderlen, was present at the audience with the Kaiser. From the official documents it does not appear why Kiderlen apparently remained completely in the background in this momentous question of foreign politics, although he fully perceived how highly significant it was. But in the now published literary remains of Kiderlen we find an answer to the question as to his attitude in the case of Haldane's mission, and it fairly bristles. It reads as follows :

" Stuttgart, February 1912. I am an opponent of Tirpitz because I am afraid that his policy will get us into war with England. I consider Tirpitz "—here follows an outburst of wrath which cannot be repeated. Later on : " Berlin, February 1912. I am furious that they received Haldane in Berlin while I was absent on leave in Stuttgart, and had parleys with him without informing me. I gave the Chancellor a good piece of my mind, and wrote

236 THE WORLD POLICY OF GERMANY

this night, about three o'clock, to His Majesty to request an audience in order to explain affairs as I see them. I wish he would part with Tirpitz." Further, it appears, from a letter of the Kaiser to Kiderlen dated February 24th, that the Kaiser believed he had cause to admonish Kiderlen because the latter had attempted in a conversation in the Navy Department to make clear to Secretary of State von Tirpitz that if the three ships of the line that were demanded were left in the Supplementary Law it would be impossible to bring about an understanding with England.[1]

We do not know why Kiderlen was kept out of the way during the conversations with Lord Haldane, nor whether the Kaiser or the Chancellor did not desire his presence, perhaps on account of the gruff antagonism existing between the two autocrats, Tirpitz and Kiderlen. At any rate, it was a scarcely comprehensible error not to make use of Kiderlen's great diplomatic skill during Haldane's mission.

Lord Haldane carried back to England a copy of the formulated but not yet published Supplementary Naval Act. His report seemed to make a rather favourable impression on the Cabinet. Grey went so far as to tell Metternich that he was "immensely impressed" by Haldane's account of his conversations with the Chancellor, and that he would do his best to further this cause. But before long the English Ministers began to feel all sorts of scruples. The Colonial Secretary made reservations to Haldane's promises; and the Admiralty, after closer scrutiny of the German Supplementary Naval Law, discovered that besides the three dreadnoughts there was provision for the increase of the personnel from 5,000 to 15,000, from which they must infer a far greater preparedness in the whole Navy. Immediately the old suspicion cropped up again that Germany was stealthily exceeding her naval programme. In the question of a neutrality clause, Grey was first and foremost anxiously seeking to avoid creating any ill-humour in Paris and St. Petersburg. From the

[1] Ernst Jäckh, *Kiderlen-Wächter, der Staatsman und der Mensch*, Stuttgart, Berlin, and Leipzig, 1924, pp. 155 *seq.*

beginning he had kept the Russian Ambassador, Count Benkendorv, and the French Ambassador, Paul Cambon, posted concerning the Haldane mission, and had also advised them of his own formula, which only promised not to make an unprovoked attack on Germany and to abstain from an aggressive policy towards Germany. From the Isvolsky papers it may even be concluded that Grey acquainted Paris with Germany's extensive formula also. According to a report of Isvolsky, the French Prime Minister, Poincaré, stated in March 1912 that if England signed such an Anglo-German Agreement of Neutrality the result would be to bring about the end of existing Anglo-French relations.

At this same time Bethmann-Hollweg, who still hoped for a favourable conclusion of the matter, made another attempt to start up again the negotiations that had come to a standstill. Ballin was once more hastily sent to London. From his conversations with Metternich, Haldane, and Churchill, he brought back the impression that the English Cabinet and the King wanted to continue the negotiations, but that the chief obstacle lay in the great increase in the personnel, and that the Admiralty took exception also to the large number of torpedo boats and submarines.[1] From the Kaiser he learned that there could be no further reductions in the provisions in the Supplementary Law. The Grand Admiral had triumphed over the Chancellor. Shortly afterwards, Metternich was sent into the wilderness. He had been tireless in his warnings, and in his official reports had unswervingly held the view that unless Germany were willing to forgo the Supplementary Naval Law she would be unsuccessful both in the neutrality question and in regard to her colonial ambitions. Even before this the Chancellor, Bethmann-Hollweg, had almost been driven from office.

The Chancellor Crisis came about in this way. Since there had been no definite result from the Haldane mission the Kaiser, apprehensive lest the diplomatic negotiations in London might possibly necessitate still further reductions

[1] Huldermann, *Albert Ballin*, p. 265.

in the Supplementary Naval Law, became increasingly impatient to have it published and thrashed out as quickly as possible in the Reichstag. It was just the opposite with the Chancellor, who was deeply interested in seeing that the negotiations should not be interrupted by any public discussions either in England or in Germany. Tired of the long delay, on March 5, 1912, from Wilhelmshaven, where he had been present on the occasion of swearing-in recruits, William II telegraphed to the hesitant Chancellor that if the Army and Navy Bills were not published at once, he would order Tirpitz and Heeringen, the Minister for War, to publish them. Up to this time the Army and Navy Bills, together with the plan for meeting the cost they would entail, had never been brought before the Bundesrat. The Chancellor could not but see in this command the sabotaging of his endeavour to come to an understanding with England and a serious contravention of his responsibility to the Constitution, and he replied to the Kaiser's command by tendering his resignation and at the same time sharply criticizing his sovereign lord's action. There is no record of this offer of resignation of March 6th among the documents in the Foreign Office, but it is to be found in the literary remains of Kiderlen.[1] The Kaiser had not expected that the Chancellor would go to such lengths, and he summoned him to Wilhelmshaven. In the audience Bethmann-Hollweg allowed himself to be appeased, since the Kaiser renounced his intention of immediately publishing the laws. However, the *Kölnische Volkszeitung* was already in a position by March 8th to give the chief contents of the Supplementary Naval Law.

So we see that the enterprise that Ballin and Cassel, Bethmann-Hollweg and Haldane, had started with such high hopes ended in nothing but smoke.

The neutrality formula proposed by Grey ensured Germany only against an unprovoked attack by England, but not against England's espousal of the cause of Dual Alliance in case of a Franco-Russian attack on Germany. The

---

[1] Ernst Jäckh, *Alfred von Kiderlen-Wächter*, p. 156.

negotiations were frustrated by Grey's refusal to agree to the clause the Chancellor wanted to add to the effect that England would observe benevolent neutrality if war should be forced upon Germany. Although in clauses like this the spirit of the parties mattered much more than the wording of the text, and on England's part the spirit was obviously weak, still the question arises whether it would not perhaps have been better not to allow the negotiations to be wrecked on Grey's formula. After all, it did contain the promise not to enter into any agreement whose object was to make an unprovoked attack on Germany. There was the prospect that the inner strengthening of the Triple Entente would immediately ensue as the inevitable consequence of a complete failure of the attempt at an Anglo-German *détente*.

That was the second great turning-point in Anglo-German relations. In 1901 Germany refused an *entente cordiale*, and England subsequently withdrew from her old friendship with Germany. In 1912 Germany missed the chance of a fresh rapprochement with England, and there followed an enormous increase in the English naval estimates and the conclusion in writing of engagements of honour between England and France as to common measures to be taken in case of an unprovoked attack by a third Power. An exaggerated determination to possess naval power on Germany's part led her to rush blindly past the second turning-point, which nevertheless might have offered auspicious prospects for a better future for the Empire.

*　　*　　*　　*　　*

Finally, we must go back and consider an undertaking of the greatest economic and cultural significance, references to which appear in many places and in various connections in the official German documents, and which therefore deserves a comprehensive treatment by itself : a railway traversing the Near East from Bagdad to the Persian Gulf. Even during Lord Haldane's mission, among the various matters whose adjustment was to bring about friendlier relations between England and Germany, there was that of some agreement about the completion of the Bagdad Railway.

The endeavours of the Deutsche Bank under the directorship of its gifted founder, Georg von Siemens, to acquire a concession for the building of a railway in Asia Minor can be traced back to the Chancellorship of Bismarck. Bismarck had approved the undertaking, which in its beginnings already contained material for conflicts with French and English competitors, with the proviso, however, that Germany's Turkish policy must remain subordinate to her Russian policy.   Later, especially after the Bosnian Crisis, Austria-Hungary took Russia's place.   The imposing plan of providing Turkey with closer connection between Anatolia, the old homeland, and Syria, Mesopotamia as far as Persia, Arabia, and Egypt, and of thus bringing about the revival of the once fabulously fruitful Anatolian uplands by means of a transverse line, was conspicuously different from the French and English schemes.   It sought to establish a unified system of railways, whereas the other Powers merely built short lines within their spheres of interest.   Helfferich exactly characterizes the German plan when he says its railways were to serve to develop the country, while the railways of the other projects were aimed at its exploitation.[1]

On September 24, 1888, the Sultan granted the first concession for the building of a railway from Haider-Pasha to Angora.   This line of about 360 miles in length was completed in 1892, and other grants followed shortly, such as that for the railway from Eskishehr to Konia, a stretch of 275 miles.   The extension of the line through Siwa to Bagdad had already been provided for in the first concession.

After he had founded in 1889 the Anatolian Railway Company, with the co-operation of three German banks and with the assistance of several Austrian banks, Siemens succeeded in pushing the scheme farther and farther by means of difficult negotiations in which he had the splendid

[1] Cf. Karl Helfferich, *Die deutsche Turkenpolitik*, Berlin, 1921.

BEATUS ILLE, QUI PROCUL——

" Just look under the bed and see if Tirpitz is there ; I cannot believe in such good luck as not hearing any war trumpet for a few weeks."

(O. Gulbransson in *Simplizissimus*, April 15, 1912.)

support of the German Ambassador at Constantinople, Baron von Marschall, and the good will of the Kaiser, whose personal efforts were, however, not always to the best interests of the undertaking. Vast economic perspectives appeared to open up for Turkey's future and actually even began to be realized after the conclusion of the Turko-German Commercial Treaty of 1890. However, the Anatolian Railway Company always insisted, whenever extravagant ideas were expressed about it, that it had neither political nor colonial ends in view. There was a small amount of English capital invested in it, but the French and the Russians viewed the undertaking with distrust. So long as the policy of the other Powers was the preservation of Turkey, the enterprise progressed vigorously.

The financing of the railway that was to be built in sections depended to a large extent on the high politics of European Governments, on the changing alinement of the European Powers. As the political barometer rose or fell, so rose or fell the prospects for the realization of the enterprise. Naturally, the Bagdad Railway was a thorn in the flesh of those Powers who aimed at weakening Turkey; this was especially true of Russia. As long as England was strongly interested in the integrity and prosperity of Turkey, there was no fear that the work would be interrupted. But when Lord Salisbury in 1895 was considering the plan for the partition of " rotten " Turkey, and there was again a repetition of Armenian atrocities, then, for the time being, England's friendly support could not be reckoned on. Not until the period of the attempted Anglo-German rapprochement did the prospects of English co-operation become brighter.

In 1899 an agreement was reached between the Deutsche Bank and the French group in the Ottoman Bank, and in London, too, the feeling became more favourable towards the Bagdad Railway. But at the beginning of the year 1901, directly after the failure of the negotiations dealing with England's offer of an alliance with Germany, England

stated she would absolutely oppose the extension of the
railway to the proposed terminus of Koweit, the only good
harbour on the north shore of the Persian Gulf. The
British Government also notified the Porte that due to
treaties with the Sheik of Koweit their position was a special
one in regard to this territory. Further attempts to fix
the terminus failed.

In 1903, shortly before the conclusion of the Entente
Cordiale, Balfour in the English Parliament and Delcassé
in the French Parliament made statements to the effect
that only by abandoning this project could Germany obtain
the co-operation of England and France. Then when the
French group in the Ottoman Bank held on to their interests
acquired in 1899, the French Government prohibited
trading in Bagdad Railway shares. Russia seconded this,
exerting pressure on the French Government and the Porte.

Not until the Entente net was completed by the Anglo-
Russian Agreement concerning the countries contiguous to
the Persian Gulf, and England's predominance was assured
in Southern Persia, could there be any hope of an adjustment of the conflicting interests of England and Germany
in the Bagdad Railway Question. During his visit to
London in November 1907, the Kaiser declared that he was
ready to cede to England " the gateway of India "—that
is to say, the approach to the northern coast of the Persian
Gulf—and the Secretary of State, von Schön, discussed the
matter in detail with Sir Edward Grey without, to be sure,
reaching any acceptable proposal. In the same year the
stoppage in the construction of the railway finally came
to an end. The finances of Turkey had so improved that
the Porte could advance an additional sum for the building
of the railroad without increasing the customs duty, for
which the consent of the Great Powers would have been
necessary. As a result, treaties were concluded for the
construction of an additional stretch of 525 miles. Now
the Taurus and the Amanus Mountains could be crossed,
connection with the Mersina-Adana line would be effected
and thus communication established with Alexandretta.

But the Young Turk Revolution and the consequent closer relations of Turkey with the Western Powers seemed to jeopardize once more the whole enterprise.   Nevertheless, the witty remark that Djavid Bey, the Young Turk Minister for Finance, made when he was in London : " *Londres ne veut pas, Berlin ne peut pas,*" was not substantiated.   There was utter amazement when the loan that Djavid Bey was seeking for Turkey was made, not by a French but by a German consortium, thereby assuring once more the building of the Bagdad Railway.

Furthermore, in connection with the meeting of the Tsar and the Kaiser at Potsdam, the Russo-German Agreement about the branch line, Bagdad–Chanekin–Teheran, was reached in 1910, so that henceforth from Russia, too, no difficulties were to be expected.

The negotiations over the final stretch, Bagdad–Basra–the Persian Gulf, dragged on until shortly before the outbreak of the World War.   On February 5, 1914, the Berlin Foreign Office could at last arrange in paragraphs the rough drafts of a treaty.   To achieve the realization of this draft, great concessions had to be made on Germany's part to her enemies of the morrow.   The German Bagdad Railway Company relinquished its claim to build the final section from Basra to the Persian Gulf, as well as that to create ports at Bagdad, at Basra, and on the Persian Gulf. A Turkish company, with 40 per cent. of the stock English, was to build ports at Bagdad and Basra.   Furthermore, Germany was to establish no railway station on the Gulf without a previous understanding with England, and was to recognize the rights conceded to an English company in 1913 for navigation of the Euphrates and the Tigris. England's chief concessions consisted in her obligation not to build any railways to compete with the Bagdad Railway.

The treaty was never formally ratified, for the war dragged the parties from the conference table.   But it was the provisions of the Treaty of Versailles that robbed Germany of any chance of reaping the fruits of her long years of preparation and of economic and financial effort. All that was left to her was the honour of having created in one generation's time a technical and cultural enterprise which offered a wide scope for her own interests, and which was of great advantage to other nations.

BOOK VI

CONCLUSION

THE CHIEF DEFECT IN THE KAISER'S WORLD POLICY

UNDER a monarch who wanted to be his own Chancellor, and who was called by Article 11 of the Constitution drawn up by Bismarck to be the sole international representative of the Empire, and who as such was able to get the direction of international relations into his own hands, Germany's foreign policy could not but reflect certain peculiarities of the Kaiser's psychology; such as his inclination to ostentatious participation in international politics, his aversion to patient waiting and weighing, and in place of creative intuition his lively imagination that confused fond dreams with actualities. Still it was not in the least on account of this sort of strain that the Kaiser's World Policy was doomed to collapse. William II, and Germany along with him, suffered shipwreck chiefly because this policy, to some extent following a zigzag route, took the wrong course. The misunderstandings and the mistakes are all traceable to the one fundamental defect which then for the first time made the policy dangerous. This was the mistake in the treatment of the Power on the Western flank. Germany's isolation among the World Powers, that ultimately led to the coalition of all the World Powers against her, would have been impossible if the grandson of William I and his counsellors had for years sought as earnestly for England's friendship as for that of Russia.

Bismarck's legacy as Chancellor did not contain the mistake of discrimination in the treatment of Great Britain. Even with very close examination, and taking into consideration the experiences of the war, it would be hard to prove that in international problems he would have overvalued Russia and

undervalued England.   Still less did the usual continental
standards tempt the first Chancellor to undervalue England
as did Pan-Germans in their consciousness of power.   There
were as yet within Bismarck's field of vision no vital interests
of Germany that brought her into opposition with England.
The idea of jeopardizing relations with the strongest naval
Power for the sake of building a German fleet of battleships
would have seemed a risky adventure to him as accountable Chancellor.   His countrymen's ardour for colonies was
always repugnant to him, on account of their having stupidly
disturbed Anglo-German relations.   On the contrary, those
who are acquainted with his policy know that he sought
England's help as a protection against the threatening
activities of the Slavic Colossus.   There is no trace in
Bismarck's political psychology of any idea that Germany,
by acquiring power overseas under Russia's protection, was
to lessen England's great position in the world, or even to
bear her any ill-will.   For him any change in Germany's
bearing in Europe, and especially outside of Europe, could
not but be of less importance than the ever-present need of
preventing any irritation or friction on Germany's part
that might make England susceptible to France's desires
for a rapprochement.

This respect and prudence in dealing with London increased in proportion as the anti-German currents flowing
between Paris and St. Petersburg began, even in Bismarck's
time, to merge into one another.   It was in direct continuation of his policy that his first successor, Caprivi, wished
to further Germany's overseas aspirations and the development of her Navy while preserving, and not running counter
to, the good relations with England.   The increasing rivalry
of the two nations in mercantile policies and international
commerce did not of itself need to lead to political discord,
if only commerce and industry, whose needs led them
normally to throw the decisive weight of their influence
on to the scales for the preservation of friendly relations,
had continued to do so.   But Germany abandoned her
early willingness to follow Bismarck's example of pursuing

her overseas aims while keeping in touch with England as far as possible. By adopting an extensive naval policy she entered upon a path that led away from a peaceful understanding with the strongest naval Power. After this, more and more, there was an inclination for an effective alliance of the continental Powers against England's ascendancy ; that is, for the isolation of England. In proportion as a deep Anglo-German antagonism, earlier non-existent, developed into a question involving the fate of Europe, while the Anglo-French and the Anglo-Russian antagonisms were diminishing, the Kaiser's policy with its idea of a continental alliance against England acquired the significance of a *carte forcée*. It must have seemed to him the only way of keeping England and the Franco-Russian Dual Alliance apart, at least as far as Europe was concerned, after repeated opportunities to set up an opposition Anglo-German group had been allowed to slip.

Feeling that Germany through her growing alienation from England was throwing away a flank protection difficult to retrieve, the Kaiser tried to grasp the hand, now of France, now of Russia. Friendly moves in the direction of the neighbour in the West—which took the French by surprise when they were not feared as being political traps —become more intelligible, if considered as part of this endeavour to unite the Continent against England. The Russo-German Two-Emperor Agreement of July 1905, the so-called " Treaty of Björkö," contained nothing that could endanger the Franco-Russian Alliance. On the contrary, it assumed that France would join the Kaiser's new peace policy, and a rapprochement between the Triple Alliance and the Dual Alliance, as far as the form went, would indeed have ushered in the alliance of the Great Powers of the Continent. The moves in Germany's policy that ran counter to William II's wooing of France, such as the visit to Tangier and the *Panther's* spring at Agadir, as we have previously shown, did not originate with the Kaiser, but emanated from those in control in the Berlin Foreign Office at the time. Therefore it may be said that

William II showed a pertinacity in this notion of a continental alliance that is not to be found elsewhere in his ideas.

From the point of view of *Realpolitik*, the continental alliance was a creation with no vitality. This opinion has not been formed only *ex post facto* from the teachings of the World War. The belief in the possibility of a continental agreement against the Island Empire that lay at Europe's door rested on the failure to appreciate France's aims at ascendancy, about which there ought never to have been any permanent misunderstanding. It is incomprehensible that Lord Haldane, in his book *Before the War*, should be in any doubt about the fact that France in her policy was striving for *la revanche*. After the death of Gambetta, the " great European " who aimed at bringing about a reconciliation between France and Germany based upon Germany's voluntary dis-annexation of Alsace-Lorraine in return for compensation from French colonial possessions, but especially after the time of Boulanger and Delcassé, dozens of Ministers, generals, deputies, and scholars made the plainest allusions to the war of revenge, and characterized a military reconquest of the provinces lost in 1871 as the task of the future absorbing all Frenchmen, intellectually, morally, and martially. Moreover, there was plenty of proof in the official school-books and military literature of France that behind *la revanche* there still existed the old hankering of the Louis and Napoleon after the Palatinate, the Saar territory and the left bank of the Rhine from Mainz to Cologne. A General Staff officer in active service, Molard by name, as far back as the beginning of the nineties in the last century, stated in a book treating of the military efficiency of the various European States : " French policy has always had only one end in view : the reconquest of the left bank of the Rhine usurped by the Germans. . . . On either side of this frontier barrier for two thousand years the Gauls and the Germans have been enemies. That is what we have been, what we are, and what we always will be—hereditary enemies." This entire chapter of history antecedent to the World War was suppressed by persons in power intoxicated with victory. It cannot be disregarded by impartial scholars and fair advocates of the right of national self-determination. And lastly, we come across this longing for the left bank of the Rhine in the secret negotiations of Ribot and Poincaré with Russia and other Powers. We even see the Versailles Treaty attacked by a whole school of French statesmen because it disappointed France in what she wanted to get on the Rhine ; and we have lived to see that even after the conclusion of peace, cities in the Main district were occupied, and the Ruhr entered and occupied for a long time, as a threat to German territory.

With traditional aims of this sort, which until 1914 were usually concealed, the men in France who were directing or inspiring her policies could not but treat the notion that their country should participate in a continental grouping of Powers to protect Germany against England as a piece of ridiculous nonsense, especially since they had been successful in their continual and sanguine efforts in making preparations for the great coalition that had always been Bismarck's nightmare. Therefore it is doubtful, to say the least, whether it would ever have been possible for Germany, a Great Power established firmly on both banks of the Rhine, to have enlisted France for this scheme. But beyond a doubt it would have been possible not to lose England completely.

It will not do to make English commercial jealousy responsible for the gradual change for the worse that took place in Anglo-German relations. Undoubtedly this jealousy had repeatedly disturbed the relations of the two peoples, and had helped to hinder and impede a return to relations of mutual confidence. But if this had been a prime motive in England's policy, the doors in all England's possessions would scarcely have remained open to the German merchant, as was actually the case. Directly after the very strong outburst of hostile feeling against German competition occasioned by the Krüger Telegram, there followed a period of friendly understandings between London and Berlin relating to the Portuguese colonies, to Samoa, to common interests in the Far East. England also attempted to reach a formal alliance with Germany, or at least to arrive at an agreement concerning Morocco. And, shortly before the World War, was not a treaty put on paper which would have assured to the German Empire a wide scope for economic activity in Asia Minor as far as the Persian Gulf ?

The chance of not entirely losing England was not therefore ruined by Germany's disturbing economic competition. Nor was it so much frustrated by the increase itself in the German Navy as by the preference shown for building battleships, and by the political propaganda that was let loose, and which very soon could not be restrained by any consideration of the need of cultivating good relations with England. Germany was threatened as a result of the union of French and Russian forces in Europe, and she should have kept her needs arising from this fact ever before her mind when she was building her Navy. This would have been possible without injury to conditions essential to her national existence.

But the naval propagandists could or would not admit that there was anything for Germany in the future except either to build a fleet of battleships of which England would be afraid in her home waters, or else to sink into wretched dependence, both political and economic, on the Island Kingdom. England's demeanour proves to the sober observer of political facts that she conceded to Germany her strong position on the Continent, and with it her temporarily sufficient share in the development of international commerce, a share which was capable of expansion as time went on. The chances for Germany to expand oversea, which admitted of a timely commercial agreement with England for the German competitor, such as might have been had, and which might, indeed, have led to new possibilities, were intentionally disregarded because they interfered with the anti-English rudiments of the naval propaganda. Germany powerful on the sea or England's vassal—in this "either—or" policy there was no third possibility, no middle way. A large part of the German public was pleased that in the agitation for battleships England, the "mortal enemy," as well as France, the "hereditary enemy," was taken into consideration.

Therefore we must understand that when, in answer to Hardinge's proposal in Friedrichshof in 1908 to limit naval armament, the Kaiser referred to duties towards the German nation, King Edward and the English Government were convinced that England was threatened. That the exaggeration of Germany's claims to sea-power actually brought about the Anglo-German estrangement, and as a further consequence, France's long-desired reckoning with Germany under circumstances unfavourable to the latter, is proved by the exact parallel that existed between Germany's naval preparations and England's increasing political and military intimacy with the Dual Alliance. This connection becomes especially evident if we compare Germany's fleet laws in chronological order with England's attitude towards Germany at the time, especially during the Morocco Crisis.

1904 : After the conclusion of the Colonial Treaty dealing with Morocco and Egypt, speeches were made in both Houses of Parliament expressing the desire that treaties of a similar sort should be concluded with other rival countries, including Germany. Shortly afterwards, during King Edward's visit to Kiel, there were, besides, friendly after-dinner speeches about the pacific designs of both flags.

1905 : The British Lion is aroused against the German Sea-Eagle. Lee, the Sea Lord, has the idea of suddenly pouncing on the German Navy. The building of dreadnoughts. Germany wants, with indisputable right, to be assured of the Open Door in Morocco. English propaganda for Minister Delcassé, and his disclosure about the landing of 100,000 English on the Schleswig or on the Franco-Belgian coast.

1906 : Shortly after the new German naval law with its demands for six armoured cruisers, Grey's statement that England would support France's claims at the Algeciras Conference at all costs, and the first verbal secret alliance with Paul Cambon about the Military and Naval Staffs of both countries keeping in touch with one another. The British Military Attaché, Barnardiston, communicates to the Chief of the Belgian General Staff the plan of sending a corps of marines to Belgium, if war should break out.

1908–9 : The German Supplementary Naval Law providing for the replacement of antiquated battleships by new ones. The Anglo-Russian plan for operations in the Near East. In the summer of 1908, Lloyd George's speech against the Two-Power Standard, and the first attempt at an Anglo-German naval agreement in Friedrichshof. After its frustration, the support of Russia in the Bosnian Crisis and eight new dreadnoughts.

1911 : In contradiction to the Act of Algeciras and the Franco-German Agreement of 1909, the French advance on Fez ; Germany's really justifiable claims for compensation for France's protectorate over Morocco ; nevertheless, Grey's public encouragement of the march on Fez, and Lloyd George's threatening speech against Germany ; English preparations for war disclosed by Captain Faber.

1912 : Haldane's mission to Berlin. The frustration of the second attempt to limit competition in naval armaments, followed by the decision of the English Government to increase the naval expenditure to fifty-one millions sterling. In September an Anglo-French Naval Convention ; then, after the conclusion of the Franco-Russian Naval Convention, Grey's verbal statement to Sazonov, that England was bound to support France both on land and on sea against Germany (as Sazonov had shortly before already learned from Poincaré in Paris), and that in case of an armed conflict between Russia and Germany " he would do his utmost to deal a good sound blow to Germany " (according to Sazonov's report to the Tsar). Finally, on November 12th, Grey's agreement with Paul Cambon, recorded in letters, that England was " in honour bound " to protect the French coasts in case of a war with Germany.

At the opening of the century, Germany refused to enter into a close alliance with England, by which she could have realized what Bismarck in 1889 characterized as the end and aim of his policy, namely, England's entry into the Triple Alliance. By the repeated refusal of England's proposal for a reciprocal limitation of naval armament, or, more exactly, of the building of large battleships, England became Germany's bitterest and most dangerous opponent —something else that was in opposition to a fundamental idea of Bismarck's policy. For whence came his constant " *cauchemar des coalitions* " ? From the oppressive fact that " millions of bayonets are polarized, generally speaking, towards the centre of Europe, so that there is this additional reason beside that of all European History, that we in the centre of Europe are especially exposed to a coalition of other Powers." These are the words Bismarck used in 1883, when he was being reproached with being militaristic, in order to explain why Germany needed a strong Army. A similar weight rested on the statesmen of the British Isles. They could with justice speak of England's *cauchemar de la flotte allemande*. At all events, it would have been in line with the fundamental idea of Bismarck's policy not to allow this nightmare to grow into the reality of a bitter enmity. The frequent reference to the fact that England, centuries in the past, had sought to destroy the strongest Power of the time, first Spain, then Holland, then Napoleonic France, cannot mean that it was now Germany's business to wreak Europe's vengeance on Albion. Wedged in between two strong military Powers bent on war, the youthful German Empire should rather have learned from the brutal instinct of self-preservation displayed for centuries by the old Kingdom of the British Isles her duty towards herself, which was to follow Bismarck's wise example of preventing the rivalry with England from becoming a question of destiny for Germany.

The courting of the Tsar by the Kaiser did not compensate for the loss of England's friendship. The efforts to make the traditional store of sentiments existing between the Hohenzollern and Romanov Houses yield security for Germany might perhaps have succeeded if in both Russia and Germany a ruler with a dominating personality had been at the helm, and if two strong monarchs could have turned their personal sympathy for each other to the service of the great common interests of their peoples. For want of all this, William II's attempts to erect a German World Policy on his personal friendship with the Tsar, which had been especially cultivated between 1895 and 1905, was doomed to failure from the very start. The exchange of demonstrations of friendship between the two Courts found no echo among the two peoples, who followed their own respective inclinations, which were not easily reconcilable with those of the other nation. Besides, leaving out of the question the anti-German influence of France on Russia, the mind of the Russian people with its predominant Slavic sentiment, especially after the appearance of Neo-Slavism, was more and more completely alienated from the German neighbour, who at the same time, in case of necessity, must come to the rescue of the Danube Empire of many nationalities. Open hostility was kindled also by details in Turko-German relations, according to which the Kaiser could be represented to the Orthodox masses as the military defender of the Sultan, the ruler of Constantinople and the Straits. The personality of Nicholas II was powerless to stem such floods of passion. After the effect of the Russo-Japanese War on affairs within his Empire, he could not but be in a constant tremble at the thought that, if there were another military gale, the Tsardom itself would go down in the sea of internal restlessness within the great Russian nation.

*   *   *   *   *

Finally, we must touch upon one more question, which we frequently hear, especially from the lips of foreigners: How was it possible that the German people put up so long with the personal rule of a man whose acts proved to be harmful for the country and the people?

In the first place we must not overlook the fact that the work of national unification was personified in the person of the Kaiser, and so remained unshaken up to the outbreak of the World War. In spite of exasperation at single acts of his personal rule, the leaders of the working masses knew well that any attempts that might be made to overthrow the Constitution in peace-time would be doomed to frustration from the outset, as long as the Crown was preserving peace with the outside world and order at home. But chiefly it was the economic boom, and the general comfort in Germany resulting from it, which stood in the way of bringing about successful revolution. When delegates from the Russian Revolution once spoke to Bebel in the lobby of the Reichstag about a speedy revolution, the old party chief said roundly : " Our people are not sufficiently badly off ; revolutions do not occur unless there is general distress." If it had not been for the disorganizing consequences of the war, which created a very real general want quite new in Germany, attempts to overthrow the monarchy or the monarch would certainly have ended in failure.

The official German documents bear witness that William II had an innate dislike of war and shrank from military enterprises. Even during the Russian War in Eastern Asia, when the opportunity to make an aggressive war against France on account of her policy of *la revanche* was tempting favourably, the idea of war never entered his head. Even Karl Kautsky, the severest critic of the notorious marginal notes of the Kaiser, has had to admit that Germany did not systematically work for a World War, and ultimately sought to avoid it. Of all the rôles which William II has played, probably that of Peace Kaiser is the truest. There was a deep-rooted conviction among the ranks of labour, both before and after the Kaiser Crisis of November 1907, that in spite of the impression he himself had created by his many threatening speeches, William II would never plunge his people into war, either from lust of conquest or through recklessness.

R

INDEX

Cowes, 64, 65
Cranborne, Lord, English Under-
Secretary, 107, 124
Crete, 172
Crispi, Italian Prime Minister, 221

Daily Telegraph interview, 216–
18
D'Amada, French General, 220
Daudet, Léon, 156
Delagoa Bay, 67, 70–1, 82, 91
Delarey, Boer General, 139
Delbrück, Clemens von, German
Secretary of State, 184
Delcassé, 88, 91, 102, 122, 125,
128, 131–2, 140, 144, 148–53,
155–6, 159–61, 168, 170, 242,
250, 253, 256
Derby, Lord, 181
Devonshire, Duke of, 64
De Wet, Boer General, 139
Diedrichsen, von, Admiral, 61
Dikov, Russian Minister for the
Navy, 192
Dillon, E. J., 176 *n.*
Djavid, Bey, Young Turk Fi-
nance Minister, 243
Dogger Bank incident, 158
Dreyfus, French Major, 132
Dual Alliance, 49 *seq.*, 74, 92,
108, 122, 124, 134, 159, 166,
194, 200–1, 249, 253
Ducarme, Belgian General, 156
Dupuy, French Minister, 153

East Asiatic Triple Alliance,
55 *seq.*, 58, 59, 72, 73, 121,
123, 140, 160
Eckardstein, Baron von, German
Ambassador at London, 103,
108, 113, 118, 119
Eckardt, Julius von, Consul
General, 45 *n.*, 125 *n.*

Edward VII of England, 92, 112,
113, 134, 146, 162, 163, 174,
176, 177, 194–6, 181, 201–2,
220, 253
Ejnem, von, Prussian Minister
for War, 180
Engels, Friedrich, 38
England's offer of alliance,
103
Entente Cordiale, 140 *seq.*, 164,
169, 173, 177–8, 180, 194,
213, 230, 242, 253
Eugénie, ex-Empress of France,
201
Eulenburg, Prince, German Ambassador at Vienna, 40 *n.*,
223

Faber, English Captain, 254
Fashoda, 77, 87–8, 133-4
Faure, Jules, French President,
133
Fisher, Lord, English Admiral,
93, 162, 185, 194
Fitzgerald, retired English Ad-
miral, 161
Formosa, Island of, 54, 57
Francis Ferdinand, Heir to
Austrian Throne, 192, 206
Francis Joseph, Emperor of
Austria, 36, 72, 111, 135–6,
201–2, 226
Franco-German Agreement, 219,
222
Franco-German Treaty, 220
Franco-Italian Treaty, 132,
224
Franco-Russian Military Conven-
tion, 132
Franco-Russian Naval Conven-
tion, 252
Franklin, Benjamin, 186
Frederick the Great, 114, 134,
186